SANCTIONS

WHAT EVERYONE NEEDS TO KNOW®

SANCTIONS

WHAT EVERYONE NEEDS TO KNOW®

BRUCE W. JENTLESON

OXFORD
UNIVERSITY PRESS

OXFORD
UNIVERSITY PRESS

Oxford University Press is a department of the University of Oxford. It furthers the University's objective of excellence in research, scholarship, and education by publishing worldwide. Oxford is a registered trade mark of Oxford University Press in the UK and certain other countries.

Published in the United States of America by Oxford University Press 198 Madison Avenue, New York, NY 10016, United States of America.

"What Everyone Needs to Know" is a registered trademark of Oxford University Press.

Library of Congress Cataloging-in-Publication Data
Names: Jentleson, Bruce W., 1951- author.
Title: Sanctions : what everyone needs to know / Bruce W. Jentleson.
Description: New York, NY : Oxford University Press, [2022] |
Includes bibliographical references and index.
Identifiers: LCCN 2022018920 (print) | LCCN 2022018921 (ebook) |
ISBN 9780197530320 (paperback) | ISBN 9780197530313 (hardback) |
ISBN 9780197530344 (epub)
Subjects: LCSH: Economic sanctions. | International economic relations.
Classification: LCC HF1413.5 .J46 2022 (print) | LCC HF1413.5 (ebook) |
DDC 327.1/17—dc23/eng/20220609
LC record available at https://lccn.loc.gov/2022018920
LC ebook record available at https://lccn.loc.gov/2022018921

DOI: 10.1093/wentk/9780197530313.001.0001

1 3 5 7 9 8 6 4 2

Paperback printed by Lakeside Book Company, United States of America
Hardback printed by Bridgeport National Bindery, Inc., United States of America

To my Bridging the Gap Colleagues

CONTENTS

ACKNOWLEDGMENTS

I wrote my early 1980s Cornell PhD dissertation on economic sanctions, in fact on Cold War sanctions against Soviet energy pipelines to Western Europe. Finishing this book amid the bevy of sanctions against Russia for its 2022 invasion of Ukraine, including the Nord Stream 2 natural gas pipeline, has made for a mix of irony, symmetry, and reflection.

In the years since I've written numerous journal articles, book chapters, commissioned studies, and the like on various aspects of economic sanctions. In the last few years, two projects really reconnected me with colleagues working on sanctions and related issues. One was the early 2019 sanctions workshop our Bridging the Gap New Voices in National Security program ran in collaboration with the Center for a New American Security in Washington, DC. This both got me more focused on recent scholarly work on sanctions and more directly engaged with the sanctions policy community. The other was the "weaponizing interdependence" conference Dan Drezner, Henry Farrell, and Abe Newman ran later that year at Tufts Fletcher School and the follow-on book they edited to which I contributed an article.

I also have had the opportunity to work on sanctions issues while serving in government, including the Clinton administration Tiananmen Square sanctions against China and the Obama administration Iran sanctions. As on other issues, I've benefited greatly from the theory-policy praxis: in some cases confirming ideas, in others calling them into question, either way learning experiences that made me a better scholar, teacher, and practitioner.

Writing a book for the Oxford What Everyone Needs to Know series struck me as an opportunity to build on the knowledge I had and experiences I'd gained. Thanks to David McBride for being receptive to the initial idea and then providing his expert editing along the way. Thanks also to his Oxford University Press colleagues Holly Mitchell and Emily Benitez and the Newgen Knowledge Works team for their roles in bringing the book to publication. Special thanks to my Duke research assistants: Andrew Trexler for his work on key methodological and conceptual sections as well as historical cases, Mochen (Phil) Ma who RA-ed a related project, and especially Elise Bousquette for her work on many aspects of the book over the last three years. Bryan Early, Erica Moret, and Jordan Tama provided very helpful feedback on draft chapters. Colleagues at Australia National University, College of Asia and the Pacific, where I held the 2020 Desmond Ball Visiting Chair, were gracious hosts, as were Robert Litwak and other colleagues at the Woodrow Wilson International Center for Scholars where I have been a 2022 Distinguished Fellow. Duke University and the Sanford School of Public Policy have continued to be my valued home institution.

Since my last book, Felix has been added to the Adam-Britt-Danny family and Lorelei to the Katie-Matt-Mabel family. More than anyone else, Barbara can see the links back to those dissertation days. My thanks and love for our family.

Previous books have been dedicated to family members. This one I dedicate to my Bridging the Gap colleagues. To all those participants who have come through our programs and have been going on to make your own contributions to academic-policy world bridging. And especially to our Bridging the Gap leadership team with whom it has been so great to work toward our shared goals and with much-valued collegiality.

INTRODUCTION

PUZZLES POSED FOR INTERNATIONAL RELATIONS THEORY AND FOREIGN POLICY STRATEGY

As I was finishing this book in early 2022, Russia invaded Ukraine. Sanctions were a major part of the US-led counterstrategy. As Chapter 5 discusses and the Appendix delineates, they were by many measures the most extensive sanctions ever imposed. They received broad global support. Major multinational companies that typically resist sanctions initiated their own. International sports organizations like FIFA and the Paralympics joined in. So too did cultural organizations. While not the "overwhelming" impact Biden administration officials originally touted, the Russian economy was hit hard.[1] Whether or not these costs helped coerce Russia to end the war remained (as of this writing, early May 2022) to be seen.

At the same time, the Russia Ukraine case was going on, debate raged over the sanctions against now Taliban-controlled Afghanistan. Should the sanctions be lifted or at least reduced so as to provide relief to the Afghan people? Or would that teach the Taliban the wrong lesson that they can rule as brutally as they want and still get international support? And what about Burma/Myanmar? How could sanctions not be imposed given the military's brutal coup? Yet the military and other powerbrokers insulated themselves while the Burmese people were feeling the pain.

Tough questions—and plenty of other cases posing their own versions. Indeed, for a number of years it's been hard to browse the news without seeing reports of yet another set of sanctions:

- The United States (US) currently also has sanctions against Iran, Venezuela, Russia, North Korea, China, Syria, Libya, Yemen, Mali, Central African Republic, Burma, Sudan, Nicaragua, Cuba, and a number of other countries. It has sweeping human rights legislation authorizing sanctions against offenders in any country. It sanctions thousands of "specially designated" individuals and companies including drug traffickers, terrorist organizations, and individuals in positions of economic and political power.[2]
- European Union (EU) sanctions, while not as long a list, include many of the same countries and individuals as the US list plus some others. So too the British one. And the Canadian one.[3]
- The United Nations (UN), which only imposed sanctions four times in its first two decades (1945–1965), has done so over forty times since then.[4]
- Russia has repeatedly imposed sanctions against former Soviet republics, as well as retaliatory ones against the US and the EU.
- China has been developing its own approach, with some sanctions targeted against other countries (e.g., Norway for awarding the Nobel Peace Prize to dissident Liu Xiaobo, South Korea for deploying a THAAD missile defense system) and others "cued" to Chinese social media against companies such as the Swedish retail giant H&M for refusing to buy cotton from the Xinjiang region because of atrocities against the Uighurs and organizations like the National Basketball Association (NBA) for tweeting in sympathy with the summer 2019 Hong Kong protests.

And not just by major powers:

- Japan and South Korea sanctioned each other over historical legacies of colonialism and World War II occupation.
- Pakistan and India against each other over Kashmir.
- Saudi Arabia and other Gulf Cooperation Council (GCC) members against Qatar because of differences over Iran and support for the Muslim Brotherhood.
- The African Union (AU) against Mali, South Sudan, and other African countries.
- And many others. . . .

While economic sanctions take many forms—such as trade, finance, and aid—and can be targeted against whole countries, key economic sectors, or designated individuals, all involve using economic relations for foreign policy and other political objectives. Their use goes way back in history, as with Athenian sanctions against Sparta in 432 BC and Napoleon's 1808–1814 Continental System. But it wasn't until the second half of the twentieth century that their frequency started significantly increasing. From 1915 to 1940 there were only eleven sanctions cases, averaging out to well less than one case per year. During the Cold War (1945–1990) there were 610 cases, a 13.5 annual average; from 1990 to 2005, this further increased to 802 cases, a 53.5 annual average.[5] While data since then are less systematic, the examples cited suggest a continuing robust rate.[6]

With such frequency of use, you'd think sanctions were a surefire weapon. Yet there is plenty of debate over their success rate. One study puts it at 22 percent, another at 34 percent—and one flat-out sees sanctions as bringing to the coercion table "little independent usefulness" compared to military force.[7] Even when they do impose some "political pain," they can also inflict that "civilian pain" with humanitarian consequences so severe as to raise fundamental ethical questions.[8] On the other hand, there is a view among some scholars that sanctions success gets "systematically underestimated" by studies that "accentuate the negative and downplay the positive aspects."[9] I know from my own experience serving in the US State Department and in other policy roles that policymakers often see sanctions as a weapon of choice.

Even if all the conceptual and methodological problems are worked out and a consensual success rate reached, the question remains, Measured against what? What percentage of success is needed for sanctions to be considered an effective strategy? In baseball, a batter who hits .300—that is, three successes out of ten tries—is considered to have had an excellent year. In football, a quarterback needs a passing completion rate of more than 50 percent to have even a good season. In basketball, free throws need to be made 70–80 percent of the time.

So some initial puzzles:

Why do sanctions get used?
How to measure success?
What key factors affect success?
What lessons can policymakers derive for why, how, and when to wield sanctions?

These and related questions are well suited for an Oxford University Press What Everyone Needs to Know book.

The book is structured in two sections. Part I focuses on the academic literature and scholarly challenges involving major concepts, theoretical debates, and methodological issues:

Chapter 1 defines core terminology of *what* the different types of sanctions are, *who* the key actors are, *why* sanctions are imposed in terms of the policy objectives being pursued, and *how* sanctions are supposed to achieve their objectives.

Chapter 2 tackles the "do sanctions work" question. It goes into more detail on the various scorecards, and probes methodological issues of what actually constitutes a sanctions case and what metrics best measure success. It then addresses ethical issues, taking humanitarian effects into account in assessments of success.

Chapter 3 focuses on the explanatory side of when, how, and why sanctions do or do not succeed. Among the questions examined: Is economic impact the key factor? Is a reciprocity strategy, sanctions and inducements together, most effective? Do multilateral sanctions work better than unilateral ones? Are democracies more vulnerable to sanctions, non-democracies less so? Are targeted "smart" sanctions, particularly financial ones, more effective than more general ones? Is the type of objective for which sanctions are being used the key factor?

While these Part I chapters bring cases in illustratively, Part II provides case studies of major sanctions policy cases organized by major sanctions sender and analyzed within the Part I what-who-why-how framework.

Chapter 4 provides historical perspective. It includes seven cases, starting with the 432 BC Athenian sanctions against Sparta amid the Peloponnesian Wars; Napoleon's early nineteenth-century Continental System blockade against Britain; and the League of Nations' 1935–1936 sanctions against Italy over its invasion of Ethiopia (Abyssinia). Four are post–World War II: the 1956 Suez crisis US sanctions against Britain; the UN sanctions against Rhodesia, 1966–1979; the Arab League and OPEC 1973 sanctions against the US and Europe; and UN and US sanctions against South Africa, 1977–1994.

Chapter 5 focuses on the US as the most frequent sanctions wielder. This was true during the Cold War and has been true since, the Biden administration included. Various aspects of the what, why, and how questions are addressed in the context of American domestic politics and overall foreign policy strategy. Cases include Iran, various sanctions against the Soviet Union/Russia (including those in 2022 related to Ukraine), various ones against China, North Korea, Venezuela, and counterterrorism.

Chapter 6 examines China's use of sanctions. Once an ardent critic of US and other sanctions as extensions of Western imperialism and violations of its sovereignty, over the past decade-plus China has been wielding its own sanctions. We first analyze its general pattern of use, both officially promulgated formal sanctions and informally cued ones. Case studies include Taiwan (elections, US arms sales), France and Tibet, Norway and the 2010 Liu Xiaobo Nobel Peace Prize, South Korea THAAD missile defense, Australia "anti-Chinese" domestic politics, and the NBA and the Hong Kong democratization protests.

Chapter 7 is on Soviet and Russian use of sanctions. Three sender state cases are examined: Soviet sanctions against Tito's Yugoslavia, 1948–1955; Russia against other Commonwealth of Independent States in the 1990s; and Russian countersanctions against the US and the EU over Ukraine (from 2014 on). Three other cases involve Soviet/Russian oil and natural gas pipelines to Western Europe—the early 1960s Friendship Oil Pipeline, the early 1980s Siberian natural gas pipeline, and the contemporary Nord Stream 2 pipeline—and debate over whether European energy dependence would give Moscow sanctions leverage.

Chapter 8 addresses multilateral sanctions authorized by the UN Security Council and EU sanctions as an example of the role regional organizations play. UN sanctions show both the advantages and the problems for multilateral sanctions. Cases are the Iraq 1990s comprehensive sanctions that were part of the overall post–Gulf War strategy, and Liberia (1992–2016) and Côte d'Ivoire (2004–2016) targeted sanctions dealing with armed conflicts. The EU section focuses on the what, why, and how effective of its sanctions, and the mix of consensus and tensions with the US.

The concluding section has two main objectives. It ties together the case evidence in Part II with the concepts and propositions laid out in Part I as contributions to the development of scholarly theory about economic sanctions. And it draws out insights and findings identifying key factors for sanctions efficacy as a working template applicable to policy strategizing going forward.

Part I

SCHOLARLY DEBATES AND CHALLENGES

1

ECONOMIC SANCTIONS

WHAT, WHO, WHY, AND HOW

This chapter sets out definitions of key terms and establishes an analytic framework of

- *What* are the different types of sanctions?
- *Who* are the key actors?
- *Why* are sanctions imposed in terms of the policy objectives being pursued?
- *How* are sanctions supposed to achieve their objectives?

Working our way down the conceptual ladder, economic sanctions can be seen as a species of the genus economic power. In his classic *National Power and the Structure of Foreign Trade*, Albert Hirschman looks at how foreign trade in all its forms can be an economic source of national power. David Baldwin's concept of economic statecraft encompasses most any use of economic means by one state to influence another state or international institution in pursuit of objectives not strictly economic in nature. "Weaponized interdependence" as developed recently by Henry Farrell and Abraham Newman is the ability of states to use "global economic networks" to achieve geostrategic objectives.[1]

Focusing in more particularly on economic sanctions, my baseline definition is *"the actual or threatened denial of economic*

relations by one or more states [sender(s)] intended to influence
the behavior of another state or non-state actors [target] on foreign
policy and other political issues."[2] While some scholars include
sanctions used for trade wars and other economic objectives,
in my view the policy and political dynamics vary sufficiently
based on whether core objectives are political or economic to
warrant separate study and strategizing.[3]

What Are the Different Types of Sanctions?

Sanctions can be of a number of different types, including:

- Trade: embargoes of exports to and boycotts of imports from
  target states, the most commonly used sanctions;
- Finance: freezing assets held within the sender state's financial systems, limiting or banning commercial banking financial transactions, and limiting or banning investment in the
  target state;
- Foreign aid: limiting or terminating economic, military,
  and other government-to-government aid unless certain
  conditions are met;
- Travel: prohibiting travel by target state individuals to the
  sender state(s) and restricting travel by its citizens to the
  target state;
- Sports: banning target state athletes from international
  sports such as the Olympics and FIFA Football (soccer) and
  Rugby World Cups;
Cultural: banning artists and performers from the target state.

They also can have different scopes:

- Comprehensive: seeking to prevent virtually all trade, akin
  to economic warfare. As Queen Elizabeth I put it back in
  the sixteenth century with regard to Philip I of Spain: "The
  stopping hindrance and impeaching of all commerce and
  traffick with him in his territories of Spain and Portugal will

quickly in all likelihood give an end to these bloudie unnatural warres which disturb the generall peace and quiet of all these parts of Chirstendom."[4]

- Sectoral: aimed at key parts of the target's economy. Arms embargoes, of which there have been over 100 (some multilateral by the UN and some by the US, EU, and others), are one example.[5] Energy sanctions are another, some as oil producer export embargoes (OPEC 1973) and some by energy consumers (boycotting Iranian oil, blocking Soviet/Russian oil and natural gas pipelines).

- Targeted: often dubbed "smart sanctions," stylized as the economic equivalent of precision-guided munitions, seeking to impose costs on designated high-value targets—individuals, businesses, non-state actors, other entities—while limiting collateral damage to the civilian population. The calculation is that such direct costs can push those targeted to cease their actions and/or exert pressure on the regime for policy change. The US Specially Designated Nationals and Blocked Persons (SDN) List targets individuals, companies, and other entities "acting for or on behalf of, targeted countries" as well as "terrorists and narcotics traffickers designated under programs that are not country-specific." The EU's Consolidated Financial Sanctions List and UN Security Council Consolidated List, while less extensive, have similar intent.[6]

- Secondary: imposed by the sender state on third parties outside its own national jurisdiction to coerce their cooperation. The US has been the lead invoker of secondary sanctions claiming extraterritorial application of its laws to foreign subsidiaries of US-based multinational corporations making goods that the US embargoes but the host country does not, foreign companies using US-made parts or US-licensed technology, and banks and companies anywhere in the world continuing to do business with the target through dollar-denominated transactions. Clashes between American assertions of extraterritorial reach and European defense of sovereignty have sparked tensions in such cases as Iran sanctions and Soviet/Russian pipelines.

Another distinction is between formal and informal sanctions. Formal sanctions are ones explicitly mandated by a government or an international institution. In the US these may be by congressional legislation or by presidential executive order. For the UN, Security Council action is required. Informal sanctions are ones that government authorities cue businesses and individuals within their countries to impose without officially promulgating them. China is the main practitioner of informal cued sanctions, as with consumer boycotts of the South Korean company Lotte over the 2016–2017 deployment of a US THAAD anti-missile system, and fanning social media outrage against the National Basketball Association for one of its officials having tweeted support for the 2019 Hong Kong protesters.

Who Are the Key Actors?

Here I work with a threefold categorization—sender, target, third parties—with distinctions within each.

Sender

Unilateral sanctions are those imposed exclusively or primarily by a single country. The US has long been the most frequent unilateral sanctions sender, in 68 percent of cases in one study, 52 percent in another.[7]

Multilateral sanctions can have various degrees of "multi-." Coalitional sanctions are ones on which an alliance or other group of states act collectively: for example, Cold War sanctions imposed by COCOM (Consultative Group-Coordinating Committee, comprising NATO plus Japan and Australia) on military-related exports to the Soviet Union and its allies.[8] Sanctions may also be through regional organizations: for example, EU, African Union, Organization of American States. Fully multilateral sanctions are ones imposed by the UN Security Council, of which there have been over forty cases. In its day, the League of Nations had four cases.

Target

Sanctions typically are targeted at a particular country or countries. In addition, the US SDN List and European and UN counterparts as noted include sanctions singling out particular individuals, businesses, and other entities within target countries as well as terrorist groups (e.g., ISIS, al Qaeda) and criminal organizations (e.g., the Mexican drug ring Zetas, Eastern European criminal ring Brothers' Circle).

Third Parties

"A country menaced with an interruption of trade with a given country has the alternative of diverting trade to a third country" is how Hirschman captures the role played by third parties and the problem posed for senders and opportunity for targets.[9] Third parties may be of four types: economically motivated by trade with the target, politically motivated as rival of the sender, neighboring states with porous borders, and non-state actors reaping profits from sanctions busting.

Why Are Sanctions Imposed in Terms of the Policy Objectives Pursued?

Doing some synthesizing and aggregating from other studies, I distinguish between primary and secondary objectives, and identify three subtypes of each:[10]

Primary objectives seek to use sanctions to change a target's objectionable policy in three ways:

- Limit military capabilities: prevent a target from aggression by denying or at least reducing its military capabilities: for example, arms embargoes, Iran and North Korea nuclear nonproliferation sanctions, technology export controls against Russia during its 2022 Ukraine war.
- Foreign policy restraint: deter or compel change in aggressive or otherwise threatening foreign policies; for example, UN

1990–1991 sanctions against Iraq over Kuwait invasion, 1980 US sanctions against Soviet Union over Afghanistan, 2016–2017 China sanctions against South Korea over THAAD missile deployment, 2014 and 2022 sanctions against Russia over Ukraine.

• Domestic political change: promote democratic elections and protect human rights, as with EU and US against various authoritarian regimes, and in their most extensive form incite regime change (Cuba, Venezuela).

Secondary objectives are efforts to signal resolve beyond the immediate issue of target policy change in one or more of the following ways:

• Target deterrence: deter further objectionable action by the target even if immediate policy change is not compelled.
• Third party deterrence: deter other international actors from taking action comparable to what the target did.[11]
• Symbolic action: affirm core international norms and national values when atrocities are committed, human rights violated, or democracy repressed.

One can find various combinations of these secondary objectives in almost every case.

How Are Sanctions Supposed to Achieve Their Objectives?

Initial power balance factors like trade dominance-dependence and relative military strength are useful starting points. But whether sanctions achieve their objectives depends on the strategic interaction of sender, target, and third parties each playing out its strategies.

Sender Strategy

What is the overall strategy of which sanctions are a part? Sanctions are rarely the only instrument by which a sender seeks to achieve its objectives. An ambassador may be recalled, offers made to negotiate, other diplomatic initiatives taken. Military force may be threatened or used. Covert operations may be launched. In none of the cases that follow were sanctions the only action the US, China, Russia, or other sender states took. Nor for the UN, whose sanctions were almost always accompanied by diplomacy and mediation and often by peacekeeping.

How does the sender manage its domestic politics? What is the mix of sanctions support and opposition at home? Even if there is little chance of achieving primary or secondary objectives, there may be domestic political benefits in avoiding don't-just-stand-there-do-something criticism. British political opposition leader David Lloyd George, hoping to make the Conservative Party government's inaction over Mussolini's 1935 Abyssinia (Ethiopia) invasion an issue in the upcoming election, lamented that the League of Nations sanctions "came too late to save Abyssinia from subjugation by Italy, but they are just in the nick of time to save the British Government."[12] A study using data from US presidential approval ratings shows "playing to the home crowd" political benefits even when sanctions were not expected to succeed.[13] In some cases the politics are directed at special interest constituencies (e.g., Cuban Americans). On the other hand, sanctions can backfire politically, the classic case being the 1980 Soviet grain embargo as a factor in President Jimmy Carter's re-election loss to Ronald Reagan. Non-democracies also can have their own domestic politics to manage if the imposition of sanctions significantly damages the interests of elites key to the regime's grip on power, as we'll see more in Chapter 3.[14]

Target Counterstrategy: Even when senders have major economic advantages, target states can have five main counterstrategies to reduce costs incurred from the sanctions. One is import substitution and shortage management. Rhodesia increased domestic manufacturing from 602 products when UN sanctions were first imposed in 1965 to 3,837 five years later.[15] By so weakening the Iranian currency (the rial) and making imported goods so expensive, sanctions were what *The Economist* called "a boon for [Iranian] manufacturers serving the home market of 83 million."[16]

Another is to cushion influential elites so that they act as "circuit breakers" not "transmission belts."[17] To the extent that their interests are served by resisting the policy change sought by the coercer state, elites break the external pressure circuit. This, for example, is what happened in Haiti, as recounted by a UNICEF official at the time: "The Haitian army, by seizing control of the black market in embargoed goods, especially fuel, was also able to realize huge windfall profits, [and] . . . produce resources the army needed to create and maintain the paramilitary group . . . to carry out its massive campaign of terror, rape and murder against the population."[18] If, on the other hand, elites' interests are significantly damaged or otherwise served by making the policy concessions demanded, they serve as transmission belts passing on and even intensifying the pressure on the regime to comply. The circuit breakers–transmission belt shift in elite interests over time was a key factor in US and UK sanctions against Libya and Muammar Qaddafi, eventually leading to the 2003 agreement settling some major terrorism cases and dismantling weapons of mass destruction programs in exchange for the lifting of some sanctions.[19] We also see this in the South Africa anti-apartheid sanctions case in which the economic costs as well as the banning from international sports prompted an increasing number of Afrikaners to transmit pressures internally "to abandon apartheid and to opt for a negotiated transition to democracy."[20]

Spurring nationalist will to resist can be another counterstrategy. "The best means for preserving a state, to prevent rebellion . . . and to maintain the good will of subjects," as an old adage has it, "is to have an enemy."[21] This can be true in democracies no less than autocracies. The latter of course also are more apt to turn to outright political repression.

Countersanctions against the target may also be used. Russia tried this against the US and the EU in the two Ukraine cases, the 2014 limited intervention and annexation of Crimea and the 2022 massive invasion. This is what the 2020–2021 tit-for-tat between the US and China was all about. In some instances the countermoves cross over into other domains, as with Iran's September 2019 attack on two Saudi oil processing facilities retaliating for the Trump administration's increased sanctions.

Most of all, targets look for third parties able and willing to be alternative trade partners.

Third Parties: Third parties are most likely to cooperate with the sender state when sanctions also serve their interests. To the extent that interests diverge, they are less likely to do so. Those interests may be economic motivations, avoiding the loss of trade that would come with joining the sanctions, as well as potential gains for trade by moving into markets the sender state leaves. They may be political, as with the Cold War geopolitical protector role the West took on with Tito's Yugoslavia amid Soviet sanctions and the Soviets did with Castro's Cuba amid American sanctions. Neighboring states may also play a role, as the Dominican Republic did in the Haiti sanctions and Liberia, Sierra Leone, Côte d'Ivoire did for and against each other.

Even when there is formal agreement for sanctions cooperation, enforcement against sanctions busting can be difficult.[22] Syria managed to set up shell companies in the Virgin Islands, Lebanon, and elsewhere to break through the sanctions against the Bashar Assad regime. The Myanmar military kept accessing imports for its own luxuries and found dealers to keep selling its "king of woods" teak in Europe. Iran devised schemes to get its oil out via late night secret transfers at sea.[23] Russian oligarchs sanctioned in 2022 found safe havens for their superyachts and other assets in a number of countries.[24] And these are just a few examples. Black markets remain abundant and tempting, and now with cryptocurrencies even more manipulable.

* * *

This, then, is the What, Who, Why, and How of economic sanctions. With key terminology defined and the analytic framework delineated, we turn in the next chapter to questions of how to measure sanctions success.

2

DO SANCTIONS WORK?

MEASURING SUCCESS

No, many argue, sanctions don't work. Time and again they have proven "unsuccessful as a means of influence in the international system."[1] Compared to military force, covert action, and other such classically hard power instruments, sanctions have "little independent usefulness."[2] Yes, others argue, they do work, their utility gets "systematically underestimated" by studies that "accentuate the negative and downplay the positive aspects."[3] Indeed, two experienced policymakers write, for the US they are "a robust—and improving—geoeconomic tool."[4]

In Chapter 3 we discuss different theories explaining why and how sanctions do or don't work. First, though, we need to take up three main questions for measuring whether or not there is success:

- What actually constitutes a sanctions case?
- Which metrics best indicate success?
- Are sanctions ethical?

Case Counting: What Constitutes a Sanctions Case?

There is no agreed definition of what constitutes a sanctions case. The major sanctions databases provide differing case counts.[5] A number of factors come into play.

Scope of objectives: While some studies include sanctions used principally for trade wars and other economic objectives, I keep the focus on sanctions principally geared to foreign policy and political objectives given the varying political and policy dynamics noted in Chapter 1.[6]

Sanctions threats: Studies also differ on including cases in which sanctions achieved their objectives through threats without having to actually be imposed. Encompassing threats can correct for negative skewing of success scores, both sender and target often having incentives to agree before further escalation. The question remains, though, of the parameters of such a threat. Drezner poses it as "an articulated demand."[7] But articulated by whom: a head of state, other top foreign policy official, a senator or member of parliament? And articulated largely rhetorically, say an off-the-cuff tweet (or the pre-Twitter rough equivalent), or having to be embodied in a démarche or other formal diplomatic mechanism?[8] Even then, as in many areas of strategic bargaining, the most effective threats may be through quiet diplomacy and thus less noticeable.

Single case or episodes: Should different sets of sanctions imposed over time against the same target count as a single case or be analytically separated out as "episodes" differentiated by changes in the combinations of sanctions imposed, shifting objectives, and broader strategic context?[9] On the one hand, there is some value in breaking down into discrete episodes and assessing the impact of particular sets of sanctions within particular slices of timeframe in pursuit of particular objectives; for example, the varying impacts of different sets of UN sanctions in the Liberia and Côte d'Ivoire cases to be discussed in Chapter 8. On the other hand, there can be a cumulative effect better gauged by single-case treatment;

for example, US, UN, and UK sanctions against Libya over a number of years finally culminating in the 2003 agreement to dismantle its weapons of mass destruction (WMD) programs and reduce terrorism.[10]

Individually targeted sanctions: Targeted sanctions singling out particular individuals, companies and other entities present another counting problem, especially with their increasing use. The US Treasury Office of Foreign Assets Control Specially Designated Nationals and Blocked Persons (SDNs) List has included over 15,000 entries. Cases like Iran, Venezuela, North Korea, Russia, and China show one SDN designation after another, as do non-country-specific ones such as narcotics trafficking and terrorism. Similar dilemmas arise with the EU Consolidated Financial Sanctions List and UN Consolidated Security Council List. It wouldn't make sense to treat each individually targeted sanction as a discrete case, but how best to aggregate and separate is open to interpretation.

Third-party deterrent effects: While US nuclear nonproliferation sanctions often have failed to get the states against which they are targeted to stop ongoing nuclear weapons development programs, their "secret success" has been in their secondary objectives of deterring some other states from initiating nuclear weapons development.[11] Yet these third-party indirect effects tend not to be counted as sanctions cases.

Informal cued sanctions: Should informal sanctions like the ones China frequently uses, cued more than promulgated, be counted? To the extent that they are included, how to count them: when coinciding with formal sanctions, keeping them separate or bundled; targeted company by targeted company, which may show differential effects but can end up quite a long list?

Civil society–initiated sanctions: What about cases like Gandhi's 1930 salt boycott intended, as he put it, for "shaking the foundations of the British Empire?"[12] Global consumer boycotts of rainforest timber targeted at Brazil's policies as well as at Weyerhaeuser and other lumber companies?

The New York City Metropolitan Opera cutting ties with a Russian soprano, Eurovision banning Russian contestants over Ukraine? World Rugby and World Cricket banning South Africa over apartheid?

Summary

Since it does not seem possible to singularly define the universe of cases, three caveats are in order. First, researchers need to be explicit about their definitions and criteria for inclusion. Second, be particularly conscious of possible case/data selection effects on the validity of empirical findings and especially the generalizability of analytic conclusions. Third, comparable tempering applies to policy lessons as to when and how sanctions can be effective.

Which Metrics Best Measure Success?

A 2019 US Government Accountability Office (GAO) Report was unusually frank about how thin the operative definition of success is within a government that uses sanctions as much as the US does. Impact typically gets measured in economic terms with few "assessments of the effectiveness of sanctions in achieving broader U.S. policy goals."[13] True, some success is inherent in the very imposition of costs. The regime has more burdens to bear. Targeted sanctions hit its supporters' bank accounts. Regime allies, who may also be adversaries of the sender, get pinched by having to ante up more support.[14] But even substantial economic costs have often not led to policy compliance. Pakistani prime minister Nawaz Sharif defiantly declared that his people would absorb sanctions, even "eat grass," rather than give up its nuclear weapons. Sanctions against North Korea have imposed plenty of costs, but its nuclear weapons programs have grown ever bigger. President Trump's "maximum pressure" pushed Iranian oil exports down from over 2 million barrels per day to less than 300,000,

GDP tanked by −10 percent, and the rial had to be so devalued that the regime renamed it the *toman* with unit revaluation 10,000 to 1—but Iran refused to comply, indeed escalated on a number of fronts. Cuba has borne American sanctions for over half a century, yet the regime has stayed very much in place. In some cases it's even been senders that conceded despite having imposed substantial costs on the target.[15]

Five additional factors have to be wrestled with in measuring sanctions success: degrees of success, net assessment, relativity to other policy options, timeframe for assessment, and false positives/false negatives.[16]

Degrees of success: For all the rhetoric about getting a target to "say uncle," sanctions have rarely if ever coerced such full policy compliance. There is no sanctions equivalent of unconditional surrender. Various studies thus have developed scales for degrees of success; for example, TIES' total acquiescence by the target, partial acquiescence, negotiated settlement, stalemate, and capitulation by the sender.[17] Account also needs to be taken of whether secondary signaling objectives are achieved even if primary ones are not. Do sanctions provide leverage against further objectionable action by the target even if the immediate issue is not resolved? Is there a deterrent effect on third parties? Does a target get meaningfully stigmatized, international norms affirmed, and national soft power enhanced by standing up for principles whether policy gets changed or not?

While these can be valid gradations, two further considerations have to be taken into account. One is prioritization of objectives and relative weight of each. While sanctions shouldn't be deemed a total failure just because the primary objective is not achieved, success can't be claimed just because they weren't a total failure. That may be de rigueur for political speeches, but analytic attribution has to take into account which objectives had what relative importance.

Second is not accepting declaratory claims at face value and assessing whether signals sent were the ones received.

Sanctions that have less impact than advertised can weaken deterrence directed at both the target and third parties. Symbolic action can be more self-actualizing, garnering immediate credit for standing up for what's right, although less so if the sender doesn't also impose sanctions against allies that commit flagrant violations of their own.

Net assessment: Even when objectives are achieved, net assessments need to be made taking into account four types of costs potentially incurred: backfiring, misfiring, cross-firing, and shooting in the foot. Backfiring means having effects counterproductive to the intended target state policy change. A study of ninety-five countries for 1981–2000 shows how sanctioned regimes often cracked down even more on human rights including torture and political killings.[18] These include Cuba, which has repeatedly manipulated US sanctions as rationales for further repression, and China, which responded to the sanctions imposed for the 1989 Tiananmen Square massacre by strengthening the People's Armed Police and intensifying policing of the Internet.[19]

Misfiring gets at humanitarian effects of hitting the populace not just the regime, the "civilian pain" even if there is "political gain." In a number of cases, sanctions worsened life expectancy, infant mortality, child malnutrition, women's health, overall public health, poverty, clean water and sanitation, and refugees and internally displaced persons.[20] "The regime elites continue to flourish, they continue to get luxury goods, they continue to do their shopping trips," a former top US sanctions official observed. "It is generally the people of the jurisdiction that pay the ultimate penalty from the poverty inflicted on that government."[21] We come back to issues of humanitarian impact in the next section as not just an instrumental net assessment but as a fundamental ethical question.

Cross-firing entails negative effects on third-party states that are allies or partners of the sender. In cases such as Iran and Soviet/Russian energy pipelines, sanctions at times have been contentious issues in US-European relations.[22] American ally Colombia has borne heavy burdens from the Venezuela sanctions, Jordan and Turkey from the Iraq and Syria ones.

Shooting in the foot entails self-inflicted costs from forgoing trade and other economic interests with the target. In some instances the willingness to bear costs can be, as in Thomas Schelling's formulation, "a standard indicator of the intensity of one's resolve" and thus in certain situations "a desirable attribute."[23] In other situations, not. Napoleon's 1806–1810 Continental Blockade seeking to weaken the British economy as part of his war strategy proved very costly to his own economy.[24] The US-China sanctions-countersanctions tit-for-tat that began in the Trump administration and continued into the Biden administration prompted one former US trade official to remark that "You want to find sanctions that hurt the perpetrators of the law without shooting yourself in the foot, and it's a difficult exercise."[25]

Taking such consequences into account may well lead to a net negative net assessment, with sanctions not just carrying costs but worsening the very objectives for which they are intended. *Relativity to other policy options:* What sanctions did or did not achieve and at what cost also must be assessed relative to other possible policy options.[26] Policymakers emphasize this point. If not sanctions, then what? Business as usual has a derogatory ring strategically, politically, and normatively. But sanctions shouldn't be resorted to as the default option based more on the negatives of other options than persuasive analysis of sanctions' own probable efficacy.* Not-as-bad-as-the-others must not preclude assessment of its own feasibility and utility.[27]

---

*. I know from my own experience in government that framing the sanctions option in ways that satisfy the appearance of doing something tough and in the moment can crowd out potentially more effective policy options. No "darn bureaucrats" slur here, as I've written those memos myself—just an empirical point.

Timeframe for assessment: Most studies of anti-apartheid sanctions against South Africa before Nelson Mandela's 1990 release from political prison deemed them a failure. Analyses since then almost all see South Africa as a success story, indeed for many an iconic case.[28] On the other hand, a timeframe can't be so open-ended as to keep giving sanctions more and more time to achieve their objectives, as defenders of close to a half-century of US sanctions against Cuba keep falling back on.

Availability of information can be another timeframe assessment issue. Objectives may be being achieved but the target regime prevents confirming information from getting out. Or sender state policymakers with more far-reaching objectives do their own obfuscation and denial. The 1990s UN Security Council sanctions against Iraq for its invasion of Kuwait and accompanying international inspections to ensure dismantlement of its WMD development programs is a case in point on both counts. Having the belief out there that he still had WMD served Saddam's purposes both for internal prestige and his own version of deterrence. Post-9/11, it became a useful pretext for the Bush administration's 2003 invasion of Iraq—he must be developing WMD or why else would he have kicked the UN inspectors out back in 1998? Once the US military occupation began, it became clear that sanctions had been a key factor stopping Saddam from developing WMD.[29]

False positives/false negatives: Given that sanctions are part of a broader strategy inclusive of a number of other policy instruments—for instance, diplomatic actions such as ambassadorial recall or expulsion, covert action, threats or uses of military force—how to get at their particular effectiveness or ineffectiveness?[30] The challenge is to avoid either false positives or false negatives. False positives are cases in which success is attributed to sanctions when other parts of the overall strategy warrant the causal credit. False negatives are cases in which sanctions did their job but other parts of the overall strategy were flawed, or ones in which sanctions could have succeeded had mistakes of policy design and/or implementation not been made. Policymakers need to be both leery of false positives overestimating sanctions efficacy and discriminating within bottom-line strategy failure assessments in which sanctions were or could have been effective.

Are Sanctions Ethical?

Even if sanctions come through the instrumental metrics as a success, if they impose major humanitarian consequences on target populations are they ethical? What about that civilian pain that may accompany political gain? The 1990s Iraq sanctions, while succeeding in disarming Saddam's WMD programs, hit the populace as "sanctions of mass destruction" with thousands of deaths from malnutrition, lack of necessary medical supplies, inadequate drinking water, and poor sanitation.[31] In Serbia, while sanctions helped bring Slobodan Milosevic to the negotiating table, they pushed close to 80 percent of the population below the poverty line.[32]

Add to these cases in which there has been even less political gain yet quite substantial misfired civilian pain. Iran: "Iranians' access to essential medicine and their right to health is being negatively impacted . . . thereby threatening the health of millions of Iranians." North Korea: "Sanctions are impeding the ability of the country and of international aid organizations to meet the urgent and long-standing humanitarian needs of the most vulnerable parts of the population. . . . Lifesaving aid is being fatally obstructed by delays, red tape, and overcompliance with financial sanctions."[33] In Haiti a former US ambassador assessed the sanctions as having set back the already impoverished Haitian economy another fifteen years, with the poor bearing the bulk of the burden while the regime and supporters were minimally affected. This led to such takeoffs in Creole on *anbago* (embargo) as *anba gwo*, meaning "under the heels of the rich and powerful."[34] "The economic situation in #Syria is at breaking point," a Syrian journalist tweeted in June 2020. "Medicine is very scarce, hunger is becoming a

normality, poverty is at the worst-point ever, people even selling their organs to survive."[35] "An avalanche of hunger and
destitution" is how the UN World Food Program characterized
the situation in Afghanistan as the 2021–2022 winter set in,
with anti-Taliban foreign sanctions a major cause.[36]

Targeted sanctions were designed to resolve this with their
ostensibly precision-guided capacity to hit the regime and
not the people. But their effects also often have proven difficult to confine just to those explicitly targeted.[37] From his
experience as Special Rapporteur of the UN Human Rights
Council, Idriss Jazairy observed how sanctions that start out
targeted over time get piled on one after the other to the point
of becoming "sector-wide measures that will inevitably have
society-wide repercussions."[38] Chilling effects ripple through
the economy as firms facing prohibitive due diligence costs
to ensure compliance and fearing the consequences of an ac-
cidental violation "de-risk" in ways that also cut off NGOs
doing humanitarian work.[39] Proposals have been made for
striking a balance by having policymakers considering the
use of sanctions take into account the impact on target state
domestic politics, establish procedures and authority for accountability, carve out humanitarian exemptions, and commit
to post-sanctions reconstruction and development.[40] The Swiss
Network of International Studies has a project on better man-
aging de-risking and mitigating humanitarian consequences.
In my own discussions with NGOs, some have conveyed
strategies for making humanitarian exemptions work and still
getting assistance to the people.

Even if such mechanisms can be devised, some nevertheless
see the negative consequences of sanctions as so unavoidable
and so disproportionate in their civilian pain as to be inherently "morally impermissible."[41] Others counter that the goal
of removing or limiting the power of brutal rulers like Fidel,
Saddam, Milosevic, Central African Republic dictator Bokassa
I, the Myanmar military, the Taliban, and the like has its own
ethical value. Each in their own way privileges intentionalist

ethics over consequentialist ones. Pro-sanctionists stress the responsibility not to be bystanders to leaders and regimes so dangerous to their own people and to the international community but are left with the humanitarian consequences of doing so. Anti-sanctionists stress the intention not to hurt civilians but are left with the consequences of continued repressive and brutal rule.

* * *

Measuring sanctions success thus poses conceptual and methodological challenges. These can't be singularly resolved, but they can be managed. Scholars need to be clear about constructs and measures being used, and explicit about the bases for as well as the limits of analytic conclusions and empirical findings. Policymakers need to take these criteria and differentiations into account, and ethical issues as well, in deciding whether to impose sanctions and assessing success and failure.

The follow-on question is how to explain when, how, and why sanctions do or do not succeed. That's for Chapter 3.

3

EXPLAINING SANCTIONS SUCCESS/FAILURE

Building from Chapter 2's focus on measuring sanctions success/failure, we next consider key factors explaining those outcomes. For scholarly research this is the independent variables question, identifying factors that have a high probability of determining sanctions success or failure and theorizing patterns of causality. For policymakers it's about matching the most important factors with the particular case at hand to formulate a viable strategy.

Seven main questions structure this chapter:

- Is economic impact the key factor?
- Are sanctions more effective if backed by threats or use of military force?
- Is a reciprocity strategy, sanctions and inducements together, more effective than sanctions alone?
- What about regime type, with regard to both sender state and target state?
- Do multilateral sanctions work better than unilateral ones?
- How effective are smart sanctions, and particularly financial sanctions?
- Does success vary with the type of objective?

Is Economic Impact the Key Factor?

Necessary but Not Sufficient

Sanctions that don't have much economic impact obviously have little chance of coercing policy compliance or signaling credibility. Some success is inherent in the very imposition of costs. The target's economy gets burdened; leaders and supporters get punished. But there is no one-to-one correlation demonstrating that the greater the economic impact, the more likely is policy compliance.[1] This holds even when the target has high economic dependence on the sender.[2] Initial costs may be high, but target states can bring to bear counterstrategies both economic (import substitution, alternative trade partners, sanctions busting) and political (cushioning elites, mobilizing nationalist will to resist, outright repression). We see various versions of the economic impact–policy compliance discrepancy in cases that follow, including Rhodesia, Iran, North Korea, Iraq, and Côte d'Ivoire.

Are Sanctions More Effective If Backed by Threats or Use of Military Force?

Less So Than One Might Think

"Diplomacy without arms," as the old adage attributed to Frederick the Great conveys the basic logic, "is like music without instruments."[3] Yet there is no consistent causal pattern in the sanctions literature. In the case of Rhodesia, it was in part the 1966–1979 UN sanctions but mostly the guerrilla war that ended white minority rule. If Russia is forced to end its 2022 invasion of Ukraine, it will be because of the combination of sanctions and Ukrainian military resistance supported by US and NATO weapons and other assistance. In one multi-case study, though, while fifteen of twenty-four sanctions successes involved military force, so too did seventeen of thirty-nine ineffective cases.[4] While favorable balances of military capabilities appeared to advantage sanctions sender states, these often have been offset by greater target state resolve to resist. Moreover, a relative military power advantage actually can be strategically counterproductive, as it can be an allure to make greater demands than a target is likely to agree to.[5] In this regard the American penchant for using sanctions to coerce regime change in any number of militarily weaker countries (Cuba, Venezuela, Iran) not only failed to achieve that objective but missed opportunities to achieve more limited objectives (as, for example, Spain did with freeing some Cuban political dissidents).

Is a Reciprocity Strategy, Sanctions and Inducements Together, More Effective Than Sanctions Alone?

Yes, with Some Caveats

Interviews of American and Iranian negotiators who had key roles in the 2015 nuclear nonproliferation agreement (JCPOA, Joint Comprehensive Plan of Action) speak to this point. The American side stressed the costs imposed by sanctions as key to Iranian concessions. Iranian diplomats said they had only been willing to come to the table "when sanctions were coupled with economic, technological and political rewards."[6] The Libya 2003 case shows a similar pattern, credible diplomatic assurances that sanctions would be lifted if concessions were made on terrorism and WMD as key to agreement.

Given that sanctions, like other forms of coercive diplomacy, are a strategy for influencing not denying the target's choices, there must be some reciprocal terms of exchange. The negotiating strategy has to avoid both undershooting with inducements too little too late or for too much in return, and overshooting with too much too soon or for too little in return. On the one hand, the linkage to inducements has to be sufficiently definite and robust that the target does not think it can get the benefits without having to reciprocate. In the early

1990s Haiti case, for example, the carrot of reduced sanctions was offered before the military junta had sufficiently complied.[7] Conversely, if the target is too unsure that reciprocal measures will follow, it may question whether the concessions being demanded are worth the return. This is a problem for those US sanctions on which Congress limits presidential discretion to lift them without its consent. Some UN and EU sanctions have had similar policy design issues.[8] Negotiating strategy thus has to avoid both undershooting with inducements too little too late or for too much in return, and overshooting with too much too soon or for too little in return.

Even if the sanctions–inducements linkages are well-crafted, some regimes remain "hard targets," as Stephan Haggard and Marcus Noland characterize North Korea.[9] Given the severity of the North Korean economic situation at various points over the past twenty-five-plus years, including the staggering 1990s famine death toll of an estimated 3–5 percent of the population, one might have thought economic inducements would have worked especially well. It is not for nothing that North Korea is known as the "Hermit Kingdom." Haggard and Noland raise the paradox that perhaps the only inducements that could have worked would have been benefits that went directly to the regime and were of quite ample magnitude, not exactly a politically palatable strategy. Similar debates continue to play out today.

What about Regime Type, Democracies Compared to Non-democracies?

Some Tendencies but No Set Pattern

Democracies' greater openness to political contestation and public pressure would seem to make them more vulnerable to sanctions targeted at them than non-democracies. A number of studies do show democracies' susceptibility to sanctions.[10] Others show autocracies' resistance.[11]

But in three respects these are more tendencies than set patterns.

First, in some cases where the general tendency does hold, separating regime type causality from other factors is analytically difficult. Prior sender–target relations is one such factor. Various studies show sanctions against allies or friends can be more effective than those against adversaries. We see this in the Chapter 4 case study of the Suez 1956 crisis in which US sanctions were a key factor pressuring Britain—a fellow democracy but also security-dependent on the US—to withdraw from its Suez Canal military intervention. Work on US nonproliferation sanctions shows greater compliance coming from countries that were democracies but also security-dependent allies.[12] Such cases raise possible false positivity in attributing sanctions efficacy to regime type rather than to other aspects of relations.

Second, even when the economic costs have been quite substantial, democracies have not always complied. Take the 1973 OPEC oil embargo, often cited as a main example of democracies' susceptibility to sanctions. No question the American economy was hit hard. Gasoline prices skyrocketed over 400 percent. Supplies were rationed based on matching auto license plate numbers to odd and even dates for fill-ups. Inflation and unemployment simultaneously ratcheted up (stagflation). Yet American Middle East policy only changed partially, and at that in ways Secretary of State Henry Kissinger deemed consistent with shifting American geopolitical strategy. Nothing close to getting the US to OPEC's stated objective to "compel Israel to relinquish our occupied territories" was achieved.[13]

Third, the notion that non-democracies can just "hunker down and withstand the effect of sanctions" ignores the ways non-democracies have their own versions of interest group politics.[14] The circuit breakers/transmission belts distinction made in Chapter 1, whether key elites see their interests as best served by blocking the impact of sanctions or by pressuring for policy change, applies to both democracies and non-democracies. This was another factor in the Libya 2003 case as key elites shifted from circuit breakers to transmission belts as their interests were increasingly damaged by sanctions. The

1960–1962 US sanctions against Dominican Republic sugar exports that were an economic base for elites that had been supporting the Trujillo family dictatorship and 1977 military aid sanctions against the Argentine and Brazilian military juntas show similar dynamics.[15]

Do Multilateral Sanctions Work Better Than Unilateral Ones?
Yes, but Not without Their Own Problems

A number of studies do show higher success rates for multilateral sanctions. These reflect three advantages.[16] One is economic, reducing if not eliminating potential alternative trade partners and thus increasing potential economic impact. Second is political, the enhanced normative legitimacy that comes with multilateral action. Third is geopolitical, taking away possible "safe haven" protection from an adversary of a sender state.[17]

Multilateralization, though, does not guarantee success. The nature of the objective still matters; for example, UN sanctions have been more successful for secondary signaling objectives than primary policy compliance ones. So too do Security Council politics: even when sanctions get initially approved, ongoing commitments are susceptible to US-Russia-China tensions. Any number of countries may succumb to incentives to defect, particularly if sanctions busting can be done quietly. UN enforcement mechanisms, while helping somewhat, have been under-resourced.[18]

Chapter 8 goes more into the advantages as well as limits of multilateral sanctions and provides some case studies.

How Effective Are Smart Sanctions, and Particularly Financial Sanctions?
Somewhat, but Less Than Proponents Claim

The shift to smart sanctions was in part a reaction to the devastating humanitarian effects of comprehensive sanctions in

Iraq, Serbia, and Haiti. The logic is to focus on key parts of a target's economy and home in on high-value targets (offending regime, its supporters, and complicit entities), directly limiting capabilities for further proscribed action and motivating transmission belt pressure by those bearing the heavy costs while shielding the broader populace. The US made many of its sanctions "smart," the EU and UN most of theirs.

The record, though, is mixed. A study of UN 1990s targeted sanctions assesses those against Libya and Cambodia as successful, but not those against Liberia, Rwanda, Sudan, Angola, and Sierra Leone. Another UN sanctions study identifies unintended consequences in 94 percent of their episodes, including corruption and criminality in 58 percent, and target regimes becoming more authoritarian in 35 percent.[19] The 2016 US and EU sanctions against President Joseph Kabila and other top Democratic Republic of the Congo (DRC) officials helped get them to step down but the political system stayed undemocratic.[20] In a number of instances, humanitarian exemptions have proven both too much, exploited to weaken the sanctions, and too little, not enough for basic health care and other humanitarian needs to be met—in effect, not so smart, not so targeted, ethical in their intentions but not in their consequences.[21] Overall the best that could be said was that while not often successful for human rights protection, smart sanctions at least tended to be "less detrimental" than more extensive sanctions.[22]

What, though, of financial sanctions? Aren't they especially "smart," targeting financial assets and transactions? And quite impactful, especially for US sanctions given the dominance of the dollar in international finance? Whereas for many goods-based sanctions third-party incentives are to trade with the target state and reap the profits from black market pricing, a US threat to use secondary sanctions to cut off access to the global financial system dwarfs whatever short-term profits can be made with the target state. Juan Zarate, the first to hold the position of Assistant Secretary of the Treasury for

Terrorist Financing and Financial Crimes (2004), titled his book *Treasury's War: The Unleashing of a New Era of Financial Warfare*. Others since then have posed financial sanctions as a "force multiplier," a "new tool for economic warfare," one of the main weaponizable interdependences.[23]

Here too, though, the results have been mixed. Reducing terrorism financing to al Qaeda, ISIS, and others limited their capacity but did not eliminate them.[24] The Obama Iran strategy combining financial sanctions with reciprocal diplomacy worked well, but Trump's even more severe financial sanctions did not. The Myanmar military hid many of its financial assets before sanctions could freeze them. The North Korean regime has turned to Bitcoin and other cryptocurrencies for alternative financing. The Panama Papers, leaked by investigative journalists, documented numerous cases of drug traffickers, crime bosses, oligarchs, and others from a wide range of countries evading targeted sanctions.[25] And a number of financial sanctions have misfired as banks, oil companies, shippers, and others deemed it "safer to simply withdraw altogether from doing business with a sanctioned country," indeed even with humanitarian NGOs trying to aid the people in targeted countries."[26]

The Russia 2022 financial sanctions show both the scope and the limits of financial sanctions. The impact was greater than any prior financial sanctions, including those imposed after Russia's 2014 Ukraine intervention and annexation of Crimea were routinely evaded. "Oligarchs Got Richer Despite Sanctions" was how a *New York Times* story on the 2014 sanctions was titled. One oligarch still had over $90 million in various holdings in the American economy. Another increased stakes in at least seven companies in European offshore tax havens. Other had money "pinballing around the globe."[27] In 2022, though, the oligarchs were more tightly targeted. One was forced to divest ownership of the British football club Chelsea. Another had his superyacht and private jet seized in Germany. Both Putin and Foreign Minister Sergei Lavrov were directly sanctioned. Other measures hit the Russian economy broadly. Main Russian banks were cut off from the SWIFT system (Society for Worldwide Interbank Financial Transactions) through which most international dollar-denominated transactions flow. The Putin government had built up a $640 billion-plus hard currency war chest, but then had its access blocked. The ruble initially had to be devalued to the point of being worth less than a penny. Everyday Russians had to wait on long ATM lines, only to run into caps on personal account withdrawals. Even Switzerland, long known for its secret bank accounts and foreign policy neutrality, joined in the financial sanctions. So too did major banks such as Citibank and German Commerzbank and financial services companies like Goldman Sachs and JP Morgan Chase. Britain seized assets from Russian oligarchs living in London.

Yet think of what it took to mount such a massive and broadly collaborative effort. This was a brutal and blatant invasion of a small country by a big one, not just some "small war." It was in the heart of Europe, a geopolitically vital region and with echoes of World War II. And, yes, most of the people bearing the humanitarian toll were white and Christian, not of color or non-Western religions.[28] I make these points as explanation not justification, part of why these sanctions were so much more widely supported than those against atrocities in other parts of the world and reasons why their generalizability is limited.

All that support notwithstanding, even these sanctions have had their limits. Russia still has had counterstrategies to play. The Russian Central Bank imposed capital controls and other measures that brought the ruble back up in value. Some assets were hidden. Others were protected by loopholes: for example, American and European art dealers and auction houses lobbied for fine art to be exempted.[29] If over time these and the other sanctions do help end the war—as of this writing (May 2022) it is still going on—lessons will need to be carefully drawn.

Does Success Vary with the Principal Objective Being Pursued?

Yes, Limited Objectives Are More Achievable Than Extensive Ones

Limited objectives being more achievable than extensive ones is the most consensual pattern in the sanctions literature.[30] This is a matter of ends-means proportionality, which as with any coercive strategy success is most likely when the scope of objectives pursued is kept proportional to the severity of the means used. Bold rhetoric notwithstanding, sanctions do not cripple economies. No sanctions target has ever said uncle. Counterstrategies can't offset all the economic impact, but they typically can keep it sufficiently limited as to be better matched with a limited policy objective. If the stakes for the target are greater than those for the sender, the coercive effort is working against an unfavorable balance of interests.[31]

This pattern of limited objectives being more achievable than extensive ones holds across the different types of policy objectives. In cases like the Central African Republic, while not ending civil wars, arms embargoes had enough limited impact on military capabilities to help make these wars shorter and less intense.[32] Nuclear proliferation sanctions have done better at preventing acquisition (e.g., Iran) than in de-proliferating weapons already possessed (e.g., North Korea, also India and Pakistan). While arms control regimes such as the Wassenaar Agreement on conventional weapons and dual-use technologies and the Nuclear Suppliers Group on nuclear weapons–related goods and technologies have not been perfect, all have had substantial success in limiting the designated arms from being acquired by designated countries.[33]

With regard to foreign policy restraint, limited policy change has been achieved in such cases as the American-British sanctions getting Qaddafi's Libya in 2003 to reduce although not end terrorism, and China's 2016–2017 sanctions getting South Korea to agree not to deploy additional THAAD missile defense systems but not dismantle the existing one. More extensive objectives such as the League of Nations' 1935–1936 sanctions pressuring Mussolini to withdraw from Ethiopia/ Abyssinia and the US 1980 sanctions against the Soviet Union for its invasion of Afghanistan were not achieved. When invasions have been reversed, as with the British 1956 Suez invasion, sanctions were combined with diplomatic and security measures.

Domestic political change does have two cases, Rhodesia and South Africa, in which sanctions helped bring about the equivalent of regime change. But as these Chapter 4 case studies show, the array of factors that came together in each were very much the exception. Regime change failures as in Cuba, Venezuela, and Iran are more the rule. As to more limited objectives of promoting democratization and protecting human rights, the evidence is mixed. Some studies see a significant degree of success, citing aggregate data showing a greater degree of democratization by sanctioned authoritarian regimes (although even that only as a degree and not to the point of becoming democracies).[34] Others find that sanctioned regimes crack down further with even greater repression.[35]

Given their nature as preventing actions not yet taken and symbolically affirming principles, inherently more limited objectives than compelling change in actions already taken, secondary signaling objectives tend to have more success than primary policy change ones.[36] Still, such signaling can't just be taken at face value. Target and third-party deterrence are not just matters of declaratory policy. They have to be assessed as strategic interaction taking into account whether the signal sent is the one received. Sanctions that are less than advertised can be seen by the target as signs of weakness not strength. Third-party adversaries may not be much deterred nor allies much reassured by a threat to hurt a target that doesn't actually hurt it very much. And while some success comes with the very affirmation of human rights and other international norms, ethical issues raised by any backfiring and misfiring in worsening human rights conditions on the ground also have to be net-assessed.

* * *

No single factor explains sanctions success or failure. We can, though, establish patterns and tendencies that provide some theoretical framework and policy parameters. Summing up:

- Economic impact, actual or the credible threat thereof, is necessary but not sufficient for sanctions success, often leaving a high economic impact–low policy compliance gap.
- Military superiority and military force do not consistently add to sanctions success.
- Reciprocal diplomacy linking sanctions and inducements is more effective than sanctions on their own.
- Regime type differences between democracies and non-democracies show some tendencies but no set pattern of either relative vulnerability as sanctions targets or relative effectiveness as sanctions senders.
- Multilateral sanctions have some advantages over unilateral ones, although with their own constraints.
- Smart sanctions have a mixed record, financial sanctions included.
- Limited objectives are more achievable than extensive ones for reasons of ends-means proportionality and balance of interests.

Part II

MAJOR CASES, THEORY
APPLIED, POLICY ANALYZED

4

HISTORICAL PERSPECTIVE

LESSONS FROM PAST SANCTIONS CASES

This chapter applies the Chapter 1 why-what-who-how sanctions analytic framework to seven cases, some from centuries past and others more recent history, selected with three main criteria in mind: demonstrate the complexities inherent to the use of sanctions; vary the principal sender states; and reflect debates over success and failure applying key measures and ideas from Chapters 2 and 3.[1] The seven cases are

- Athens-Sparta, Megarian Decree, 432 BC
- Napoleon's Continental System, 1808–1814
- League of Nations, Italian invasion of Ethiopia, 1935
- Suez crisis, US sanctions against Britain, 1956
- British and UN sanctions against Rhodesia, 1966–1979
- OPEC sanctions against the US and global markets, 1973
- Anti-apartheid sanctions against South Africa, 1962–1994

The concluding section draws out cross-case patterns along the lines of the analytic and methodological challenges raised in Chapters 2 and 3.

Athens-Sparta, Megarian Decree, 432 BC

This tends to be the earliest case cited in the economic sanctions literature. The Megaran Decree was a set of economic sanctions issued in 432 BC by Pericles, the fabled leader of Athens in its golden age of democracy and its Delian League empire of over 300 city-states and islands, against Megara, a small city-state allied with Sparta in its Peloponnesian League.

WHY Did Athens Impose Sanctions against Megara?

The historical record is unclear on the direct precipitating event for the Megarian Decree. Thucydides does not discuss it in his *History of the Peloponnesian War*. Yale historian Donald Kagan points to Megara's support for Corinth's attacks against Athenian ally Corcyra, a foreign policy restraint objective in our terms. Oxford historian Sir Alfred Zimmern sees it as a show of resolve to deter Sparta and its allies from further attacks.[2] The ancient Greek playwright Aristophanes quite colorfully cites counter-kidnappings of prostitutes, first of a Megaran courtesan by Athenian "young drunkards" and then by Megarans of "two harlots" related to Pericles' lover Aspasia.[3]

WHAT Types of Sanctions Were Imposed?

Megara was banned from trading with Athens and all the Delian League empire. The sanctions were comprehensive with no exceptions for any individual commodities.

WHO Were the Key Actors?

Sender (city-)state: Athens, Athens-controlled Delian League
Target (city-)state: Megara
Third parties: Megara's patron Sparta and other Peloponnesian allies.

HOW Did the Sanctions Play Out?

Kagan attributes major economic impact to the decree. Megara's northerly position on the Isthmus of Corinth put much of its trade flow within territories under Athenian control, and limited the utility of turning to alternative trade partners among the Peloponnesian League. It did not, though, deter war. The Peloponnesian Wars broke out the following year. They lasted twenty-six years, with a six-year truce intertwined. Sparta won, Athens surrendered, and the golden age of Athenian democracy gave way to an oligarchy imposed by Sparta. Henry Bienen and Robert Gilpin are quite harsh in their assessment of the sanctions as having boomeranged, precipitating the war and leading "to the weakening of Greek civilization and its eventual conquest by Macedonian imperialism."[4] Thucydides, though, sees Pericles as having sought a middle ground between attacking Megara and doing nothing, trying to deter but not provoke, but with the causes of war running deeper to the rivalry between an established power and a rising power.[5]

Case Assessment

While following Thucydides in not attributing principal causality for the Peloponnesian Wars, the Megaran Decree sanctions still warrant a failure assessment. It may well be, as David Baldwin argues, "the probability of war was fairly great to begin with; and perhaps nothing he [Pericles] could have done would have avoided it."[6] But the very deterrent objectives that Baldwin stresses were not achieved. The Megaran Decree may not have been a major cause of the war, but it did not succeed in avoiding war—and the consequences for Athens were enormous.

Napoleon's Continental System, 1806-1814

In 1806 as a further measure in his wars to conquer Europe, French emperor-general Napoleon Bonaparte imposed sweeping economic sanctions against principal rival Great Britain. British exports to the vast swath of continental Europe that Napoleon had conquered (Belgium, Netherlands, much of Italy, Austria, much of Germany, Poland, Spain) were boycotted, and continental exports to Britain embargoed—thus the name "Continental System." In addition, neutral country ships coming directly from Britain or its colonies were first banned from European ports and then threatened with seizure. While substantial costs were imposed on Britain, the combination of self-incurred economic costs, British retaliatory measures, and counterproductive effects on Napoleon's overall military position made the Continental System a significant factor in Napoleon's ultimate defeat in 1814.

WHY Did Napoleon Impose Economic Sanctions against Britain?

"England is lost," Napoleon believed, if he could "enforce a prohibition on her industrial products in Europe, for to destroy her trade is to deal her a blow in the heart."[7] His Grand Army of England, some 100,000 troops, was ready to invade. Short of that, he sought to bring the British to the negotiating table in such a weak position that they would have to accept the French continental empire. Either way, the objective was to compel Britain into foreign policy restraint.

WHAT Types of Sanctions Were Imposed?

Principally trade sanctions. British exports to continental Europe were boycotted, including re-transited goods from British colonies. Continental European exports to Britain were embargoed. Finance effects followed from the inability of Britain to have gold inflow in payments for its manufactures—although without British purchases, less gold also flowed into Napoleon's treasury and the coffers of his conquered countries.

WHO Were the Key Actors?

Sender state: France. Its vassal states and allies, with varying degrees of willingness, joined the Continental System in waves: Spain, Italy, and Holland at its inception in 1806; Russia, Denmark, Portugal, and Prussia in 1807; Sweden in 1810.

Target state: Britain

Third parties: Russia and the US

HOW Did the Sanctions Play Out?

Substantial costs were imposed on Britain. British exports fell from £40.8 million in 1806 to £35.2 million in 1808, with further declines in ensuing years. Food supplies were especially hard hit, plummeting grain imports coming amid bad harvests. Lower demand for British manufacture exports caused wages to fall and unemployment to rise, feeding a wave of labor strikes in 1811.

But France incurred quite substantial costs of its own. Napoleon's envoy in Hamburg, for example, felt compelled to circumvent the import sanctions to procure considerably cheaper British clothing to supply France's own army. Within France itself, some industries highly dependent on overseas trade suffered, while less-efficient ones lacking a competitive advantage saw gains under the protectionist regime. These competing interests at times forced Napoleon to weaken or circumvent his own Continental System in response to domestic industrial demands. The system of licenses for trade with Britain favored French commercial interests over those of the rest of the continent, breeding resentment across the empire including among elites deprived of luxuries like coffee, sugar, tobacco, and cocoa from British colonies. These resentments are frequently cited as a reason Napoleon's allies eventually abandoned him. And all along there was plenty of smuggling, aided by continued British naval dominance. As economic historian

Eli Heckscher nicely puts it, "to keep the English away from the Continent by blockade without possessing fleets is just as impossible as to forbid the birds to build their nests in our country."[8]

The US, hit hard by the sanctions against neutral country ships, retaliated with the Embargo Act of 1807 prohibiting American ships from trading with either Britain or France. While this denied Britain cotton for its mills and grain for its food supply, and France the raw materials for its economy and war machine, the fledgling American economy also incurred substantial costs.

By 1810, both because of its dependence on British trade and due to its geopolitical concerns about Napoleon gaining too much power too close to its borders, Russia started reducing cooperation with the Continental System. In June 1812, Napoleon made the fateful decision to launch his Moscow Campaign, which had disastrous consequences. Less than six months later, the toll of Russian resistance and the early onset of a brutal winter killed over 50 percent of his 700,000 soldiers. Another 100,000 were captured. Napoleon was forced to retreat. He did so amid, as Carl von Clausewitz wrote in one of his earliest treatises, "the utter destruction of his army. . . . Besides himself, his principal generals, and a couple of thousand officers, he brought away nothing of the whole army worth mentioning."[9]

On another front, Britain stepped up its support for Spain in its fight against Napoleon's brother Joseph Bonaparte, who had been installed on the Spanish throne. Under the command of Lt. General Sir Arthur Wellesley (who later would become the 1st Duke of Wellington), British forces won key battles and retook Madrid. In the winter of 1813–1814, French forces were forced to retreat across the Pyrenees.

Case Assessment

"I have come once and for all to finish off these barbarians of the North," Napoleon declared to his top military advisors at the start of his 1812 invasion of Russia. "The sword is now drawn. They must be pushed back into their ice, so that for the next 25 years they no longer come to busy themselves with the affairs of civilized Europe."[10] But it was he, Napoleon, who in April 1814 would be forced into exile. Many factors contributed to his fall, the counterproductive consequences of the Continental System sanctions clearly being one of them.

League of Nations, Italian Invasion of Ethiopia, 1935

On October 3, 1935, led by "Il Duce" Benito Mussolini, Italy invaded Ethiopia (also known as Abyssinia) seeking to add this African country to an expanding Italian empire. According to Article 16 of the League of Nations Covenant, any nation that committed aggression against any League member was "ipso facto . . . deemed to have committed an act of war against all other Members of the League." Accordingly, members were "immediately to subject it to the severance of all trade or financial relations, the prohibition of all intercourse between their nationals and the nationals of the Covenant-breaking state, and the prevention of all financial, commercial or personal intercourse." With Britain and France playing key roles, the League did impose sanctions against Italy—although well short of severance of all trade. Oil, coal, and steel were among the strategic commodities excluded. The diplomatic message also was quite mixed, punishing Italy albeit with some elements of appeasement out of concern that Mussolini would react by allying more closely with Hitler's Germany. While some economic costs did get imposed, a combination of third-party alternative trade partners (Hitler's Germany and League non-member US in particular) and other counterstrategies allowed Mussolini not to comply, indeed instead intensifying the warfare including resorting to chemical weapons against Ethiopian resistance.

*WHY Did the League of Nations Impose Economic
Sanctions against Mussolini's Italy?*

Foreign policy restraint was the principal objective, compelling Mussolini to end the war, although not necessarily
to fully withdraw from Ethiopia. The Hoare-Laval Plan,
developed secretly by the eponymous British and French
foreign ministers, offered to appease Italy with two-thirds
of Ethiopia's territory, leaving Ethiopian emperor Haile
Selassie not much more than a corridor to the sea. Public
outcry once the plan was leaked caused it to be withdrawn,
but the damage already had been done to any compellent
credibility.[11]

WHAT Types of Sanctions Were Imposed?

The trade-related elements of the sanctions included a boycott
on imports from Italy and an embargo on arms sales and certain exports that could be considered vital to Italy's war efforts
including horses, rubber, and some ores and metals—although
not oil, coal, or steel. On the financial side, the League sanctions
prohibited loans and credits to Italy.[12]

WHO Were the Key Actors?

> Sender states: League of Nations, with Britain and France
> playing lead roles.
> Target state: Italy
> Third parties: Germany and the US, both non-League
> members

HOW Did the Sanctions Play Out?

The sanctions did have substantial initial economic impact.
Italian exports fell 61 percent, imports 44 percent, gold reserves 23 percent. The lira had to be devalued 25 percent.[13]
Hufbauer, Schott, and Elliott estimate an $86 million welfare
loss, or 1.7 percent of Italy's gross national product.[14]

But while planning in advance for his Ethiopia invasion and anticipating League sanctions in response, Mussolini had been stockpiling key resources. He had enough oil to supply military action; the exclusion of oil from the League sanctions and the increased US supply took care of the rest of the economy. For many Italians, household income actually increased as the state drew down unemployment by enrolling men in military service and increasing employment in autarchic war-related industries.[15] Politically, Mussolini manipulated sanctions "to intensify statism and to consolidate personal rule . . . (they were) transformed by the Italian government into a case for rapid intensification of . . . nationalism."[16] The stakes of the war were cast as nothing less than Italian honor and glory. To support it was to be a patriot, as, for example, with the Day of the Wedding Ring during which women donated their gold wedding rings to the national cause, ostensibly to augment Italy's dwindling gold reserves (yet these rings were never actually melted down).[17]

Mussolini also shrewdly played on British and French fears of escalation. Mussolini never announced a more pro-Germany foreign policy but frequently hinted at that possibility. Adolf Hitler and Mussolini were not yet fully allied; their "Axis" would be sealed by Mussolini's September 1937 visit to Berlin and Hitler's May 1938 visit to Rome. But they were moving in that direction. The 11.7 percent increase in German exports to Italy helped offset the League sanctions with coal exports of particular value.

The mid-1930s Neutrality Acts passed by the US Congress cut both ways. The total prohibition on arms exports fit with the League arms embargo. But neutrality also meant not imposing other sanctions. The 10.8 percent increase in American exports to Italy included oil going from 6.5 percent of Italian oil imports to 17 percent as American oil companies saw an opportunity to expand global market share.[18]

Austria, Hungary, and a few other League members refused to comply with the sanctions and also played third-party alternative trade partner roles, albeit on a more limited basis both economically and strategically. Romania and the Soviet Union conditioned compliance on all other League oil producers doing so, which Venezuela refused to do.[19]

Britain and France had military options such as closing the Suez Canal or providing arms to Ethiopia, but they never even threatened to take such action, not even when Mussolini resorted to poison gas to hasten his victory. By May 5, 1936, Mussolini's troops had captured Addis Ababa, Ethiopia's capital. On June 7, Emperor Haile Selassie appealed to the League for "justice for my people." On July 4 by a vote of 44–1, claiming the war was over and in effect acknowledging Italian colonial acquisition of Ethiopia, the League lifted its sanctions.

Case Assessment

Years later reflecting in his diary Anthony Eden, British foreign minister at the time, wondered: "Looking back, the thought comes again, should we not have shown more determination in pressing through with sanctions in 1935, and if we had could we not have called Mussolini's bluff and at least postponed this [Second World] war? The answer, I am sure, is yes."[20] Along these lines, Mussolini is alleged to have said to Hitler that had his oil supply been embargoed, "I would have had to order a withdrawal from Abyssinia in a week . . . It would have been an unmistakable catastrophe for me."[21] Given our Chapter 3 emphasis on means-ends proportionality by which sanctions show little success in compelling military reversal, both Eden's reflections and Mussolini's musings seem a tad hyperbolic. Still, the sanctions failed. Indeed, on top of other crises like the 1931 Japanese invasion of Manchuria in which the League could not even agree to impose any economic sanctions, the Mussolini Ethiopia case was one of the last nails in the coffin of League-based collective security.

Suez Crisis, US Sanctions against Britain, 1956

On July 26, 1956, Egyptian president Gamal Abdel Nasser nationalized the Suez Canal from British control. Nasser, who came to power in a 1952 military coup against the Egyptian monarchy, had emerged as an influential leader across the Arab World and more broadly in the Third World. He justified the move as retaliation for colonial exploitation and also as providing revenues to finance the megaproject Aswan Dam for which Europe and the US had refused aid. With neither side doing much more than going through the motions diplomatically, Britain, France, and Israel planned coordinated military action. Israel invaded on October 29, Britain and France two days later. Amid the Cold War, Third World decolonization, and the Arab-Israeli conflict, risks of escalation were high. Two main factors averted escalation and led to resolution of the crisis. Skilled diplomacy led by UN Secretary-General Dag Hammarskjöld was one.[22] American sanctions imposed by the Eisenhower administration against Britain, embargoing oil and blocking financial support, was the other.[23]

WHY Did the US Impose Sanctions on the UK, One of Its Closest Allies?

Foreign policy restraint, compelling an end to the military invasion, was the principal objective. While President Eisenhower shared concerns about the Canal nationalization and other Nasser actions, the British-French-Israeli invasion threatened American strategic interests in four respects. First, too close an association with European colonialism hurt American standing among other newly decolonizing independent countries. Second, the Soviets were exploiting the Suez crisis for gains in Cold War competition in the Arab world and Third World broadly. Third, American criticism of the Soviet invasion of Hungary, which occurred at the same time, wasn't very credible with its close allies in the middle of their own invasion. Fourth, at a time when Americans viewed the UN largely

positively, it was important to show that it could peacefully resolve conflicts. When the invasion occurred despite American
entreaties and without warning, the Eisenhower team was left
with a sense that they "had been lied to for weeks by America's
closest allies."[24]

WHAT Types of Sanctions Were Imposed?

Between Nasser's closure of the Canal blocking oil tankers
from transiting and Syrian-Iraqi oil pipelines getting blown
up, Britain lost about two-thirds of its oil imports. Eisenhower
rebuffed appeals to offset these shortages with more American
produced oil, in effect embargoing anything more than the
limited oil the US had been providing pre-crisis.

Various financial sanctions also were imposed. Requests for
American loans were denied. American leverage within the
International Monetary Fund blocked multilateral lending. At
the same time a $2 billion loan if troops were withdrawn was
offered as an incentive.

WHO Were the Key Actors?

Sender state: US
Target state: UK, and to a lesser extent France and Israel
Third parties: not many. The US dominated global financial
    markets. Saudi Arabia and other Arab oil producers also
    embargoed oil.

HOW Did the Sanctions Play Out?

The Suez Canal was one of the crown jewels of the British
Empire, an engineering feat when built in 1858–1869 and crucial to commerce ever since. Symbolically no less than substan-
tively, Nasser's nationalization "struck at the jugular vein of
the British Empire." "What's all this nonsense about isolating
Nasser and 'neutralizing' him," Prime Minister Anthony Eden
vented. "I want him destroyed, can't you understand? I want
him removed."[25]

Along with the American concerns noted earlier, the UN had its own credibility called into question by having two permanent members of the Security Council invading another UN member. Secretary-General Hammarskjöld, who in his four prior years had never publicly criticized member states let alone permanent Security Council members, got 64–5 support in the General Assembly for a resolution calling for an immediate ceasefire and withdrawal of all foreign troops, and empowering him to take further action. Recognizing Secretary-General Hammarskjöld's crucial role, President Eisenhower pledged to ensure that the US "do nothing that could possibly delay his operations, impede them, or hurt them in any way."[26]

The sanctions hit Britain hard. Hufbauer, Schott, and Elliott estimate a 5 percent aggregate welfare loss (annualized rate). Oil shortages forced petrol rationing. The financial sanctions pushed gold and dollar reserves dangerously low. "We cannot continue to lose reserves at the present rate, and continue at the same time to hold sterling at its present value," the British Treasury and Bank of England warned raising the prospect of devaluation and suspension of currency convertibility.[27]

The combined diplomatic and economic pressures were so great that just a few days after having launched military operations, Britain accepted the UN proposal for a ceasefire. It still stalled, though, on withdrawing its troops. So the US kept the economic pressure on. Historian Diane Kunz quotes Eisenhower as strategizing "that the purposes of peace and stability would be served by not being too quick in attempting to render extraordinary assistance."[28] Working with Canadian foreign minister and also UN ambassador Lester Pearson, Hammarskjöld developed a plan for a UN peacekeeping force to supervise the ceasefire. Within a month, Britain agreed to withdraw. Robert Bowie, a top Eisenhower aide, cites Chancellor of the Exchequer Harold Macmillan as saying that "the strain was greater than the economy could bear. . . . The need for US assistance for the pound and for oil was too great to resist."[29]

With the withdrawal commitment made, the US started lifting the sanctions. Within seventy-two hours, American oil exports were on their way to Britain, and by Christmas almost $2 billion in US-backed loans had been made.

Case Assessment

While not the only factor—UN diplomacy also was key—the causal connection between the sanctions and the policy change was strong. Oil and financial sanctions hit British economic vulnerabilities hard. Few alternative trade partners were available. Substantial economic incentives were on the offer if policy compliance was agreed to. The context of broader British dependence on the US for security and partnership was also a factor.

British and UN Sanctions against Rhodesia, 1965–1979

On November 11, 1965, anticipating British plans to establish a multiracial government, the white minority of the colony of Southern Rhodesia (located in southern Africa, and now known as Zimbabwe) led by Prime Minister Ian Smith unilaterally declared independence (UDI). Britain imposed economic sanctions. These were reinforced and extended the following year by the UN Security Council to comprehensive global sanctions. While initial economic impact was highly disruptive, political and economic counterstrategies at home as well as alternative trade partners from apartheid South Africa and neighboring Portuguese colonies Angola and Mozambique, and from 1971 to 1977 from the US, reduced the impact. By the late 1970s, though, alternative trade was getting pinched. The civil war led by anti-regime guerrilla movements was raging. In 1979 the British-mediated "Lancaster House" agreement was reached for official independence with black majority rule and the renaming of the country as Zimbabwe. All sanctions were lifted.[30]

WHY Did Britain and the UN Impose Economic Sanctions against Rhodesia?

Domestic political change, nullifying the white minority UDI and establishing democratic majority rule, was the principal objective. Concern was not only about Rhodesia itself but the effects on decolonization broadly. Between 1957 and 1965, twenty-nine African countries gained independence: eleven formerly British colonies, fifteen French, and three Belgian. All the new governments were established through formal processes based on the UN Charter and with black majority rule. Prime Minister Smith's UDI was both illegal and a major diplomatic challenge to Britain's standing particularly within its Commonwealth of former colonies now treated as partners. Indeed, British prime minister Harold Wilson had just made a trip to Rhodesia stressing "our insistence that guaranteed and unimpeded progress to majority rule should not be frustrated."[31]

For the UN, decolonization was second only to Cold War issues on its agenda. Rhodesia was an outright challenge to the UN's authority and credibility.

WHAT Types of Sanctions Were Imposed?

Within days of the Rhodesian UDI, Britain cut off foreign aid, froze Rhodesian financial assets in London banks, and suspended Rhodesia from trading and currency preferences granted to members of the Commonwealth. The following month it embargoed key exports including oil, and boycotted most imports from Rhodesia.

The initial sanctions imposed by the UN in 1965 urged but did not require member states to follow suit. It wasn't until over a year later, in December 1966, that the UN made sanctions mandatory although still only on certain exports (e.g., military arms, oil) and imports, and limited to not signing new contracts. Two years later, the sanctions were made comprehensive.

WHO Were the Key Actors?

Sender states: Great Britain, UN

Target state: Rhodesia

Third parties: South Africa, neighboring Portuguese colonies of Angola and Mozambique, and the US

HOW Did the Sanctions Play Out?

Initial economic impact was substantial. In 1966 and 1967, Rhodesian exports fell 20 percent, imports 30 percent. The tobacco industry was particularly hard hit, with estimated income falling from £33.8 million (1965) to £13.7 million (1969). The index of manufacturing production fell 7 percent in 1966. Gross domestic product, on the rise the previous year, dropped 5 percent.

But Prime Minister Wilson's prediction that the Smith government would fall "within weeks, not months" proved much too optimistic.[32] Rhodesia was the case on which Johan Galtung based his theory of sanctions' politically integrative effect. Galtung maps out "Homo rhodesiensis," for which white minority rule was transformed into a transcendent civilizational cause against black Africans. Domestic substitution also tempered the economic effects. Buoyed by an almost doubling of the rate of domestic capital formation, the index of manufacturing production increased 88 percent, import substitution taking the range of manufactured products from 602 in 1963 to 3,837 in 1970. By 1975, GDP had increased 87 percent from its initial fall.[33]

Those alternative trade partners also helped a lot. Using 1964 levels of import volume as an index = 100, imports fell below 100 through 1970, but by 1971 reached 102.7 and by 1974 114.6. This included sufficient oil to allow the Smith regime to lift gasoline rationing in 1971; the 33 percent increase in motor vehicle registration was a telling statistic. South Africa also was supplying military aid and training.[34]

In 1971 the US Congress enacted the Byrd Amendment authorizing breach of UN sanctions for the import of strategic resources, chrome in particular. Three factors were in play: anti-communism, both in the Rhodesia sanctions creating greater dependence on chrome imports from the Soviet Union and the Marxist leanings of some of the anti-UDI guerrilla groups; solidarity with the white regime, as exemplified by Senator Harry F. Byrd Jr., the amendment's principal sponsor having been a longtime segregationist; and corporate lobbying, given chrome's use in stainless steel products ranging from home appliances to automobiles. The Byrd Amendment not only added to the alternative trade relief, but as a rebuff of sanctions first mandated by one of America's closest allies and as defection from a UN Security Council action it had a powerful geopolitical effect. It was, the *Rhodesian Herald* editorialized, "a wonderful boost for Rhodesian morale and a bitter setback to those who still seek the country's collapse . . . the American move is at least a signal to the world that sanctions are not important enough to warrant serious sacrifice."[35]

In 1977, Congress repealed the Byrd Amendment, and Carter administration officials led by UN Ambassador Andrew Young became outspoken critics of the Smith regime. Rhodesian economic conditions plummeted—for example, the import index fell to 66.9 in 1979. And the balance of military power shifted to the guerrillas as Angola and Mozambique, now independent black majority–rule countries, provided basing grounds and other support to the Rhodesian guerrillas.

The British launched new negotiations. In December 1979 the Lancaster House Agreement was reached (named for the historic London building where it was signed). In April 1980 the country was granted independence under its traditional African name Zimbabwe. Elections were held resulting in a black majority government led by former guerrilla leader Robert Mugabe.

Case Assessment

A number of studies deem the Rhodesia sanctions a failure.[36] Military force not sanctions ended UDI, contends Robert Pape. Others see it as a success. Hufbauer, Schott and Elliott give it a positive success score. Baldwin disaggregates component objectives and argues for degrees of success.

I come down on partial credit for partial success.

Partial credit: for a decade, Rhodesia's target state counterstrategies reduced and managed the costs and resisted even limited policy compliance. When third-party calculations shifted, the toll from sanctions became less absorbable. Even then it's unclear whether sanctions would have sufficed for regime change without the shift in the military balance and the gains guerrilla forces were making. But here too the sanctions had their own weakening effect as well as a legitimization without which, given their Marxist allegiance, the guerrilla forces would have been less accepted.

Partial success: UDI and its intent to maintain white minority rule was defeated. Zimbabwe was decolonized and a democratic political system set up. Yet Mugabe would stay in power for almost forty years, ruling increasingly repressively, destroying the economy, and driving ever deeper fissures into the society. While such longer-term developments can't be directly attributed to sanctions, it's hard to deem the outcome as fully successful.

OPEC Sanctions against the US and Global Markets, 1973

On October 6, 1973, Egypt and Syria attacked Israel, setting off another Arab-Israeli war. The Organization of Petroleum Exporting Countries (OPEC) imposed economic sanctions in support of the Arab cause. OPEC cut global oil supplies, imposed full embargoes on the US and other major supporters of Israel, and increased world oil prices by close to 400 percent. While the US and others in the international community did not compel Israel to withdraw from occupied territories taken in previous wars, they did increase pressure on Israel on issues key to the 1973 war ceasefire and disengagement. The reasons for this degree of success, and for the failure of the prior 1967 oil embargo as well as of other 1970s commodity cartels, trace to such factors as the limited availability of alternative trade partners and the economically strategic nature of oil.[37]

WHY Did the Arab League Mandate and OPEC Impose Economic Sanctions against the US and Western Europe?

Foreign policy restraint was the proximate objective, OPEC wielding the oil weapon "until such a time as the international community compels Israel to relinquish our occupied territories."[38] The longer-term reason, going back to OPEC's founding in 1960, was to exercise cartelistic power to raise prices and otherwise reshape global oil markets for terms of trade more favorable to producer countries.

WHAT Types of Sanctions Were Imposed?

Oil supplies were cut and prices hiked globally. All countries were impacted by oil shortages and the over 400 percent price shock. Exports were totally embargoed to the US. The Netherlands also was singled out for full embargo for being more pro-Israel than other European states, and also because its port of Rotterdam was the hub for the overall Western European oil distribution network.

WHO Were the Key Actors?

Sender states: OPEC members, including both Arab state members (Algeria, Iraq, Kuwait, Libya, Saudi Arabia, United Arab Emirates), other Muslim countries (Indonesia, Iran), Nigeria with a large Muslim population, and Venezuela

Target states: US and Netherlands, world oil markets

Third parties: Some but few

HOW Did the Sanctions Play Out?

Oil sanctions had actually been tried before during the June 1967 Arab-Israeli war, also targeted at the US and other supporters of Israel. But those sanctions were only imposed by the Arab members of OPEC (the OAPEC, Organization of Arab Petroleum Exporting Countries, subgroup). Iran, Muslim but Persian, stepped up its oil production by 23 percent in the second half of 1967. Venezuela also increased its oil production. The US, at that time still the world's largest oil producer, had enough excess capacity to increase its own production by one million barrels per day. Israel defeated the Arab armies in what came to be known as the Six-Day War. The oil embargo was lifted, the Saudi oil minister lamenting "it hurt the Arabs more than anyone else."[39]

In 1973, though, all OPEC members largely stuck together. American oil production had been falling since 1970, and only a 100,000 barrels-per-day increase could be mustered. The two factors together meant that whereas in 1967 OAPEC oil constituted only 1.6 percent of American oil consumption, OPEC oil now amounted to 26.7 percent share. For Western Europe, the percentages went from 64 percent to 87.3 percent, and for Japan from 56.3 percent to 93.8 percent. Gasoline rationing had to be imposed in the US with long lines at the gas pumps. The price per gallon skyrocketed over 400 percent.

Some OPEC members did not fully cut their supplies by the agreed amounts. Major oil companies maneuvered some supply reallocations within their global networks. And, interestingly, as part of the early 1970s US-Soviet détente, the Soviet Union quietly provided the US with some additional oil, increasing from $7.5 million in 1972 to $76.3 million in 1973 and $37.3 million in the first two months of 1974 (an annual rate of $200 million).[40] But these only slightly softened the economic impact. Huge oil import bills left major balance-of-payments deficits in one country after another, further shaking an international monetary system trying to adjust to the end of the gold standard a few years before. Worldwide recession took hold.

While the full conditions of the original Arab League resolution were not met, policies toward Israel did change. Britain embargoed arms and spare parts to all belligerents in the war, a policy that primarily hurt Israel. West Germany protested the American use of German ports for loading military cargo bound for Israel. No European country other than Portugal allowed the US to use its bases for airlifts. On November 6, the European Economic Community (forerunner to the EU) foreign ministers issued a communiqué adopting a pro-Arab interpretation of the 1967 UN Security Council Resolution 242 land-for-peace formula. OPEC cited this as a reason for canceling the additional production cutbacks scheduled for December. In November and December 1973, a high-level Japanese delegation visited eight Arab states offering various assistance. Some thirty African nations severed diplomatic relations with Israel. Beyond the Arab-Israeli conflict, many developing countries saw the OPEC actions "as redressing the economic injustice inflicted for over a century by the raw-material consuming West on the raw-material producing East."[41]

While still maintaining a close alliance with Israel, the US started placing higher priority than before on amicable relations with the Arab world. Secretary of State Henry Kissinger's 1973–1976 "shuttle diplomacy" seeking to end the war and lay bases for peace included pressure on Israel as well as the Arabs. One leading scholar characterizes Kissinger's assessment of the Israeli leadership as "shortsighted, incompetent, weak." President Gerald Ford initiated a sweeping "reassessment" of US-Israeli relations, including suspending new military and economic agreements.[42] While other factors came into play, the OPEC oil weapon—including concern that it could be wielded again—was a major one.

Case Assessment

While Arab League maximal objectives of getting the US and others to "compel [Israel] to relinquish [Arab] occupied territories" were not achieved, Israel did come under increased international pressure that was highly unlikely to have been exerted without the OPEC oil sanctions. More of a peace brokering role was taken on first by Kissinger and then by every succeeding administration in which the US worked with Arab states while at the same time maintaining and indeed increasing support for Israel. Coercing militarily superior and economically richer countries into high-level policy change even to this degree was no small achievement. Both global oil markets and the geopolitics of the Middle East were dramatically transformed in ways that have persisted for close to a half-century. OPEC's success set off a wave of other attempted cartels by other developing world natural resource and primary products producers such as bauxite and coffee. None, though, was as economically strategic as oil.

Anti-Apartheid Sanctions against South Africa, 1962–1994

South Africa had a long history of white settler dominance going back to the first colony established by the Dutch East India Company in 1652. In 1948 the "apartheid" system was formalized by the white Afrikaner government with segregation and oppression of the black African majority taken to an extreme. The anti-apartheid movement within South Africa, building for many years, was further spurred in 1960 by the Sharpeville massacre (named for the township where it occurred), killing sixty-nine protesters and wounding over 200 others at the hands of the South African police. The apartheid regime cracked down even further, including in August 1962 making Nelson Mandela, a young African lawyer emerging as a leader of the anti-apartheid African National Congress (ANC), a political prisoner. Later that same year the UN imposed partial trade sanctions. The June 1976 police killing of over 1,000 student protesters in the Soweto township and murder the following year of student leader Steve Biko prompted the UN Security Council to elevate the arms embargo from partial and voluntary to full and mandatory. Over the next decade-plus, with the anti-apartheid movement gaining more and more transnational support, one country after another, including the US, imposed harsher sanctions. Pressure also came from "bankers' sanctions," refusals of international banks to grant South Africa additional loans because of mounting financial risks. Under these and other pressures, President F. W. de Klerk agreed to begin dismantling apartheid. On February 11, 1990, after twenty-seven years as a political prisoner, Mandela was released. Over the next four years he led negotiations with de Klerk paving the way for a largely peaceful transition to multiracial democracy with Mandela as president, a Truth and Reconciliation Commission established, and a new constitution. Most sanctions were lifted.[43]

WHY Were Sanctions Imposed on South Africa?

Ending apartheid was the main objective, in our categorization domestic political change so extensive as to be regime change.

Stopping South African military intervention in support of other white minority regimes in the region, particularly Namibia, was another objective (foreign policy restraint).

WHAT Types of Sanctions Were Imposed?

This case had many different types of sanctions. The principal ones:

Arms embargo: voluntary as initially mandated by the UN in 1962, made mandatory in 1977.

Oil sanctions: Norway and Britain embargoed oil from their North Sea production. OPEC targeted South Africa although Iran continued supplying over 95 percent of South Africa's imports until its 1979 revolution. After that, Saudi Arabia and other OPEC members evaded their own sanctions with some oil supplies via the black market.

Numerous other trade sanctions.

Investment sanctions: The "Sullivan Principles," developed in 1977 by a private sector–civil society coalition led by African American Rev. Leon Sullivan, established a voluntary code of conduct for international companies investing in South Africa requiring workplace and other practices contrary to strict apartheid. Local-level divestment activism pushed American state and local governments to use their pension funds and universities their endowments to pressure companies to divest from South Africa. Countries such as Sweden passed laws prohibiting their companies' investments.

Financial sanctions: These were both governmental prohibitions on official loans and trade credits, and the mid-1980s bankers' sanctions.

International sports boycotts: Starting in 1964, South Africa was banned from the Olympics. Bans followed from FIFA (world football/soccer) in 1976, from the first ever rugby world cup in 1987, and from cricket tours in the 1970s and 1980s.

Cultural boycotts: Bono, Tina Turner, Elton John, Bruce Springsteen, and other celebrities refused to perform in South Africa. Meanwhile, concerts and other major events in support of the anti-apartheid movement were held around the world, for example the July 1988 "Freedom at 70" concert in London commemorating Nelson Mandela's seventieth birthday, drawing over 70,000 attendees and reaching 200 million viewers in sixty countries via BBC broadcast.

WHO Were the Key Actors?

Sender states: India was actually the first to impose sanctions (1946). Other senders included the UN, the

US (particularly after 1986), Great Britain and the British Commonwealth, the EU, and others. In this case we also use "state" to include individual American states and other local governments that imposed divestment and other of their own sanctions (see Chapter 5). Social movements deserve special mention for the anti-apartheid pressure they brought on governments, the UN, and other entities such as universities.

Target state: South Africa

Third parties: Just as South Africa provided alternative trade for Rhodesia, so did Rhodesia provide alternative trade for South Africa, at least until 1979 and 1980 when it became black majority Zimbabwe. The US did as well during much of the Cold War and during the Reagan administration. Other countries also did so at various times (e.g., defecting states as in the OPEC example), as did companies via black markets.

HOW Did the Sanctions Play Out?

Initially, like Rhodesia, South Africa was able to offset the economic impact and channel the global outrage for politically integrative solidarity among the white Afrikaner community. Export embargoes were manipulated for import substitution industrialization. Oil was stockpiled. Nuclear power plants were developed as alternative sources of energy. Arms were still obtained in the black market. Premiums were paid and GDP growth was hampered, but until the mid-1980s the economic impact was kept within manageable levels.

By then, though, the mounting toll of sanctions had South Africa carrying an estimated $24 billion in external debt, two-thirds of which was short-term with higher interest rates and recurrent renewals. "We felt that the risk attached to political unrest and economic instability became too high for our investors," a Chase Manhattan Bank executive stated in July 1985. "We decided to withdraw. It was never the intention to facilitate change in South Africa, the decision was taken purely on account of what was in the interest of Chase and its assets."[44] London-based Barclays cited customer pressure for its version of bankers' sanctions. The divestment movement was ratcheting up pressure on companies with direct investments in and major trade with South Africa. In 1986 and 1987 more than 100 American companies sold off their South African subsidiaries. No longer believing that the change brought about by the principles bearing his name was extensive or rapid enough, Rev. Sullivan came out for firmer sanctions.

For South African whites the toll was not just economic but also the sense of being seen in many parts of the world as pariahs. They were banned from the Olympics, from FIFA football/soccer, from world rugby, and from world cricket. Fewer and fewer entertainers performed at their theaters and other cultural venues. Their South African passports were not welcome even for personal travel in a growing list of countries.

And now even the US was moving away from them. For much of the Cold War the ANC's connections to the South African Communist Party and to Marxist groups in Angola and Rhodesia were prioritized over apartheid in keeping the US largely supportive of the South African government. While the Carter administration saw the relationship more in human rights terms, the Reagan administration shifted back to "old friends . . . getting together again."[45] Foreign policy vetoes rarely get overridden, so when Congress did override Reagan's veto of the 1986 Comprehensive Anti-Apartheid Act, and with a 78–21 vote in the Republican-majority Senate, the message was a powerful one. The anti-apartheid movement was bipartisan. Outrage transcended party lines when celebrities like tennis star Arthur Ashe, the first African American to captain the American Davis Cup team, were among those arrested for protesting at the South African embassy in Washington. Meanwhile, intensifying police brutality and other racist violence in the streets of South Africa were coming across the television airwaves.

On February 11, 1990, with South Africa under ever-increasing pressure, Nelson Mandela made his "walk to freedom." A transition period began in which Mandela led negotiations with Afrikaner President de Klerk. On May 10, 1994, in the first genuinely democratic elections ever held in South Africa with multiracial participation, Mandela was elected president.

On October 12, 1993, the UN General Assembly passed Resolution A/Res/48/1 stating

> that all provisions adopted by the General Assembly relating to prohibitions or restrictions on economic relations with South Africa and its nationals including the areas of trade, investment, finance, travel and transportation, shall cease to have effect as of the date of the adoption of the present resolution, and requests all States to take appropriate measures within their jurisdiction to lift the restrictions and prohibitions they had imposed.

The following month American sanctions, partially lifted in 1991, were fully repealed.

Case Assessment

As Neta Crawford and Audie Klotz aptly put it, "nearly every theoretical argument about the potential impact of sanctions on a target was made with respect to South Africa."[46] Many different sanctions were used over three-plus decades. Some effects were intended, some unintended, and some consequences persisted long after sanctions were lifted. A host of other factors came into play. While acknowledging such factors, it is difficult to imagine Nelson Mandela getting out of jail and South Africa peacefully transitioning to a multiracial society without economic sanctions.

Conclusion: Some Cross-Case Patterns

These cases show a number of patterns manifesting analytic and methodological issues laid out in Chapters 2 and 3.

Success tends to be more a matter of degree and net assessment than crying uncle or unconditional surrender.

None of the successes came without some downsides. The Eisenhower administration succeeded in getting the British to withdraw from Suez, but not in preventing them from launching the invasion in the first place. The length of time it took to force change in Rhodesia gave Mugabe time to strengthen his position over alternative black leaders, positioning him for close to forty years of repressive and destructive rule. OPEC shifted US and European Middle East policies, but not to the point of extensive pressure on Israel.

Failure can end up not just the absence of success but making a bad situation worse.

While historians are mixed on the extent to which the Megarian Decree led to the Peloponnesian Wars, it clearly did not have a deterrent effect and prevent war. The Continental System didn't just fail to bring Britain to its knees. It pushed Russia to defect from the sanctions and resume trade with Britain, which in turn prompted Napoleon to invade Russia, and instead of "finishing off those barbarians of the North" suffer major military defeat, which ultimately led to his own downfall. The gap between the sanctions threat embodied in the League of Nations Charter and the actual sanctions imposed on Italy was so gaping as to make Mussolini even more boldly aggressive, using poison gas in Ethiopia and moving closer to the full Axis alliance with Hitler.

Sanctions were not the only key factor in either the successes or failures.

In the Suez 1956 case the American sanctions were in the context of broader British dependence on the US for security and partnership. In Rhodesia, while it was unlikely that regime change would have occurred without the toll taken by the guerrilla war, the sanctions were important not only for their own coercive impact but also for their legitimizing effect partially offsetting the guerrilla force's Marxist allegiances. Napoleon didn't have to respond to the Russian defection from his anti-Britain sanctions by invading. There were other options available. Sanctions didn't make that choice inevitable, although they did play into it. Relatedly, had Britain and France turned to available military options against Mussolini like closing the Suez Canal and supporting the Ethiopians, the League sanctions might have had more impact.

Oil and finance were the most effective sanctions.

The Suez case had both oil and finance sanctions. OPEC 1973 was the iconic oil weapon case. The banker sanctions in the South Africa case, while based largely on commercial risk, added to the more politically driven sanctions by the US, UN, and others. Conversely, the omission of oil from the League of Nations sanctions was a key part of their coercive weakness.

Multilateral sanctions had some advantages but not to the extent of being a decisive factor.

In the Rhodesia and South Africa cases, the UN imprimatur carried important normative value. But while this facilitated global cooperation and compliance, states and companies still did some sanctions busting. In both cases when the US defected, as with the 1971 Byrd Amendment in the Rhodesia case and Reagan's re-engagement with South Africa, it was that much harder for institutionalized multilateral efforts to have impact. When the US came back into the fold, the multilateral effort was that much stronger.

All the successes were against democracies.

Britain in the Suez case, Rhodesia and South Africa in the sense of democracy within the white minority communities, US in the OPEC case. While these cases fit the vulnerable democracies theory, the sampling in this chapter was based on different criteria and not intended as representative of the regime-type debate. Refer back to the data and analysis in Chapter 3 showing regime type as less strictly determinative.

Target states had counterstrategies.

Italy (Mussolini's Day of the Wedding Ring) and Rhodesia (rally 'round whiteness) exemplified politically integrative effects. Rhodesia and South Africa also helped offset sanctions economic impact with import substitution industrialization.

Third parties played key roles.

Sparta was a key third party as protector as well as trade partner for Megara. Russia and the US were key third parties for Britain against Napoleon's sanctions. The 1930s isolationist US and Hitler's Germany were key for Mussolini against the League sanctions. Along with the shifting US role, there also was the colony-to-independence shift in Angola and Mozambique in initially supporting the Rhodesian regime but then aiding and abetting the guerrilla movements. Britain in 1956 did not have any significant third parties to turn to. Nor did the US or other oil consumer countries in 1973.

Time needed to coerce compliance varied.

Britain agreed to a Suez ceasefire within days, and a military withdrawal within a month. Rhodesia took fifteen years, South Africa close to thirty.

Carrot-and-stick inducements were a factor in some of the cases.

Eisenhower promised Britain close to $2 billion in loans and other economic assistance if it withdrew from Suez. Sanctions against South Africa began to be lifted once Mandela was out of jail and the transition was deemed credible.

5

UNITED STATES

FOREIGN POLICY STRATEGY AND DOMESTIC POLITICS

This chapter focuses on US sanctions policy. Key questions to be addressed:

- Why does the US use sanctions so much more frequently than any other country?
- What types of sanctions does the US make particular use of?
- Whom does the US target?
- Are American sanctions more successful than others?
- What are key patterns in the domestic politics and policy process?
- How does federalism and the role of state and local governments affect sanctions?
- What are some major recent/current cases of US sanctions?
- Summary: What conclusions can be drawn and challenges identified for American sanctions?

Why Does the US Use Sanctions So Much More Frequently Than Any Other Country?

The frequency of American use of sanctions is quite striking. One study had the US as sender state in 69 percent of the cases, another at 52 percent: "the go-to solution for nearly every foreign policy problem," as one analyst critiqued; "a Swiss army knife with a ready attachment just right for any foreign policy challenge," as another colorfully put it.[1]

The Bush and Obama administrations continued this frequent use trend. The Specially Designated Nationals (SDN) List of targeted sanctions increased during the Bush administration and then further in the Obama administration. For the Trump administration, sanctions were the proverbial hammer be it a nail or a screw. Its annual SDN rate was over 300 percent higher than Obama's annual rate, including a record-high $1.3 billion in penalties on sanctions violators.[2] It increased sanctions against North Korea, Iran, Syria, Venezuela, Belarus, China, Cuba, Libya, and a number of other countries. Russia also got sanctioned, although more from congressional initiative given Trump's overall coziness with Vladimir Putin.

The Biden administration quickly showed its own penchant for sanctions. In just its first 100 days it sanctioned Myanmar following the February 2021 military coup, Russia over the poisoning and then imprisonment of leading dissident Alexei Navalny, Saudi Arabia over the brutal murder of Saudi journalist-American resident Jamal Khashoggi (although excluding Saudi Crown Prince Mohammed bin Salman despite ample evidence of his having ordered the murder), China over the Uyghurs and other issues, Ukraine on corruption, a Mexican drug lord, ISIS affiliates in Mozambique and the Democratic Republic of Congo, and others. It made sanctions a major part of its strategy against Russia in the 2021–2022 Ukraine crisis.

Four main factors explain American proclivity for wielding sanctions: interests, power, ideology, and politics.

Pre–World War II, when its international interests were less extensive, the US used sanctions half as much as then-major power Great Britain. During the Cold War, with now broadly global interests, the American sanctioning rate was more than three times greater than now lesser-power Britain's, indeed comprising 67.2 percent of the world total. The rate was even higher in the 1990s, 75.8 percent, in that "unipolar moment" at which with the fall of the Soviet Union, American interests seemed global-spanning.

Its global economic preponderance has provided power with which to pursue those interests, to make trade "an instrument of national power," and to weaponize interdependence by exploiting its position as a "central node in the international networked structures through which money, goods and information travel . . . to impose costs on others."[3] We'll see in cases like the Trump sanctions against Iran how weaponized interdependence power can get overestimated; the point here is less whether sanctions succeed than why they get imposed.

Ideology comes into play in the emphasis given to democracy promotion and human rights as foreign policy goals toward which sanctions are among the tools to be put to use. Past and current cases include sanctions imposed against communist regimes (e.g., Soviet Union/Russia, China, Cuba, North Korea), military coups (e.g., Chile, Argentina, Brazil, Haiti, Myanmar), other dictatorships (e.g., Zimbabwe, Libya, Syria, Venezuela), other violators of human rights (e.g., apartheid South Africa), and Islamist regimes (e.g., Iran). The Global Magnitsky Act, passed with bipartisan support in 2016, while initially targeted at Russians involved in the death of dissident Sergei Magnitsky, has been used in the years since to target human rights violators in over twenty countries including the Dominican Republic, Nicaragua, Turkey, Saudi Arabia, China, Eritrea, and Myanmar.

By politics I mean the "playing to the home crowd" electoral and public opinion incentives for both the president and Congress, together and at times separately, both to impose sanctions and to maintain them even when they have not been effective.

What Types of Sanctions Does the US Make Particular Use Of?

Trade sanctions: As the world's largest economy, the US has had plenty to work with for trade sanctions. The global competitiveness of American manufactured goods, industrial products, and technologies makes export embargoes attractive tools for policymakers. So too the robust domestic market and consumer culture for import boycotts.

Arms embargoes: In some instances these are unilateral, the US using its position as the major arms exporter to a target country, for example, the 1970s tying of military aid to a number of Latin American countries to democratic and human rights reform. In others it has been more coalitional, as with US-European coordinated arms embargoes. In some it has been broadly multilateral, as with the Nuclear Nonproliferation Treaty.

Foreign aid: Of 103 US sanctions between 1960 and 2010, 83 involved foreign aid.[4] Part of the appeal of foreign aid sanctions is in the power imbalance of the target being weaker than and more dependent on the US. Part also is political in incurring fewer domestic interest group costs than sanctioning private sector trade.

Financial and other "smart" sanctions: With over 60 percent of global currency reserves and 40 percent of international payments transactions still dollar-based, financial sanctions have been a major part of interdependence weaponization theory; in more military terms, a "force multiplier."[5] All told, the SDN List—"individuals and companies owned or controlled by, or acting for or on behalf of, targeted countries . . . [and] individuals, groups, and entities, such as terrorists and narcotics traffickers designated under programs that are not country-specific"—runs over 1,500 pages.[6]

Secondary sanctions: The US also has been the major user of secondary sanctions. Make your choice, trade with them or with us. That's the leverage logic of secondary sanctions, threatening loss of access to the lucrative American economy if US sanctions are not abided by. These get applied to foreign subsidiaries of American companies making goods that the US embargoes but the country in which they are located does not, to foreign companies using American-made parts and technology, and to dollar-denominated transactions anywhere in the world. This chapter's Iran case study as well as others in Chapters 7 and 8 bring out the tensions between US extraterritorial claims for secondary sanctions and European allies' sovereignty rights to choose their own policy.

Whom Does the US Target?

Adversaries: Most US sanctions are targeted against adversaries: for example, the Soviet Union/Russia, China, Cuba, North Korea, Iran.

Allies: The Suez 1956 case involved sanctions imposed against Britain and France. Numerous foreign aid recipients have been sanctioned over human rights, democracy reform, and other issues. Many of the secondary sanctions, as noted, have been targeted against Europe.

Objectionables: Sanctions also have been used against countries neither adversary nor ally but which have policies considered contrary to American interests and/or values: for example, apartheid South Africa.

Non-state actors: The long SDN List is full of sanctions against drug traffickers, terrorists, criminals, and the like.

What Are the Main Objectives the US Uses Sanctions For?

US sanctions encompass the full range of objectives. Primary policy change objectives:

- Limiting military capabilities: for example, the Cold War embargo on military-related technologies to the Soviet Union and nonproliferation sanctions against Iran, North Korea, and Libya;
- Foreign policy restraint: for example, against state sponsors of terrorism, the Soviet Union for its 1979 invasion of Afghanistan and Russia for its 2014 intervention and 2022 invasion of Ukraine.

- Domestic political change: human rights protection and democracy promotion long the most frequent sanctions, as of
  2022 being applied to more than ten countries (e.g., Russia,
  China, Burma/Myanmar, Syria, Venezuela, Cuba, Iran) and
  over 3,000 individuals.

Secondary signaling objectives:

- Target deterrence, in most every foreign policy restraint
  case, seeking to deter further objectionable action even if the
  immediate one is not changed.
- Third-party deterrence; given global interests, there is little
  the US does from which signals aren't taken by third parties
  be they allies, adversaries, or others in between.
- Symbolic action, standing up for principles as a matter of soft
  power as well as broad international normative affirmation.

Are American Sanctions More Successful Than Others?

"There is no doubt that economic sanctions remain a robust—
and improving—geoeconomic tool for the United States" is the
claim two experienced policymakers make.[7] The data are more
mixed. One study found only a 33.5 percent American success rate, and only 28.2 percent when sanctioning unilaterally,
compared to 56.1 percent for other sanctioners. Another study
had a somewhat higher US success rate, but also a higher percentage of cases in which the outcome favored the target when
the US was the sanctioner (47% to 37%).

Within this general data some periodization can be
discerned. From 1945 to 1969, the years of greatest US dominance geopolitically and economically, the US success rate
was 50 percent, and even higher at 62.5 percent for unilateral
sanctions. For the period 1970–1989, when American economic
power was showing some cracks and the Cold War waning,
the overall success rate fell to 24.1 percent, even lower (19.5%)
for unilateral sanctions. For the years 1990–2000 the US success

rate was up a bit but not as high as earlier.[8] While we lack full aggregate data sets for more recent years, other analysts as well as our case studies in this chapter indicate more failures than successes.[9]

Separating out by objectives, the US record is consistent with the overall pattern of limited objectives being more achievable than extensive ones. Sanctions helped keep Iran and Libya from developing nuclear weapons but have not compelled North Korea to de-proliferate. Foreign policy restraint has been more achievable on particular policies (e.g., reducing terrorism) than compelling the end to major military actions (1979 Soviet Afghanistan invasion, 2014 Russian Ukraine intervention).[10] On human rights and democratization there has been more success in achieving a degree of liberalization than broad domestic political transformation, although not even that in the Soviet/Russia and China cases included herein—and no successes at all for regime change.[11]

Measuring success on secondary signaling runs into the uncertainties of whether message intended to be sent is message received. Did the 1980 sanctions deter Brezhnev from going into the Persian Gulf, or did he not have any such intention, Afghanistan being a particular issue, not a falling domino? While there was much debate about whether the 2014 sanctions had a deterrent effect on his going further, Putin's 2022 invasion made it more likely that he was biding his time, building his forces, looking for what he considered a right opportunity. Nonproliferation sanctions have been shown to have some third-party deterrent effect, but with some indication of these being particular to the policy area and not more broadly generalizable.[12] As to symbolic action, net assessments have to be made of any backfiring from target governments making the repression worse and misfiring with severe humanitarian consequences. Moreover, when severe human rights violations by US partner countries are left un- or much less severely sanctioned, the inconsistency runs counter to principled claims of principles.

What Are Key Patterns in the Domestic Politics and Policy Process?

As noted, domestic politics can play in as incentives for sanctions. There are exceptions like the political costs President Jimmy Carter paid for the 1980 grain sanctions against the Soviet Union, but as with many issues presidents often do get "playing to the home crowd" credit for acting firmly against objectionable foreign actions.[13]

Congress often has played its own independent role pushing some sanctions presidents have opposed and opposing others presidents have supported. In the 1970s as in so many other foreign policy domains, Congress increased its sanctions role, from involvement in less than 50 percent of cases during the prior three decades to about 75 percent of cases. A study covering 103 pieces of sanctions legislation (1983–2014) shows that almost half of those opposed by the president were still approved by Congress. In those years partisanship was not a factor: the cases spread over Republican and Democratic presidential administrations; support within Congress was bipartisan on most of the legislation.[14] These can cut both ways. On the one hand, legislatively imposed sanctions can have the immediate benefit of sending their own strong message. On the other hand, if relations with the target improve over time legislated sanctions have to be formally rescinded and thus are harder than those imposed under executive discretion to relax or lift.

Pro-sanctions political pressure often comes from interest groups. In the late 1970s, pro-Israel groups such as AIPAC (American Israel Public Affairs Committee) played a key role in getting Congress to prohibit American companies from complying with the Arab League boycott of Israel, as well as in years since then on various rounds of Iran and counterterrorism sanctions. While the Cold War was the original motivation for sanctions against Cuba, the Cuban-American lobby has thrown its political weight around to keep these going for more than fifty years. The 60 percent support among the South Florida Cuban-American community for Cuba sanctions was a key factor in the large margin by which Trump won their 2020 vote. While the same poll showed over 70 percent believing the embargo hadn't worked, its expressive and symbolic value still resonated.[15]

In other instances, domestic politics can be a constraint on sanctions. For example, in 1988 following Iraqi dictator Saddam Hussein's chemical weapons attacks on the Kurds in northern Iraq, the Senate unanimously passed an anti-Iraq sanctions bill. Yet Iraq had become a significant market for American agricultural exports. "I in no way wish to condone the use of chemical weapons by Iraq," House Agriculture Chairman E. "Kika" de la Garza (D-Texas) claimed, but "in light of the difficulties our farmers have faced over the past few years, I am deeply concerned over the possible loss of a major market." Nor was it just agricultural interests. The US Chamber of Commerce urged that the US "set aside the emotions of the moment" and ponder the costs of economic sanctions. The US-Iraq Business Forum, whose member companies included oil giants and other Fortune 500 companies, asserted that "while morality is an essential ingredient in foreign policy in a democratic society . . . morality detached from reality is stupidity." Based both on these interest group pressures and its tilt toward Iraq as part of its enemy-of-my-enemy-is-my-friend calculus against Iran, the Reagan administration also opposed the sanctions. The Senate bill died.[16]

In addition to the interbranch presidential-congressional dynamics, intra-executive branch roles are distributed across the bureaucracy. The State Department Bureau of International Security and Nonproliferation leads on sanctions geared toward weapons of mass destruction nonproliferation, its Bureau of Political and Military Affairs Directorate of Defense Trade Controls (DDTC) on conventional arms, its Bureau of Counterterrorism on the State Sponsors of Terrorism list. The Treasury Department has a lead role on financial sanctions.

Its Office of Terrorism and Financial Intelligence is headed by an under secretary and includes the Office of Foreign Assets Control (OFAC) with responsibility for the SDN List, the Financial Crimes Enforcement Network (FinCEN) with broad investigatory authority, and other sanctions-related offices. The Commerce Department Bureau of Industry and Security (BIS) is in charge of licensing for exports and technologies controlled under the Export Administration Act and other legislation. The Departments of Homeland Security and Justice (including the FBI) also have significant sanctions roles.[17] The White House–based National Security Council tries to coordinate all of this.

A March 2021 story in the *New York Times* focusing on the Commerce Department BIS illustrates some of the bureaucratic politics.[18] At the time, the Biden administration had not yet chosen the new BIS head. "China hawks" saw the pro-trade American business sector as having "too much sway over the bureau" and pushed for "a leader for the agency who would take a more aggressive approach to regulating the technology that the United States exports." Pro-business interests countered that this would hurt the American economy and pushed for a more pro-trade appointee.

And all of this is just inside Washington. . . .

How Does Federalism and the Role of State and Local Governments Affect Sanctions?

Sanctions are more affected by federalism and the national/ state/local division of power than most other US foreign policy issues. The South Africa anti-apartheid case illustrates.[19]

By the time Congress passed the 1986 Comprehensive Anti-Apartheid Act, over 150 US states, counties, and municipalities had already imposed sanctions on the regime. They did so by using their own economic leverage, restricting government procurement and divesting public pension funds from companies doing business in South Africa. Connecticut passed a partial divestment law in 1982. In 1985 and 1986, Chicago, Houston, Los Angeles, New York, Pittsburgh, San Francisco, and Washington were among the major cities taking action. Notable also were university-based cities such as Madison, Wisconsin, and Berkeley, California, spurred by the greatest campus activism since the anti–Vietnam War movement. All this bottom-up pressure was strong enough to prompt major institutional investors such as TIAA-CREF (Teachers Insurance and Annuity Association—College Retirement Equities Fund) to put their own pressure on companies whose assets they held. The cumulative effect, as one anti-apartheid movement leader put it, was to "increase US public awareness of apartheid, creating a political environment conducive to Congressional sanctions against South Africa."[20]

The Constitution does limit some state and local governments' sanctioning. The "supremacy clause" (Article VI) stating that laws passed at the federal level "shall be the supreme law of the land" means that states cannot enact laws contrary to laws and policies set in Washington. Moreover, as the Supreme Court affirmed in a seminal 1936 case,

> The broad statement that the federal government can exercise no powers except those specifically enumerated in the Constitution, and such implied powers as are necessary and proper to carry into effect the enumerated powers, is categorically true only in respect to our internal affairs . . . the federal power over external affairs [is] in origin and essential character different from that over internal affairs.[21]

Thus, in *Crosby v. National Foreign Trade Council* (2000), the Supreme Court ruled that a Massachusetts law imposing state sanctions on Burma/Myanmar for human rights violations unconstitutionally infringed on the foreign affairs power of the federal government. Other relevant cases include the 2008 judicial overturning Illinois sanctions against Sudan, and a 2012 US District Court ruling against Florida trying to counter the Obama administration's loosening of sanctions against Cuba with more restrictive ones of its own. What had made the South Africa case different was that pre-1986 the federal government had not acted, so states and cities could fill the void.

Various states and localities also applied their own sanctions in the 2022 Russia Ukraine case. Citing both fiduciary responsibilities and "our moral imperative," California governor Gavin Newsom required the state retirement systems, which together held over $970 billion, "to leverage its sizeable global investment portfolio to sanction the Russian government."[22]

What Are Some Major Recent Cases of US Sanctions?

Given the American proclivity to use sanctions, there are plenty of cases to choose from. We already discussed two past ones in Chapter 4, Suez 1956 and South Africa 1977–1994. The cases selected are both important in their own right and illustrative of broader analytic and policy points.

Iran: Obama's Coercive Diplomacy vs. Trump's Maximum Pressure

American sanctions against Iran go back to the 1979 Islamic Revolution. Release of the American hostages taken during the revolution was the initial objective. In the more than forty years since, objectives have included numerous issues of foreign policy restraint (nonproliferation, counterterrorism, countering Iranian regional intervention) as well as domestic political change (human rights, democracy promotion, regime change). Since the US has had very little trade with Islamist Iran, sanctions have been principally secondary ones aimed at other governments and private sector actors. Our focus here is comparing two contrasting strategies: the Obama sanctions as part of the coercive diplomacy strategy for achieving the

2015 nuclear nonproliferation agreement known as the Joint Comprehensive Plan of Action (JCPOA) negotiated with Iran by the P-5+1 (US, Russia, China, Britain, France, and Germany), and then Trump's withdrawal from the JCPOA and ratcheting up sanctions as part of his "maximum pressure" strategy.

WHY Did the US Impose Sanctions?

The main Obama objective was to stop Iranian development of nuclear weapons as foreign policy restraint and limiting military capabilities. Trump sought to force Iran into much greater foreign policy concessions and ultimately regime change.

WHAT Types of Sanctions Were Imposed?

Obama combined unilateral American sanctions and UN multilateral ones. UN Security Council Resolution 1929 (June 2010) tightened oil, finance, shipping, and other sanctions on a multilateral basis (Russia and China included). Prior UN sanctions had been largely confined to technology and other exports with nuclear weapons development applications. Congress passed the Comprehensive Iran Sanctions, Accountability and Divestment Act (CISADA) and Obama issued a number of executive orders expanding US sanctions beyond the UN multilateral ones. The administration pressured American oil companies to end their Iranian operations. It leveraged the centrality of the dollar to international finance for secondary sanctions against any countries or companies not abiding by the sanctions. Once the JCPOA came into force, Obama lifted many of the sanctions his administration had imposed as well as some prior ones. The UN did the same with its Resolution 1929 multilateral sanctions.

On May 8, 2018, despite intelligence reports largely confirming Iranian compliance, Trump renounced the JCPOA. He reimposed the sanctions Obama had lifted and added a host of others. These included the banking, oil, shipping, energy, and shipbuilding sectors. Entities that were previously removed from the SDN List were redesignated. Hundreds more were added. With America's European allies as well as Russia and China continuing to support the JCPOA and trade with Iran, Trump imposed secondary sanctions against them. Foreign banks conducting transactions in any way connected to Iran were barred from the US financial system. US-based property and other assets of any person or company, foreign or domestic, conducting business with Iran were blocked. All this was ratcheted up further in January 2020 following the Trump-ordered assassination of Iranian Revolutionary Guard leader Qasem Soleimani and Iranian retaliation against an American military base in Iraq. Even when Iran got hit hard by COVID-19, sanctions on medicine and other humanitarian supplies were maintained, including blocking Iran's request for a $5 billion COVID-19 relief loan from the International Monetary Fund.

WHO Were the Key Actors?

Sender state: US principally, some UN sanctions, some EU sanctions, some by other countries

Target state: Iran

Third parties: European allies as well as China and Russia. All largely complied with the 2010 UN sanctions and worked with the Obama administration on the JCPOA diplomacy. When Trump shifted policy, each in its own way took on more of an alternative trade partner role.

HOW Did the Sanctions Play Out?

The Obama strategy was economic pressure combined with diplomatic negotiations for a nuclear nonproliferation agreement with the incentive of lifting sanctions if an agreement was reached. The sanctions were a key factor in getting Iran to agree to the JCPOA. Iranian oil exports fell from 2.5 million barrels per day in 2011 to 1.1 million in 2015. The annual GDP growth rate, 5.7 percent in 2010, went to negative 1.6 percent.

Inflation approached 60 percent. The rial foreign exchange rate plummeted over 200 percent.[23] Once the JCPOA went into force and sanctions began to be lifted, oil exports nearly doubled to 2.1 million barrels per day, oil export earnings increased over 240 percent, GDP growth came back up to 3.7 percent, inflation went down to single digits, and the rial leveled off.

Trump's reimposition of the sanctions lifted by Obama and additional ones did hit hard. Iranian oil exports were squeezed way back down to less than 300,000 barrels per day. GDP dropped by 10 percent. Inflation went back up to 40 percent. Youth unemployment was close to 30 percent. The rial had to be so devalued that the regime renamed its currency the toman, with a unit revaluation of 10,000 to 1.[24] The 200 percent increase in domestic gasoline prices and supply rationing that the Iranian government was forced to impose in November 2019 as part of sanctions-induced austerity set off the most intense and widespread political unrest since the 1979 Iranian Revolution. Iranian elites, though, their own economic interests cushioned by black markets and government subsidies, had little compunction against supporting this resort to violent repression, that is, circuit breakers not transmission belts.

"The United States of America supports the brave people of Iran who are protesting for their FREEDOM," Trump tweeted. "The United States is with you," Secretary of State Mike Pompeo added. Regime change advocates inside and outside the administration felt like they could taste victory.[25] But it did not come. Nor did renegotiation of the JCPOA on the highly concessionary terms the Trump administration demanded. Nor significant reduction of Iranian involvement in Iraq, or Syria, or Yemen. Why?

Trump's secondary sanctions making foreign banks and businesses subject to losing access to the dollar for any international transactions if they did not comply did block some alternative trade. Even with the EU's August 2018 "blocking statute" seeking to protect European businesses, firms still saw greater risks in not complying with the US measures. Oil companies such as Total (French), shipping giants such as Maersk (Denmark), and insurance companies such as Allianz (Germany) pulled out of Iran. The Society for Worldwide Interbank Financial Telecommunications (SWIFT), the clearinghouse for much of international financial transactions, suspended major Iranian banks.[26] The French bank BNP was hit with a nearly $7 billion penalty for processing dollar payments from Iran.[27] Germany, France, and Britain joined with Russia and China in creating a "special purpose vehicle" (SPV) to facilitate trade with Iran by avoiding dollar-denominated transactions or other exposure to the US market. In January 2019 this vehicle was officially registered as the Instrument for Supporting Trade Exchanges (INSTEX). Yet, it was not until March 31, 2020, that INSTEX actually completed its first transaction.[28]

Despite such economic costs, Europe pushed back diplomatically. Britain and France blocked Trump efforts at the UN Security Council to invoke the "snapback" provision of the JCPOA by which multilateral sanctions would be automatically reimposed if Iran was in violation. "That the closest western allies of the US unambiguously reject the legitimacy of using the SnapBack procedure," the former French ambassador to the US and the UN tweeted, "confirms their commitment to the JCPOA, their opposition to the maximum pressure policy against Iran and says a lot about the world status of the US today."[29] China gained openings to grow closer to Iran, increasing oil imports to close to 1 million barrels per day, the highest in two years, and negotiating a long-term comprehensive strategic partnership for greater military cooperation and $400 billion in investment and trade. Russian-Iranian relations grew closer, some analysts pointing to Russia as "the winner in the U.S.-Iran showdown."[30]

Once COVID-19 hit, while the Iranian regime bore plenty of responsibility for the disease's severity in its country, American sanctions so further hindered access to drugs and medical equipment that humanitarian ethical condemnations were intensified.[31]

Case Assessment

Obama's coercive diplomacy worked, Trump's maximum pressure did not.[32]

The Obama success wasn't perfect. The JCPOA could have run into problems even without Trump's wrecking ball. But it was a substantial success and sanctions were a key part. The strategy had reciprocity in the US and the P5+1 gaining from reducing the prospect of Iranian nuclear proliferation and Iran gaining sanctions relief, and proportionality between sanctions as a limited coercive instrument and nonproliferation as a significant but still limited policy concession.

Trump's eschewing of anything close to a serious diplomatic process took away any credible bases for reciprocity, while regime change or other versions of saying uncle were totally disproportional to what even tough sanctions could achieve. The costs Trump imposed did matter. They hurt Iran. But they did not bring about significant policy change. While Iran did have to reduce support for the Assad regime in Syria as well as regional proxies such as Hizbollah in Lebanon and Shiite militias in Iraq, it continued to pose threats to American and allied interests and grew closer to China and Russia. And for all the economic costs incurred, by early 2022 *The Economist* assessed the Iranian economy as "resilient."[33]

Soviet Union/Russia: Human Rights and Military Aggression

Included are two types of objectives, human rights (domestic political change, symbolic action) and anti-military intervention (foreign policy restraint, deterrence signaling).[34] The human rights cases are the 1974 Jackson-Vanik Amendment linking Soviet Jewish emigration to trade benefits, and the 2021 sanctions protesting the poisoning and imprisonment of Russian dissident Alexei Navalny.[35] The military aggression cases are the sanctions against the 1980 Soviet invasion of Afghanistan and those against the 2014 Russian limited military intervention in Ukraine and annexation of Crimea and then the 2022 ones against Russia for its massive invasion of Ukraine.[36]

WHY Did the US Impose Each of These Sanctions?

Jackson-Vanik 1974: This was a congressional provision amid the opening of US-Soviet détente linking trade to greater emigration rights for Soviet Jews.

Navalny 2021: In August 2020, Navalny was poisoned by Russian agents. The Trump administration characteristically looked the other way. On January 17, 2021, after recovering in a German hospital, Navalny returned to Russia. He was promptly arrested. In imposing sanctions, the Biden administration spoke of "condemning" the Russian action and "to send a clear signal that use of chemical weapons and abuse of human rights have severe consequences"—that is, both to coerce domestic political change and as symbolic affirmation of principles.[37]

Afghanistan 1980: In December 1979 the Soviet Union invaded Afghanistan. No nation, "committed to world peace and stability," President Carter told the nation, "can continue to do business as usual with the Soviet Union." The objectives of the sanctions along with military and diplomatic measures were both to compel the Soviets to get out of Afghanistan and to deter them for taking similar actions elsewhere.

Ukraine 2014, 2022: In February 2014 protesters toppled the pro-Russia and highly corrupt President Viktor Yanukovych. Russia intervened with some of its own military forces and annexed Crimea, part of Ukraine. Sanctions were part of a broader US and European strategy including military and economic aid to the Ukrainian government, covert action, and diplomatic negotiations seeking to pressure Russia to withdraw its troops and proxies from Ukrainian territory and reverse its annexation of Crimea and deter it from escalating further. None of this happened.

Starting in late 2021, Russia mobilized close to 200,000 troops, fleets of tanks and other heavy equipment, and bombers at various locations along the Ukrainian border. The Biden administration threatened major sanctions along with other measures seeking to deter Russia. In February 2022, Russia invaded, massively and with wanton destruction. The extensive sanctions the US then imposed, joined not only by NATO allies but numerous other countries as well as many major multinational corporations, were intended along with other elements of the strategy (diplomatic pressure, military aid to Ukraine) to coerce Russia to end its invasion.

WHAT Types of Sanctions Were Imposed?

Jackson-Vanik: Withholding most-favored-nation status, key for Soviet exports to be price competitive in American markets, until the Soviets met a US-imposed quota for Soviet Jewish emigration was the main sanction.

Navalny: The Navalny sanctions were part of an early Biden administration package also citing Russian election interference, use of chemical weapons in poisoning other dissidents, and cyberhacking. Some were sectoral, tightening restrictions on technology and commercial exports. Some were financial including a ban on purchasing Russian sovereign debt in international financial markets. Some were targeted at key individuals and organizations closely associated with the Navalny case, although not including Putin or others in his senior leadership.

Afghanistan 1980: Grain exports were embargoed. All existing licenses for high-technology exports were suspended. Future applications to export technology were subjected to a presumption of denial, with some of the strictest standards applied to oil and gas.

Ukraine 2014, 2022: Sectoral sanctions were imposed against the Russian energy sector banning technology for oil and gas exploration and financial credits to Russian energy companies such as Rosneft and Gazprom. Financing for state-owned banks was banned. A series of Obama executive orders expanded the SDN List to include oligarchs and others in Putin's inner circle. In April 2018, under congressional pressure from legislation passed with bipartisan support and trying to deflect from revelations about Russian interference in his 2016 election victory, Trump allowed Treasury OFAC to add other Russians to the SDN List. The Biden administration imposed additional sanctions including financial ones on this and other "aggressive and harmful" Russian actions.[38] The EU added to its sanctions as well.[39]

The sanctions imposed by the US and the EU in response to the 2022 Russian invasion were sweeping. Financial sanctions hit Russian banks and dollar-based economic transactions. Technology sanctions went after imports like semiconductors key to both military industries and commercial products like cellphones and cars. Russian commercial airlines were banned from flying over Europe and to the US. They also lost a large share of their fleet when Ireland ended leases on over 200 planes to Russian carriers.[40] More Russian oligarchs as well as top military officials and Putin himself were added to the SDN List for individualized sanctions on their financial assets, travel bans, superyacht seizures, and other measures. While initially Russian oil exports were only minimally sanctioned, constrained by Europe being heavily reliant on them (about 25% of its oil imports) and American inflationary concerns of higher gas prices, as the war intensified oil also got sanctioned. The new Nord Stream 2 natural gas pipeline was blocked from completion (Chapter 7), although existing natural gas shipments were scaled back but not shut off given even higher European dependence on Russian natural gas. Sports and cultural sanctions added their own economic effects as well as a sense of isolation for Russians and their society with bans including from the World Cup (men's and women's), Wimbledon Tennis, International Ice Hockey Federation, Formula One, Cannes Film Festival, and Eurovision.

While some countries refused to join the sanctions—China and India being two major ones—international support was widespread. Even Switzerland, typically neutral in international disputes, agreed to impose similar sanctions to the EU ones. Asian allies such as Japan, South Korea, and Australia also joined in—Singapore, too, which had never before imposed non-UN authorized sanctions. UN sanctions were blocked by the Russian Security Council veto, but the General Assembly voted to condemn the Russian invasion by an astounding 141–5 vote.

In contrast to most cases in which major multinational companies resist sanctions, close to 1000 companies—oil companies like BP and ExxonMobil, retail companies like Nike and Ikea, restaurant chains like McDonald's and Starbucks, auto companies like BMW and Ford, entertainment companies like Disney, tech companies like Apple and Google, and Coinbase the largest US cryptocurrency exchange—ended or at least suspended business in and with Russia.

All told, these were the most extensive and globally supported sanctions the US had ever imposed.

WHO Were the Key Actors?

Sender: US

Target: Soviet Union/Russia

Third Parties: Jackson-Vanik was largely US-Soviet bilateral. Afghanistan 1980, Ukraine 2014, and Navalny 2021 involved American allies (NATO, EU, others). Ukraine 2022 had broad global support but with China, India, and some other countries as alternative trade partners.

HOW Did the Sanctions Play Out?

Jackson-Vanik: President Richard Nixon and National Security Advisor Henry Kissinger strongly opposed congressional efforts to make the MFN-Jewish emigration linkage. "How would it be," Kissinger asked, "if [Soviet leader] Brezhnev comes to the United States with a petition about the Negroes in Mississippi?" The Soviets actually had been increasing Soviet Jewish emigration (from 13,020 in 1971 to almost 35,000 in 1973) as part of the overall détente give-and-take and trying to signal the American Congress that no formal pressure was needed. But when formal pressure came with the passage of Jackson-Vanik and the setting of a 60,000 annual quota, the issue became, as a top Kremlin leader put it, a matter "of sovereignty and of our internal affairs." In 1975, Jewish emigration fell back down to 13,221.

Navalny: Along with other early Biden administration actions and statements, the Navalny sanctions sent the message that the post-Trump US was done looking the other way at Putin's actions. In being well coordinated with European sanctions, they conveyed revitalized alliance solidarity. They were more limited, though, than human rights activists called for. Of the thirty inner-circle Putin cronies that Navalny supporters pointed to, only three were initially included in the Biden sanctions.[41] While the sovereign debt sanctions went further, one business analyst assessed that they still could "easily be circumvented via the secondary market."[42]

Afghanistan 1980: The Soviets deepened their involvement in Afghanistan, withdrawing only in 1988 as part of President Mikhail Gorbachev's reforms. They offset much of the US grain embargo with alternative trade partners, Argentina being one of them as a major grain producer and its military government at the time subject to American sanctions on human rights issues. For Jimmy Carter, the sanctions did not play well with the American home crowd. American farmers vented their anger about the lost grain sales by voting in overwhelming numbers for presidential candidate Ronald Reagan.

Ukraine 2014, 2022: Declining oil prices, corruption, and mismanagement had the Russian economy already in rough shape in 2014. With the sanctions added, GDP fell 2 percent, the ruble close to 60 percent in value against the dollar.[43] Yet neither the overall economic impact nor the SDN hits on Putin's buddies budged Russia out of Ukraine. In keeping with Russia being, as former senior US policymaker Thomas Graham put it, "a patrimonial state, in which personal wealth and social position are ultimately dependent on the good graces of those in power," the oligarchs were more circuit breakers than transmission belts.[44] American domestic constraints further compounded sanctions impact. ExxonMobil and other oil sector companies with lucrative contracts for Russian Arctic oil and gas development lobbied to loosen the sanctions and busted them as they deemed fit their interests.[45] Even with bipartisan congressional support for the 2017 Countering America's Adversaries Through Sanctions Act (419–3 in the House, 98–2 in the Senate), with Trump there was little commitment to implementation and enforcement.

The 2022 sanctions had quite substantial economic impact on Russia. GDP, which grew 4.7 percent in 2021, was projected to contract 10–15 percent in 2022. Inflation was running at 17 percent. Unemployment was projected to exceed 9 percent for the first time in a decade. In mid-April the Moscow Mayor warned of 200,000 jobs at risk in the capital city. For the first time since the 1917 Bolshevik revolution international debt default loomed. The ruble initially depreciated from 84 to the dollar to 154. The Russian central bank got the ruble mostly propped back up but with little confidence in its ongoing value. Other counterstrategies—for example, increasing retiree pensions, bailing out some companies—offset some other costs. But Elvira Nabiullina, central bank chairwoman, warned that "the period during which the economy can live on reserves is finite."[46] Some trade came from China, India, and other alternative partners; for example, India contracted for more Russian oil in the first four months of the Ukraine war than in all of 2021.[47] But this and other alternative trade was not on a scale or of a type to substantially offset the sanctions. Even so, while the overall effect was more than what a *New York Times* editorial called "dents in both Russia's economy and its ability to wage war in Ukraine," it was less than Biden administration initial claims of "devastating" and "overwhelming."[48]

Similar mixed assessment holds for the sanctions targeted at Russian oligarchs and state officials. Some of the oligarchs got hit hard: superyachts seized, assets like the British Chelsea football (soccer) club having to be sold. Others had well hidden their assets in offshore tax and financial havens, in some instances with collusion from American financial institutions and law firms.[49]

Case Assessment

In the Soviet Jewish emigration case when pressures were kept informal and addressed as part of the overall give-and-take détente diplomacy, the Soviets did show some flexibility, as evidenced in the 1971–1973 170% increase in Soviet Jewish emigration. President Gerald Ford claimed that Soviet ambassador Anatoly Dobrynin privately gave him an oral guarantee of 55,000. But once Congress passed Jackson-Vanik, singling out the issue and making Soviet domestic political change an American demand, the crackdown came. This fits the greater success rates sanctions threats have over sanctions imposition, and when sanctions are part of reciprocal diplomacy. Moreover, because they were congressionally mandated sanctions, Jackson-Vanik stayed on the books for many years after Soviet Jewish emigration had opened up, complicating Cold War–ending diplomacy.

On the one hand, it was hard to imagine the Biden administration not acting on Navalny. Both politics and policy pointed to differentiating from Trump on Russia in particular and human rights in general. Alliance solidarity also was a factor, as Europe already had imposed its Navalny sanctions.

Yet Russia characteristically resisted freeing Navalny. While symbolic value still could be claimed for acting on principle, the failure to have significant impact took away from the credibility of American power. Arguments also cut both ways as to whether taking a stand on this issue showed a toughness that helped on other US-Russian issues or exacerbated tensions in ways that impeded other progress. Russian retaliation with its own measures also needs to be taken into account in a net assessment.

Both the Afghanistan 1980 and Ukraine 2014 sanctions did impose significant costs. This, as stressed, can be an objective in itself. That neither got the Soviets/Russians to end their military aggression is in keeping with other cases (e.g., League of Nations Italy-Ethiopia 1935–1936) that show the inherent disproportionality between the means of sanctions as a limited coercive instrument and the ends of compelling military withdrawal as a quite extensive objective.

What, though, of the secondary deterrence objectives? It's not clear Brezhnev had any intentions of going into the Persian Gulf. Moreover, to the extent that he was deterred, it's likely that it was more from US military moves such as the Carter Doctrine, launching the Rapid Deployment Force, and formation of the Gulf Cooperation Council (GCC). While it still it could be argued that the costs sanctions imposed over time were a factor in what Gorbachev called the "bleeding wound" that led to his 1988 withdrawal from Afghanistan, it was a limited one compared to the burdens of the nuclear arms race and the Soviet economy's own systemic flaws.[50]

The sanctions the Biden administration threatened as Russian forces mobilized near Ukraine starting in late 2021 were intended to deter an outright invasion. This failed.[51] Once Russia invaded, the sanctions imposed were intended to support Ukraine's defense and pressure Russia to end the war. While the economic costs paid by Russia have been considerable, thus far (May 2022) this has been another case of an economic impact-policy compliance gap. Nor have the sanctions targeted at Russian oligarchs and key government officials moved them from being circuit breakers to transmission belts. Most of the oligarchs have their assets well hidden. The few that have spoken out have paid a price—Oleg Tinkov, for example, who after an Instagram post criticizing the war was forced to dump his $9 billion bank at firesale prices, and then retreated into hiding.[52] Whatever the combination of loyalty, like-mindedness, and intimidation, military and other state officials, the so-called *siloviki*, have stayed in line with Putin.

At the same time there have been global costs and risks. With the sanctions and war adding to other economic instabilities, global GDP growth projections were cut from 4.4 to 3.6 percent. Inflation was further exacerbated in the US, Europe, and most everywhere. Poor and developing countries have been especially hard hit including by food shortages. World oil prices, about $96 a barrel pre-war, shot up to $139/barrel (highest in 14 years) with some leveling off since but still lots of fluctuation. Coal, steel, aluminum, nickel, and palladium are among the other commodities hit by rising prices and supply chain disruptions. And while Putin's calling sanctions "economic war" is in part rhetoric, the risks of horizontal and vertical escalation are very real: "horizontal" meaning to other countries (Moldova? a NATO member?) and "vertical" meaning climbing the ladder toward use of nuclear weapons.[53]

If things do get to the point that Russia concedes to ending the war on terms acceptable to Ukraine and the international community, sanctions will warrant some credit. The main credit, though, will go to the military strategy. Had the Ukrainian forces not been so skilled and courageous and the US and Europe not provided such massive military aid, no sanctions would have stopped Putin from conquest.

China: Human Rights and Geopolitical Rivalry

During the Cold War, the US and its allies imposed sanctions against "Red China" similar to those imposed against the Soviet

Union and Soviet bloc. Relations began to change with the 1971–1972 "opening" negotiated by President Richard Nixon and National Security Advisor Henry Kissinger with Chinese leaders Mao Zedong and Zhou Enlai. In 1979, President Jimmy Carter and Chinese leader Deng Xiaoping established full diplomatic relations. Trade grew to the point of being each other's top trade partners. Yet the countries have remained ideological opponents and increasingly have become geopolitical rivals. We see the former in two major human rights sanctions cases, the June 1989 Tiananmen Square massacre and the recent atrocities against the Muslim ethnic minority Uyghurs and the latter in the Huawei sanctions case.

WHY Did the US Impose Sanctions?

Tiananmen Square: In spring 1989, in part spurred by democratization in other parts of the communist world (the Soviet Union under Gorbachev, Poland led by Lech Wałęsa, Czechoslovakia led by Václav Havel), pro-democracy protests grew rapidly in China. Tens of thousands of students, workers, and others made Beijing's Tiananmen Square, seat of the government and party, protests ground zero. While General Party Secretary Zhao Ziyang felt dialogue possible with the protesters and that the changes being pushed could be accommodated, paramount leader Deng Xiaoping saw the goal as "overthrowing the regime . . . aided by hostile outside forces."[54] Deng purged Zhao. On the night of June 3–4, the government brutally cracked down, sending tanks and heavily armed soldiers into the square. Thousands were arrested. The government claimed only about 200 deaths: leaked documents estimated the death toll as high as 10,000.[55] US sanctions thus were intended to pressure China for domestic political change and as broader signaling of American principles.

Uyghurs: These sanctions also had domestic political change and symbolic signaling objectives. China has been accused of genocide and crimes against humanity for the atrocities

perpetrated against the Uyghurs in the western China region of Xinjiang. Estimates are of about 1.5 million Uyghurs
hauled into political prison camps and subjected to forced
labor. Women have been involuntarily sterilized. Surveillance
systems have been set up throughout Xinjiang, biometric data
forcibly collected. "Death is everywhere," an exiled leader of
the Uyghur World Congress reported in 2020.[56]

Huawei: Sanctions were imposed on Huawei, a leading
Chinese communications technology company producing
smartphones and infrastructure such as 5G wireless technology, for national security reasons. While formally an independent company, its close links to the Chinese government
raised significant security concerns for the US and its allies,
including espionage "backdoors" in its 5G systems. It also
was a major commercial competitor to American companies,
in 2018 passing Apple as the second-leading smartphone provider globally. Along with ZTE, another Chinese telecommunications company, Huawei accounted for about 40 percent
of global 5G infrastructure and had over ninety commercial
contracts for additional 5G equipment.

WHAT Types of Sanctions Were Imposed?

Tiananmen Square: The main issue was whether to suspend the
favored tariff treatment (most favored nation [MFN] is the technical term) on Chinese imports to the US. Prioritizing overall
strategic interests in the US-China relationship, the Bush administration imposed some sanctions but resisted suspending
MFN.[57] Getting tougher with "the butchers of Beijing" was
a resonant part of Bill Clinton's 1992 presidential campaign.
Yet once he became president, having also campaigned on
the slogan "it's the economy, stupid," Clinton somewhat
toughened the conditions but continued MFN.

Uyghurs: In 2021, with rare bipartisanship, indeed close
to unanimity (by unanimous vote in the Senate, 428–1 in the
House), Congress passed the Uyghur Forced Labor Prevention

Act. President Biden then signed it into law. This was a wide prohibition, with any goods even partially manufactured in the Xinjiang region presumed to include at least some Uyghur forced labor. Companies could appeal, but the burden of proof was with them to convincingly show that no Uyghur forced labor went into any item in their supply chain. Chinese officials and companies most closely connected to Uyghur atrocities were added to the SDN List with travel bans, assets freezes, and other measures.

Huawei: In May 2019, sanctions were announced banning Huawei from American communications networks and prohibiting its use of American semiconductor chips and technologies such as Alphabet Inc.'s (Google) Android operating system in products sold anywhere in the world. But the Trump administration was inconsistent in their implementation. For example, on August 18 President Trump spoke to national security concerns for not doing business with Huawei, only to have his Commerce Department the very next day extend temporary licenses for companies still doing business with Huawei. In May 2020, sanctions were tightened up, including secondary ones applied to semiconductors made by foreign companies using American components and technology. The Biden administration added to the sanctions and stepped up efforts to get other countries to ban Huawei from their 5G networks.

WHO Were the Key Actors?

Sender: US

Target: China

Third parties: Europe and other US allies, various China trade partners, and US and other international companies with extensive business interests in China.

HOW Did the Sanctions Play Out?

Tiananmen Square: In Congress a coalition of conservatives and liberals, combining the anti-communism of the right and

human rights advocacy of the left, pushed the Bush administration for more extensive sanctions. Clinton tried to navigate
his "butchers of Beijing" criticism of the Bush administration
and his own "it's the economy, stupid" prioritization. I was
serving in the State Department and involved in trying to
bridge our own department's differences between the Human
Rights Bureau's support for tough sanctions and the East Asia
bureau's concern about damage to overall US-China relations. The sanctions that did get added were more than Bush's
but less than many advocates wanted. For its part, Beijing
doubled down on repressiveness, strengthening the People's
Armed Police and units policing the Internet, seeking to
show what Andrew Nathan, the Columbia University scholar
who got access to the regime's secret papers, calls "resilient
authoritarianism."[58]

Uyghurs: Whereas we saw major multinational companies
cooperate with the 2022 Russia Ukraine sanctions, many
worked against the Uyghurs sanctions. "A fierce corporate
lobbying campaign" was how the *New York Times* characterized
business opposition to the Uyghur Forced Labor Prevention
Act. Tech companies were among the major contractors for
Chinese facial recognition, 24/7 GPS tracking, and other
"Orwellian state" technologies.[59] Nike, Coca-Cola, Apple,
and other companies were using Uyghur forced labor in their
supply chains. When Intel sent a letter to its suppliers once
the legislation passed instructing them to avoid sourcing from
Xinjiang, Chinese social media lit up with such uproar that it
took the letter down from its website and went so far as to
apologize to the Chinese public. This in turn set off heavy criticism back in the US.[60]

Internationally, Biden did more than Trump to coordinate
sanctions with democratic allies in Europe and Canada. Asian
allies Japan, Australia, and New Zealand, more dependent
on trade with China, gave rhetorical support but didn't impose sanctions of their own. Despite that the atrocities
being perpetrated against Muslims, the forty-nine-country

Organization of Islamic Cooperation passed a resolution praising China for "providing care to its Muslim citizens."[61] For all its claims to being the guardians of Islam's holy places, Saudi Arabia has been largely silent on the Uyghurs. In his July 2019 visit to Beijing, Turkish president Recep Tayyip Erdoğan told reporters that the Uyghur issue had been exploited to undermine Turkish-Chinese relations.[62] Demand by 180 human rights and related NGOs for a boycott of the 2022 Beijing Winter Olympics because of the Uyghurs was met by the statement from a senior International Olympics Committee official that this would be "a gesture that we know will have no impact whatsoever."[63]

Huawei: Impact of the May 2019 first wave sanctions was limited. Huawei revenues were up 17 percent over 2018, net profits up $5 billion. Loopholes and waivers allowed purchases from American companies to increase over 60 percent.[64] Once the sanctions were tightened, the economic impact increased. Fourth quarter 2020 smartphone global sales were down 42 percent, Huawei falling all the way to fifth place. Even within China, its 2021 market share fell from 23 percent to 7 percent, with Apple moving into first place. Still while 2021 revenues were down 29 percent, business adjustments and some Chinese government support had net profits up 76 percent. And innovation was kept sufficiently apace for Huawei to move up to fifth place in the number of US patents.[65]

Even more than the ban on the American domestic market, the extraterritorial application to foreign companies using Google's Android and other American technologies and parts was a key lever. China accused the US of claiming security concerns as "as a pretext for suppressing foreign business," and imposed countersanctions against American companies. Initially other than Australia and a few others, most countries resisted Huawei 5G network bans. But as China's repression at home and assertiveness if not aggression abroad fed greater security concerns, more countries—including Britain, Denmark, India, Japan, New Zealand, and Sweden—imposed at least some restrictions if not outright bans on Huawei 5G. Numerous other countries, though, have continued to strike deals with Huawei.

Case Assessment

I got an even deeper sense for how little Chinese domestic political change the Tiananmen Square sanctions had achieved during a fall 2019 Duke graduate student class discussion about the role of history in the present. A couple weeks earlier, manifesting William Faulkner's "the past is never dead, it's never even past," Spain unburied dictator Francisco Franco from the massive Valley of the Fallen mausoleum originally built to honor him, and China finally gave permission for the purged Zhao Ziyang's ashes to be buried fourteen years after his 2005 death. Two Chinese students in the class looked at me blankly. They later privately told me they didn't know who I was talking about, they'd never heard of Zhao Ziyang. It wasn't that they'd been taught he was a disgraced leader. He'd been expurgated from any mention in any schoolbook. I had had experience drawing blanks from Googling Tiananmen Square when in China, but this really drove home the depth to which China had resisted the domestic political change sanctions proponents had sought.

Like the Russia Navalny sanctions, the Uyghurs sanctions had symbolic value for Biden reclaiming human rights post-Trump. But as horrific as the atrocities against the Uyghurs have been—genocide in the view of the US and some others—sanctions have not been able to coerce policy change. While some costs have been imposed, they have not been sufficient given the imbalance of interests given Chinese stakes in resisting. China has slapped back with its own sanctions against the US as well as Canada and Europe. "They must stop political manipulation on Xinjiang-related issues, stop interfering in China's internal affairs in any form and refrain from going further down the wrong path. Otherwise, they will get their fingers burnt," the Chinese Foreign Ministry retorted.[66]

Two factors explain the Huawei sanctions getting more international cooperation than either of the human rights sanctions. One is the market dominance the US still had in key technologies. American chip makers held 47 percent of global production. Another 29 percent was offshore production in European and Asian allied countries subject to the extraterritorial reach of American secondary sanctions. There thus were few prospective alternative trade partners.[67] The other was Huawei being so closely linked to Chinese government military and intelligence operations and thus security concerns taking precedence over commercial ones.[68] While international cooperation has not been as extensive as the US wanted, it did represent a significant degree of success.

North Korea Nuclear Proliferation: Array of Target Counterstrategies

While US sanctions go back to the 1950 Korean War, it was the 1990s when the nuclear proliferation issue emerged. The International Atomic Energy Agency found evidence that North Korea was not abiding by commitments made in signing the multilateral Nuclear Nonproliferation Treaty (NPT). North Korea still did not have nuclear weapons, but was seeking to develop them. It refused to comply, insisting that its nuclear program was for peaceful energy supply. In 2003, North Korea formally withdrew from the NPT. It conducted a first nuclear weapons test in 2006. In the years since, more sanctions have been imposed, including multilaterally by the UN. But North Korea has kept increasing its nuclear weapons and ballistic missiles.

WHY Did the US Impose Sanctions?

The goals have been both to deny access to nuclear- and missile-related items and technology (limit military capabilities) and to coerce North Korea to agree to a policy of nuclear nonproliferation (foreign policy restraint). Human rights also has been a factor (domestic political change), as has terrorism (foreign policy restraint). Other incidents such as the 2014 hacking of Sony Pictures over a film that satirized "Dear Leader" Kim Jong-un have prompted additional sanctions.

WHAT Types of Sanctions Were Imposed?

The Clinton administration tried a mixed sanctions-inducements strategy offering alternative energy supplies, food aid for the massive famine then taking hold, and other benefits linked to NPT compliance. The deal fell apart. In 2005 as North Korea further developed its nuclear weapons and ballistic missiles, the George W. Bush administration ratcheted sanctions up. The Obama administration did the same. The Trump administration added to these while also launching summit diplomacy, Trump and Kim meeting twice but without significant progress.

The first UN sanctions were approved by the Security Council in 2006 in response to North Korea's first nuclear weapons test. Numerous additional Security Council sanctions resolutions were passed further tightening and expanding sanctions. South Korea and Japan also had their own additional sanctions.

WHO Were the Key Actors?

Sender: US, UN
Target: North Korea
Third parties: China

HOW Did the Sanctions Play Out?

While sanctions have been a factor, North Korea's economic problems have been mostly caused by North Korean policies. Domestic food production that did not even reach minimum human need levels, let alone normal human need, was the main factor in the mass famine that started in 1994 and lasted close to a decade. The $2.4 billion the international community provided brought some relief, but less than it would have had the North Korean government not interfered with efforts to distribute the aid on a need, not political basis.[69]

Concern about North Korea's 2003 withdrawal from the NPT was sufficiently shared that the US, China, Russia, Japan, and South Korea came together to launch the Six Party Talks with North Korea. These lasted on and off until 2010, with some progress but not enough to head off continued North Korean nuclear weapons development.

China's position has been mixed. It supported the initial 2006 UN sanctions as well as some but not others. While North Korea was a longtime ally, China did not want it to gain nuclear weapons. It was somewhat leery of the young untested Kim Jong-un when he came to power following his father's death in December 2011. But its economy, particularly in the northeastern region, relied on North Korean trade, including minerals, textiles, seafood, and labor. The foreign currency generated by these exports allowed North Korea to import Chinese goods. From 2008 to 2014, Chinese–North Korean trade grew 143 percent. After North Korea's fourth nuclear test in 2016, and with added pressure from US secondary sanctions, bilateral trade was cut by 54 percent. Even then, though, China and China-based entities engaged in sanctions busting through ship-to-ship transfers of embargoed petroleum products, allowing North Korean workers to remain in China and send earnings home, protecting North Korean hackers and providing some technological infrastructure and Internet connectivity.[70]

North Korea has also been pulling off plenty of other sanctions busting. The Singapore-based oil trader Winson Group was found to be covertly delivering oil. A 2019 UN study estimated North Korea had raised $2 billion through cybercrime, to which an investigative journalism article added "bountiful evidence to indicate that the pace and ingenuity of NK's online threat has accelerated." In May 2020 the US

Justice Department indicted shell companies and banks based in at least six different countries for laundering $2.5 billion to North Korea. Chainanalysis, a blockchain analysis company, revealed over $400 million in North Korean cryptocurrency thefts in 2021.[71]

Such measures have reduced but not blocked the sanctions' economic impact. North Korea's foreign trade plummeted from $2.9 billion in 2016 to $260 million in 2019. Its GDP fell from a growth rate of +3.9 percent in 2016 to −4.1 percent in 2018 and −4.5 percent in 2021. A UN Food and Agriculture Organization and World Food Programme report found that sanctions limiting fuel, fertilizer, and machinery necessary for agricultural production have had adverse effect on irrigation and yields.[72] At the January 2021 Workers Party Congress, Kim apologized to the country for the state of the economy. "Our five-year economic development plan has fallen greatly short of its goals in almost all sectors. . . . I am really sorry for that. My efforts and sincerity have not been sufficient enough to rid our people of the difficulties in their life."[73] But there did not appear to be any threats to Kim's leadership. While poverty has worsened and the humanitarian situation has been further exacerbated, elites continued to be well cushioned, buying odd luxury goods and all.[74]

And the North Korean nuclear weapons and ballistic missile programs have kept moving forward.

Case Assessment

The various negotiating efforts, both Six Party and US–North Korea, have tried to find a sanctions lifting–nonproliferation reciprocity formula. The sequencing and timing, how much sanctions get lifted for how many steps toward nonproliferation, have been elusive. Drawing lessons from Iraq's Saddam Hussein and Libya's Muammar Qaddafi having given up their nuclear weapons development programs and later being overthrown (more to the point, killed), Kim sees his nuclear weapons as an insurance policy against regime change. For that he is quite rational. The issue as he sees it is not just limited foreign policy restraint but the much more disproportionate risk of survival. Absorbing economic costs is preferable to giving up that insurance policy. Whatever its flaws and incompetence, North Korea has used an array of counterstrategies—keeping elites comfortable, sanctions busting, China as an alternative trade partner—to make itself, as Stephan Haggard and Marcus Noland put it, "the paradigmatic hard target."[75]

Venezuela: Regime Still Standing, the People Hurting

American-Venezuelan relations have been conflictual ever since Chávez's rise to power in the late 1990s. Tensions increased further following Chávez's death in 2013 and succession by his right-hand man, Nicolas Maduro, in an election widely seen as neither free nor fair. Maduro became increasingly repressive and the situation for the Venezuelan people increasingly dire.

WHY Did the US Impose Sanctions?

Sanctions started as pressure for democratization and human rights protection during the Obama administration. They became the pursuit of regime change in the Trump administration. Stopping support for terrorism and involvement in drug trafficking have also been objectives.

WHAT Types of Sanctions Were Imposed?

The 2014 Venezuelan Defense of Human Rights and Civil Society Act passed by Congress and the follow-on executive orders from President Obama imposed additional sanctions on top of those already in place. In another version of its maximum pressure strategy, the Trump administration intensified the sanctions to cover almost all trade and finance targeting the Venezuelan oil industry in particular. Venezuela has long been a major oil-producing country; indeed, it was one of the founders of OPEC back in 1960. For many years the US was its major customer, importing close to 36 percent of Venezuelan oil exports prior to the sanctions. In August 2017 a Trump executive order banned Petroleos de Venezuela, the main state-controlled oil company, from American and any dollar-denominated international financial markets. In May 2018 additional sanctions effectively ended the US-Venezuelan oil trade. Other sanctions froze other Venezuelan assets, including through SDN listing of Maduro, his family, and other top officials. In August 2019, secondary sanctions against non-Venezuelans involved with the Venezuelan economy were added. Canada and the EU kept their sanctions limited to ones targeting Maduro and other key leaders rather than the economy-wide US ones. Most Latin American countries applied other pressure but imposed limited if any sanctions. The Biden administration kept most of the Trump sanctions in place with a few humanitarian exemptions, such as in July 2021 allowing propane supplies to mitigate cooking gas shortages among the Venezuelan people.

WHO Were the Key Actors?

Sender state: US, EU, some Latin American countries
Target state: Venezuela
Third parties: Russia, China, Cuba, Turkey

HOW Did the Sanctions Play Out?

The combination of Chávez-Maduro mismanagement and corruption, fluctuating global oil prices, and the sanctions made for quite substantial economic impact. In 2000, the early days of Chávez, oil production was about 2.9 million barrels per day. By 2016 that measure was down to about 2.3 million and by 2020 it was less than 500,000. With oil having constituted 35 percent of GDP and 99 percent of export earnings, the overall Venezuelan economy contracted 45 percent. Inflation rose an astounding 10 million percent. By 2019, 96 percent of the population was living below the poverty line, 80 percent in extreme poverty.[76] Sanctions and hard currency shortages pushed food imports way down from $11.2 billion to $2.46 billion. Numbers of undernourished children were 400 percent higher than 2012. Clean water was tightly rationed. The close to 5 million Venezuelan refugees, about 16 percent of the prior population, was the second highest in the world yet the most underfunded, namely, $1,500 per Syrian refugee, $125 per Venezuelan.[77] The situation truly was, as a US Congressional Research Service report put it, a "dire humanitarian crisis."[78]

Yet Maduro was still in power. Russia provided financial, military, and diplomatic support. China increased imports of Venezuelan oil. Cuba provided doctors and other health sector assistance in exchange for Venezuelan oil. Iran provided some gasoline and other refined products. Turkey purchased an estimated $800 million worth of gold reserves in 2018, apparently as manifestation of autocrat solidarity from President Erdoğan. And in classic circuit-breaker fashion, assuaged economically and fearful politically, most of the police, military, courts, and bureaucracy stuck by Maduro. A combination of US unwillingness to take the diplomatic route and Maduro's resistance to compromise undermined mediation efforts by the Lima Group coalition of Latin American countries and Canada. Trump instead tried in 2017 and 2018 to cultivate a coup with some rebellious military officers. A May 2020 operation by American mercenaries, apparently blessed and perhaps coordinated by the Trump administration, was a disaster, characterized by the *New York Times* journalist who broke the story as "something out of a Hollywood script," with some of the Americans taken prisoner.[79]

Case Assessment

Principal fault for Venezuela's humanitarian crisis, indeed for the destruction of what had been one of the more robust civil societies in Latin America, lies with Maduro and Chávez. But the sanctions have also been a contributing factor.[80] The refugee flow to neighboring Colombia, Peru, and other countries has added to the burdens these countries are already facing. Perhaps the Lima Group diplomacy could have worked, at least negotiating terms for averting and alleviating the humanitarian situation, had the US supported it. What we do know is the Maduro regime was left still standing, and the Venezuelan people still hurting. Sanctions didn't just fail in the sense of not succeeding. They made a bad situation substantially worse, raising ethical issues discussed in Chapter 2.

Counterterrorism: Scope and Limits of Financial Sanctions

US counterterrorism strategy obviously has entailed a lot more than economic sanctions. The sanctions have been targeted at specific countries deemed state sponsors of terrorism, at transnational terrorist organizations, and at individuals and organizations providing links in the terrorism financing chains. Treasury's Office of Foreign Assets Control (OFAC) has been the lead agency. Commerce, State, Homeland Security, and the FBI also have been involved. UN Security Council Resolution 1373, passed right after 9/11, requires states to criminalize financial support for terrorism. The coalitional Financial Action Task Force (FATF), established in 1989 by the US and some allies, also has played a role. While originally prioritizing drug trafficking money laundering, since 9/11 FATF has been heavily focused on terrorism. It now has thirty-nine members as well as links to other multilateral organizations such as the World Bank and Interpol.

WHY Did the US Impose Sanctions?

A FATF report conveys the core rationale:

> Combatting and disrupting terrorist financing creates a hostile environment for terrorism. Lack of money limits the capability of terrorist groups to prepare or carry out

attacks; and financial intelligence can reveal the structure of terrorist groups, the activities of individual terrorists, and their logistics and facilitation networks. Financing is important for all terrorists—from large terrorist organizations which control territory to small terrorist cells.[81]

There are elements here of both foreign policy restraint and military capabilities limitation.

WHAT Types of Sanctions Were Imposed?

These sanctions have included asset freezes and seizures, restrictions on a range of types of financial transactions, aid cutoffs to organizations deemed linked to terrorists, secondary sanctions on non-US financial institutions, blocking cross-border transportation of cash, and breaking up *hawalas* with their informal method of "money transfer without money movement."[82] The counterterrorism component of the SDN List is in the thousands of individuals and organizations providing links in the financial chain.

WHO Were the Key Actors?

Senders: US, EU, FATF

Target: Countries on the US state sponsors of terrorism list: currently Iran, North Korea, Cuba, and Syria; previously Iraq, Libya, South Yemen, and Sudan. Non-state terrorist organizations such as al Qaeda, Hizbollah, ISIS, and over forty others also are targeted.

Third parties: Non-state actors such as the hawalas and charitable front organizations are the main third-party potential sanctions busters.

HOW Did the Sanctions Play Out?

SWIFT, the global financial messaging and transmission system discussed in the Iran case, is also relevant here, so much so that Farrell and Newman dub it "the Rosetta stone for

U.S. counterterrorism operations."[83] In Farrell and Newman's terms, it provided both "panopticon" effects of extensive information on money flows to terrorists and "chokepoint" capacity to block and intercept transactions. FATF's effectiveness goes beyond its formal members by having "prompted international banks to move resources away from [non-cooperating] states and raised the costs of continued noncompliance, significantly increasing the number of states with laws criminalizing terrorist financing."[84]

In its 2018 annual report, OFAC calculated $216.83 million blocked from reaching state sponsors of terrorism and $46.2 million from more than forty non-state terrorist organizations.[85] Other operations broke up quite the range of terrorist financing schemes, including $2 million in Bitcoin and other cryptocurrency, a scam website and set of Facebook pages fraudulently claiming to have N95 masks and other personal protective equipment (PPE), and an Australian-based gemstone company.[86]

Case Assessment

Yes, al Qaeda is still functioning. It's not as strong as it was pre-9/11, but stronger than it had been for a while. Its affiliates have shifted to more of a local financing strategy to get around SWIFT and FATF. Even after losing much of its territorial control in Syria, ISIS still had an estimated $100 million in financial reserves, with kidnapping ransoms among its versions of alternative financing. Hizbollah is still a force in Lebanon and Syria, and against Israel, turning more and more to its drug trade for funds. Yet terrorism would likely be even worse if not for limits imposed by financial sanctions. The assessment by then Treasury Under Secretary David Cohen strikes this net assessment balance:

We have no illusion that we can entirely prevent the flow of funds to terrorist groups. Some funds will find a

way to flow. But that does not mean the effort is futile—
far from it. What we have learned is that by deterring
would-be funders and disrupting the financial facilitation networks, we significantly impede terrorists' ability
to operate.[87]

Thus while not a full success, counterterrorism financing
sanctions can claim a degree of success.

Summary: What Main Conclusions Can Be Drawn and Challenges Identified for American Sanctions?

Sanctions are very much part of the American modus operandi. All
four factors delineated earlier in the chapter—interests, power,
ideology, politics—come through in the case studies. As a
great power with global interests, the US has many tools in
the toolbox, sanctions being one of them. American economic
preponderance and the power that is believed to come with it
have made sanctions particularly appealing. Ideological dis-
position makes human rights and democracy promotion a
frequent motivation. While politics sometimes works against
sanctions, more often it pushes toward them for presidents as
well as Congress.

Sanctions are being overused. The Biden administration has
been using sanctions even more than the Trump administration (and Trump more than Obama, Obama as much if not
more than Bush, etc.). The "Swiss army knife" metaphor well
captures this sense of sanctions as an all-purpose tool. They are
often the default option for any issue on which some coercion
is deemed needed. Yet as we've seen, their success rate does
not warrant such frequency of use.

Domestic politics has substantial impact on sanctions. Congress
has been playing an increasing role. In some instances, its support can strengthen the president's hand in making sanctions
credible. In others, it can be problematic, both in imposing

sanctions that presidents do not want and in legislating them with language that constrains presidential authority to lift them as part of negotiations. With regard to interest groups, we see pressure against sanctions (e.g., business opposition to the China Uyghurs sanctions) as well as pushes for sanctions that presidents may not favor (e.g., Jewish-Americans and the 1974 Jackson-Vanik sanctions) or want to reduce or lift (e.g., Cuban Americans on Cuba sanctions). Public opinion also can cut both ways, supportive in that "playing to the home crowd" way or opposed as with the Carter 1980 Soviet grain embargo. In cases such as the 1980s South Africa anti-apartheid sanctions, state and local governments were out in front of the federal government.

American sanctions often exemplify the economic impact–policy compliance disparity. The tendency to focus principally on sanctions' economic impact and not "sanctions' overall effectiveness in achieving broader U.S. policy goals or objectives" was a main criticism in a 2019 report by the US Government Accountability Office report.[88] Imposing economic costs, burdening target state economies, and punishing key individuals does have its own value. But even when these have been substantial, target policy change has not necessarily followed. Trump's sanctions hit Iran hard but fueled resistance not compliance. North Korea sanctions have imposed plenty of costs, but its nuclear weapons programs have grown even bigger. Other cases also speak to high economic costs (imposed or threatened) being necessary but not sufficient for sanctions success.

Given their strong security rationale and direct impact by embargoing the items involved without then having to leverage target decisions to change policy, sanctions for limiting military capabilities have been more achievable than for other objectives. The Huawei sanctions were more successful than the other China ones, effectively imposing policy change by cutting off key goods and technologies. The counterterrorism financial sanctions limited resources that impeded though did not prevent al Qaeda, ISIS, and other terrorism.

Foreign policy restraint objectives have been most likely to be achieved with some combination of diplomatic reciprocity, proportional objectives, and shared interests with key third parties. The Obama Iran sanctions were linked to reciprocating diplomacy, had proportionality as policy change not regime change, and tapped shared interests with Russia and China as well as European allies. The Trump Iran sanctions were non-reciprocating, disproportionate, and in tension with the other key countries. Ending the Soviet/Russian invasions of Afghanistan and Ukraine were more extensive objectives than sanctions as a limited instrument could coerce. Restricting Huawei was a more limited objective than some other US-China disputes and one many allies shared.

Sanctions seeking human rights protection and democracy promotion have a mixed record. None of the case studies in this category—Russian and Chinese human rights, Iranian and Venezuelan regime change—were successes. This is not to say human rights and democracy sanctions never succeed. The fact that some studies show lower likelihood still means that in some cases human rights do get protected and democracy promoted. Still, whether soft power and symbolic signaling are well served needs to be assessed rather than just assumed, including taking into account ethical considerations from any backfiring and misfiring with humanitarian consequences for the population that was to be protected.

Deterrence signaling has to be assessed as strategic interaction, taking into account whether message sent is the one received. Deterrence depends on whether shows of resolve are perceived as such. Credibility depends not just on the sender deeming signals a show of resolve but whether relevant others see them that way. Sanctions that are less than advertised can be seen by the target as signs of weakness not strength. Third-party adversaries may not be much deterred nor allies much reassured by a threat to hurt a target that doesn't actually hurt it very much. And as with Putin and Ukraine in 2022, some targets have objectives fundamentally not deterrable by sanctions.

Financial sanctions can have substantial economic impact but often still leave a policy compliance gap, risk humanitarian consequences, and raise concerns about a wasting asset. The dollar's centrality to international finance gives the US a market dominance it no longer has in most sectors of international trade. It is much harder for states targeted with financial sanctions to find alternative trade partners. But here too economic impact does not ensure policy compliance. The Trump Iran sanctions had greater economic impact than the Obama ones but lacked the diplomatic reciprocity that provided the basis for the Obama strategy to achieve policy change. Cases like Syria show the humanitarian consequences as financial sanctions end up much less targeted than claimed, with chilling effects on even legitimate trade as firms face risks and costs to ensure legal compliance and disincline even from supplying NGOs seeking to help the people. The Russia 2022 financial sanctions were the most extensive ever imposed but have not coerced Putin to end the war.

If the 2022 Russia sanctions do end up contributing to an end to the Ukraine war, concerns may be exacerbated that the US may resort to financial sanctions even more. Former Treasury Secretary Jacob Lew earlier raised the wasting asset concern that if American sanctions "excessively interfere with the flow of funds worldwide, financial transactions may begin to move outside of the United States entirely—which could threaten . . . the effectiveness of sanctions in the future." Mark Carney, governor of the Bank of England, pointed to "the growing asymmetry between the importance of the U.S. dollar in the global financial system and the increasingly multi-polar nature of global economic activity."[89] Secondary sanctions deployed to coerce international cooperation stoke resentments from allies who don't like their interdependence being weaponized, as well as countermoves by adversaries like China seeking to reduce vulnerability the next time around. It's worth noting in this regard that in its own October 2021 policy review (i.e., pre-Ukraine war) Biden's Treasury Department stressed the need to be "mindful of the risk" that "American adversaries—and some allies—are already reducing their use of the U.S. dollar and their exposure to the U.S. financial system more broadly in cross-border transactions."[90] It is not that the dollar would be replaced, but that it may finally lose its quasi-monopoly position in international finance.[91]

Overall sanctions reform requires process, analytic, and strategic elements. There is a need, as a Center for a New America Security study put it, to "strengthen the government institutions that develop and deploy coercive economic measures and continue to modernize the tool kit available to policymakers of better coordination among the various executive branch actors."[92] Indeed, some of the authors of this study came into the Biden administration and led the 2021 policy review.[93] The review sketches "a structured policy framework that links sanctions to a clear policy objective," including assessing whether sanctions are "the right tool for the circumstances." Factors discussed in this and other chapters are among the keys to making this work: recognizing the frequency of economic impact-policy compliance disparity, factoring in target counterstrategies, assessing signaling less on a declaratory basis and more as strategic interaction, net assessment weighing whatever economic impact and policy compliance achieved against costs incurred (backfiring, misfiring, cross-firing, shooting in foot), and breaking out of the tendency to treat sanctions as a default option crowding out potentially more effective policy options. This would help the US use sanctions less often but more effectively, and as such have overall strategic value for American foreign policy.

6

CHINA'S USE OF SANCTIONS

China's views on economic sanctions sure have changed. Interference in national sovereignty, extensions of Western imperialism, violations of international law—for decades the People's Republic's opposition to sanctions wielded by the US and others was, as one scholar put it, "legendary."[1] But while China continues to be resistant to being targeted with sanctions over human rights and other domestic political change issues, as its economic power has grown it has become a frequent wielder of sanctions. One study quotes a Chinese official as calling sanctions and other economic coercion "the best option between subtle diplomacy and all-out-war."[2] Two top Biden administration China policy officials, in an article written just before they assumed office, assessed China as having come to have a "preference for economic coercion."[3] A study by an Australian research institute identified nineteen cases of China-imposed sanctions between 2010 and 2020, half of which were since 2018.[4] Some Chinese sanctions have been officially promulgated by the Beijing government. Others have been more cued than formalized, signals for social media outrage and consumer boycotts against "anti-China" countries and companies, in effect China's version of smart sanctions.[5]

This chapter focuses on the following main questions:

- Why does China impose sanctions?
- What types of sanctions does it use, those informal "cued" sanctions in particular?
- What are some major cases?
- How successful have China's sanctions been?

Why Does China Impose Sanctions?

The capacity to be a sanctions sender and not just a target has been very much a part of what President Xi Jinping has called leaving behind the "century of humiliation" and asserting newfound power as well as civilizational pride.[6] At the same time that it keeps invoking principles of non-interference in domestic affairs when it has been sanctioned on issues like the Uyghurs, Beijing has imposed its own domestic political change sanctions against other countries. We include two such cases, the Taiwanese 2016 elections and 2017–2018 Australian "anti-China" domestic policies, where the objective nevertheless has been to pressure another country's domestic politics.[7]

Chinese foreign policy restraint sanctions have often been couched with (non)plausible deniability. It wasn't that Norwegian salmon was being boycotted because of the 2010 Nobel Peace Prize awarded to the dissident political prisoner Liu Xiaobao—it was that Norwegian salmon just didn't meet the more stringent sanitary inspection standards that happened to be promulgated just after Liu's Nobel award and weren't being as strictly enforced for other countries' salmon. Those South Korean–owned Lotte Mart retail stores that had been doing brisk business for a number of years all over China somehow no longer met fire code regulations once the 2016–2017 dispute broke out over South Korea's deployment of an American-supplied missile defense system.[8]

Lots of signaling played out in the 2020–2021 sanctions-countersanctions tit-for-tat with the US:

- March 2020: The Trump administration imposed restrictions on Chinese journalists in the US. Shortly thereafter, China kicked *New York Times*, *Wall Street Journal*, and other American journalists out of China.
- July: The Chinese consulate in Houston, allegedly "a hub of spying and intellectual property theft," was closed.[9] China then closed the American consulate in Chengdu.
- July: Congress passed legislation and Trump issued an executive order imposing sanctions on Chinese officials deemed responsible for the Hong Kong crackdown. In August, China sanctioned eleven Americans including Republican senators who cosponsored the Hong Kong sanctions bill and human rights organization leaders.
- August: China initiated a major policy review creating an "unreliable entity list" for which "Chinese officials made clear that while a broad category, it very much had the United States in mind."[10]
- November: China's top chipmaker SMIC and some energy companies were blacklisted as military-connected companies. In December, fourteen members of China's National People's Congress were added to the SDN List for their involvement in Hong Kong. China added more American officials and companies to its sanctions list and threatened further action.
- January 2021: On January 14, exports to the China National Overseas Oil Corporation (CNOOC) were banned. On January 16, days before leaving office, the Trump administration added six Chinese and Hong Kong officials to the sanctions list. On January 19, on the eve of the transition to the Biden administration, China imposed sanctions against outgoing Secretary of State Mike Pompeo and twenty-seven other "lying and cheating" Trump officials.[11]
- March: The Biden administration went even further with additional sanctions on twenty-four Chinese officials on the eve of its first high-level diplomatic meeting with China. European and other allies followed suit. China retaliated with sanctions against American and European officials.

And there were more. . . .

What Types of Sanctions Does China Use, Those "Cued" Sanctions in Particular?

Just as the US weaponizes interdependence through its international financial dominance, China does so through access to its 1.5 billion-person domestic market. Targeted countries' exports are boycotted, as in the Australia case. Chinese outbound tourists, at 150 million the world's largest cohort, many of whom travel on group packages that require government permits, get restricted from travel to sanctioned countries, as in the Taiwan and South Korea cases. "The patriotism button gets pushed," as a Chinese singer-songwriter put it, cueing social media outrage and consumer boycotts against designated foreign companies.[12] For example, when the Swedish fashion retailer H&M said it would stop buying Xinjiang cotton over the Uyghurs issue, three major Chinese e-commerce platforms removed H&M products. Alibaba's Sina Weibo microblogging site sent its over 450 million users pictures of an H&M sign being taken down from a mall. With its China sales down 23 percent, H&M replaced the Uyghurs-sympathetic statement on its website with one stating company policy as to "comply with local laws and regulatory frameworks in all the markets where we operate" and being "dedicated to regaining the trust and confidence of our customers, colleagues, and business partners in China."[13] Yet China also incurred shooting-in-the-foot costs. Over 600 factories that had contracts with H&M lost business. Chat rooms showed heightened curiosity and concern about the Uyghurs issues.

China's increased global economic presence may be making export and foreign aid more useful levers than in the past. China has had a lead role in creating such new international economic institutions as the Asian Infrastructure Investment Bank (AIIB) and the Cross-Border Interbank

Payment System (CIPS). With investments now upwards of $600 billion and projected to go into the trillions, far exceeding American foreign aid and other comparable programs, some analysts see the Belt and Road Initiative (BRI) as bringing China "coercion unbound."[14] On the other hand, pushbacks have been coming from BRI recipients dissatisfied with the terms of deals and concerned about Chinese efforts to leverage them.

What Are Some Major Cases?

Taiwan: US Arms Sales, Taiwanese Elections

For close to fifty years dating back to the 1972 Shanghai Communiqué "opening" between the US and the People's Republic of China (PRC) and 1979 full diplomatic normalization, relations among the US, PRC, and Taiwan have been framed by three main strategic parameters:[15]

- The US recognizes the People's Republic as the legitimate government of all of China, Taiwan included, while retaining the right to provide Taiwan with arms and other military assistance of a defensive nature. While some weapons systems can be clearly differentiated as offensive or defensive, many pose classic "security dilemma" questions of what one side sees as defensive the other sees as offensive.
- Beijing agrees to resolve its issues with Taiwan peacefully, reunification included. Various areas of "cross-straits" cooperative relations have developed including tourism, trade, and investment. But disputes also have kept recurring. While certain actions clearly are not peaceful, others may be short of war but are quite coercive in their own right.
- Taiwan was given ambiguous status as less than an internationally recognized nation-state. Taiwan has risked sanctions and other Beijing pressures when it has taken significant steps toward pursuing independence.

WHY Did China Impose Sanctions?

Arms sales: While many American arms sales to Taiwan have gone forward over the years with limited objections from Beijing, certain ones have been met with Chinese sanctions, or at least the threat thereof, with limiting Taiwanese military capabilities as the primary objective. In 2010 a $6.4 billion arms sales package prompted sanctions threats against the American companies involved, but were defused by agreement not to include certain fighter jets (F-16 C/D) Beijing considered more offensive than defensive. A similar dynamic played out in 2015, with sanctions threats followed by some (but only some) modification in the arms sale package. Between 2017 and 2020 the Trump administration ratcheted up arms sales to over $18 billion compared to $14 billion over Obama's eight years. This included an October 2020 package with missiles, drones, and rocket systems that, as one American business executive put it, tried to "masterfully massage" the definition of defensive weaponry. In Beijing's view, though, these arms "brutally interfere in China's internal affairs and seriously undermines China's sovereignty and security interests."[16]

2016 Taiwan election: The Taiwan 2016 election sanctions were about domestic political change. This was by no means the first time Taiwanese political developments had prompted PRC sanctions. For example, in 2000 Beijing targeted Acer, the Taiwanese electronics company, removing its products from mainland stores because its chairman supported the pro-independence candidate. In the run-up to the 2012 elections it tried the inducements approach of providing greater market access to Taiwanese agricultural products. In 2016 the combination of Xi Jinping now being the PRC leader with his tougher approach and Tsai Ing-wen and her Democratic Progressive Party (DPP) being quite vocally pro-independence made the 2016 situation even tenser.

WHAT Types of Sanctions Were Imposed?

Arms sales: The arms sales threats have been directly against producer companies such as Boeing, Lockheed Martin, and Raytheon.

2016 Taiwan election: In the year following President Tsai's election victory, China-Taiwan trade in goods and services declined about 15 percent. Tourism permits for mainlanders visiting Taiwan were cut 40 percent (mainlanders representing about one-third of Taiwanese tourism). PRC university athletes were banned from the 150-nation Taipei 2017 Summer Universiade. International airlines (European ones such as Air France and Lufthansa, US ones such as United and Delta, Singapore Airlines) and hotel chains (Marriott, Sheraton, Starwood) were pressured not to list Taiwan as a country destination; cues went out to boycott those that balked.[17] Diplomatic pressure got some countries that still had official relations with Taiwan to sever them. A record number of air force sorties into Taiwanese airspace added some military intimidation.

WHO Were the Key Actors?

Sender: People's Republic of China
Target: US on arms sales, Taiwan and international companies on domestic political change
Third parties: The US is pretty much always the main third party on Taiwanese politics.

HOW Did the Sanctions Play Out?

Arms sales: In addition to the offense-defense particulars of the arms packages, three other factors played in. The overall context of US-PRC relations was one. The US was more apt to push the envelope of what constituted defensive weaponry when it was seeking to send a broader message of toughening up. The PRC in turn was more apt to object to particular gray-area arms when other issues were served by its pushback message.

Second was the tension between the US taking a hard line to reassure other East Asian allies of its regional commitments, and China's incentive for taking a hard line against American companies as deterrence of European and other potential arms sellers to Taiwan. Each side's sense of economic vulnerability also played in, with Boeing and other companies concerned about losing their lucrative mainland China market on the one hand and Beijing knowing that their technology was key to China's aviation sector modernization on the other.

2016 Taiwan election: Sectors like tourism were hit especially hard. Beijing kept the pressure on. "Any actions and tricks to split China are doomed to failure," President Xi warned in March 2018, "and will meet with the people's condemnation and the punishment of history." Xi also tried inducements as with a new law promulgated just before the 2020 election opening more sectors to Taiwanese investment. Still, President Tsai won re-election. "Today I want to once again remind the Beijing authorities that peace, parity, democracy and dialogue are the keys to stability," she said in her victory speech. "Democratic Taiwan and our democratically elected government will never concede to threats. . . . I hope that Beijing will show its goodwill."[18] Beijing's response was not exactly good will. "The situation across the Taiwan Strait will be more complex and grim," a government spokesman said.[19] The combination of Taiwanese support for the 2019–2020 protests in Hong Kong and rising tensions in US-China relations added further to the dynamics.

Case Assessment

Arms sales: For all its classic security dilemma elements, the arms sales issue has been managed. Some sales have gone through that the PRC preferred not, some have not that the US preferred would have (including ones considered in the internal policy process but never officially proposed). It's also important to take into account how both the PRC and the US have used the Taiwan arms issue to deflect broader tensions in the relationship—although escalation scenarios remain a risk.

2016 Taiwan election: PRC sanctions reinforced parameters beyond which President Tsai and other pro-independence leaders have not gone, but they have not prevented Tsai from winning two elections. Backfiring is suggested in polls showing that while 52 percent of Taiwanese favor closer economic relations with China, only 36 percent favor closer political relations. Questions about identity show 66 percent saying Taiwanese and only 28 percent Taiwanese-Chinese combined, and among eighteen- to twenty-nine-year-olds an even sharper 83–13 percent split.[20]

France and Tibet (2008–2009), Norway and Liu Xiaobo Nobel Peace Prize (2010)

China has imposed sanctions numerous times on countries whose leaders have met with the Tibetan Dalai Lama, as it did against France in 2008 and 2009. The sanctions against Norway were for the 2010 awarding of the Nobel Peace Prize to Chinese dissident Liu Xiaobo.

WHY Did China Impose Sanctions?

France and Tibet: The Dalai Lama is the spiritual leader of Tibet, forced into exile in 1959 living in India and traveling the world to build support for Tibetan self-determination and human rights. China maintains that "Tibet is an inalienable part of China" and has long threatened other nations to change their foreign policies so as to not meet with the Dalai Lama or support Tibet in other ways "if they want to remain on good terms with China."[21] The French case involved pro-Tibet protests along the Olympic torch route through France in the run-up to the 2008 Beijing-hosted Summer Olympics, and President Nicolas Sarkozy meeting with the Dalai Lama a few months later. That Sarkozy at the time also held the EU rotating presidency gave the meeting added meaning to China. Deputy

Foreign Minister He Yafei accused France of "undermin[ing] China's core interest, gravely hurt[ing] the feelings of the Chinese people and sabotag[ing] the political basis of China-France and China-EU relations."[22]

Norway Liu Xiaobo Nobel Peace Prize: Liu Xiaobo was awarded the 2010 Nobel Peace Prize "for his long and non-violent struggle for fundamental human rights in China." The Nobel committee gave particular praise to his leadership in the Charter 08 manifesto calling for democracy in China, for which he had been jailed by Beijing.[23] While the Nobel Peace Prize is decided by an independent commission, China sanctioned Norway as the Nobel Peace Prize host and supporter. In 2014, while this dispute was still going on, the Tibetan Dalai Lama visited Oslo.

WHAT Types of Sanctions Were Imposed?

France and Tibet: Import boycotts and other market access denial against French goods were the main sanctions, imposed through a mix of formal policy and informal cues. Right after the Olympic torch protests, Chinese Internet chat rooms lit up with calls to boycott the French-owned chain Carrefour. When President Sarkozy also announced his intent to meet the Dalai Lama, the Chinese government withdrew a pending order for 150 planes from the France-based consortium Airbus, required that the upcoming EU-China summit be moved from Paris to another European city, and took France off the trade mission itinerary. "I looked at a map of Europe on the plane," Premier Wen Jiaobao remarked. "My trip goes around France. . . . We all know why."[24]

Norway Liu Xiaobo Nobel Peace Prize: Knowing that Liu was a Nobel Peace Prize candidate, a senior Chinese official threatened sanctions against Norway. Once the award nevertheless was made, the scheduled Chinese ministerial trade delegation to Norway was canceled. Sanctions were targeted at Norwegian salmon and other fish exports. Other measures included visa restrictions on Norwegian businesspeople and academics, a ban on Norwegian tourism advertising in China, and an overall freeze on diplomatic relations.[25]

WHO Were the Key Actors?

Sender: China
Target: France and Norway
Third parties: Other EU members in both cases.

HOW Did the Sanctions Play Out?

France and Tibet: The EU gave in on the China summit, moving it to Prague. In the trade mission that skipped France, China signed $15 billion worth of agreements with other European countries. A broader study by two German economists found that countries that hosted official visits with the Dalai Lama were hit with an average 12.5 percent drop in exports to China over the following two years.[26] The French experience followed suit. Overall trade with China fell 16 percent in the first half of 2009, the first such decline since 1996.[27] While Sarkozy resisted pressures to cancel the Dalai Lama meeting, his government issued a follow-on statement recognizing Tibet as part of China. By 2011, with diplomatic relations more smoothed out, French exports to China were up about 80 percent over 2009.[28]

Norway Liu Xiaobo Nobel Peace Prize: Two days after the Nobel was announced, British prime minister David Cameron led a trade delegation to China. Cameron "refrained from raising human rights or Liu Xiaobao in his meetings with Chinese leaders" and inked an estimated $2.7 billion in bilateral trade deals. Norway did some re-routing of its salmon through Vietnam, but salmon sales took a significant economic hit, falling by half in the first year and by an estimated $1.3 billion by 2013. Even so, this was less than 1 percent of the Norwegian fishing industry's total annual exports. And deals Beijing considered economically crucial, such as the $2 billion purchase by ChemChina of a technologically advanced

Norwegian silicon producer and Chinese purchase of a Norwegian company with expertise in deep-water oil and gas drilling, were not sanctioned.[29]

When the Dalai Lama came to Oslo in 2014 to mark the twenty-fifth anniversary of his 1989 Nobel Peace Prize, things got more complicated. Top Norwegian officials who had long been Tibet supporters refused to meet with him.[30] China eased sanctions in response. Norwegian-Chinese trade reached a new high in 2015. In December 2016, diplomatic relations were restored. While Norway didn't explicitly apologize, it went so far as to state that it "fully respects China's sovereignty and territorial integrity, attaches high importance to China's core interests and major concerns, will not support actions that undermine them, and will do its best to avoid any future damage to the bilateral relations."[31] When Liu died in July 2017 still imprisoned, Amnesty International criticized the condolence offered by Norwegian prime minister Erna Solberg (not in office back in 2010) as so muted as to being "relieved" at Liu's death.[32] The pace of trade picked up, and by December 2017 Norwegian salmon exports to China had increased 262 percent.[33]

Case Assessment

China didn't prevent the Olympic torch protests or Sarkozy's meeting with the Dalai Lama, or Liu Xiaobao's Nobel Peace Prize. It did get compromise statements and agreements like Sarkozy's recognition of China's claim over Tibet and Norway's acknowledgment of "China's core interests and major concerns." Such statements and agreements, though, also worked for the French and Norwegians, getting their trade with China going and allowing them to balance assertiveness and compromise in their diplomacy and domestic politics. Both sides thus could claim a degree of success.

The global deterrent effect on Dalai Lama meetings has been pretty striking. Between 1999 and 2002, the period just before and right as China joined the World Trade Organization and became more part of the global economy, the Dalai Lama averaged about six meetings per year with heads of state. In the years since, the annual average has been much lower, indeed with zero heads of state meetings since 2016.[34] This fits the balance of interests pattern, with China having a greater interest at stake in impeding the Dalai Lama from gaining greater international legitimation than other countries had in affirming human rights and self-determination, especially as China's economic leverage increased.

South Korea THAAD Missile Defense System, 2016–2017

In July 2016, South Korea announced that it would acquire the THAAD missile defense system (Terminal High-Altitude Area Defense) from the US as added protection against North Korean ballistic missiles.[35] In May 2017, THAAD became operational. Viewing THAAD as a threat to its own security, China imposed economic sanctions on South Korea.

WHY Did China Impose Sanctions?

This was a version of a foreign policy restraint objective. Right after the THAAD acquisition decision was announced, the Chinese Foreign Ministry expressed "its strong dissatisfaction and firm opposition." China claimed the THAAD radar system could penetrate into its territory and be targeted at its military systems. It also raised concern that the system would be expanded regionally with other American allies in the Asia-Pacific, making China's own defense vulnerable. In that first month alone, the Chinese government issued twenty-seven THAAD-related statements and the *People's Daily* ran 265 critical articles.

WHAT Types of Sanctions Were Imposed?

Korean exports with large markets in China such as cosmetics, music (K-Pop), television soaps, and online video games were sanctioned. Because back in South Korea the Lotte Mart home office allowed the government to acquire one of its golf courses as the land for THAAD deployment, its retail chain within China was targeted. Fire code violations were the alleged basis the Chinese government gave for shutting the Lotte stores down. South Korean auto companies Kia and Hyundai also were boycott-cued. Chinese tourist visits to South Korea, particularly large group package tours, were restricted.

WHO Were the Key Actors?

Sender: China
Target: South Korea
Third parties: The US pressured South Korea to go ahead with the THAAD deployment.

HOW Did the Sanctions Play Out?

The sanctions had significant economic impact. China was South Korea's largest export market, destination for about 25 percent of its total world exports, almost twice as much as to the US. Aggregate cost estimates were over $15 billion, equivalent to about −0.5 percent annual growth. Lotte was forced to close 87 of its 109 China stores at an estimated $837 million loss. Kia and Hyundai car sales were down 52 percent. Chinese tourists visiting South Korea fell from 600,000 to 250,000, group tours from 130,000 monthly to fewer than 3,000.

China's own domestic constraints did limit its sanctions scope. Semiconductors, South Korea's number one export to China, were not sanctioned because of potential disruption to China's own massive electronic manufacturing industry. A *Wall Street Journal* headline captured the costs of the Kia boycott: "Beijing Campaign against South Korean Goods Leaves Chinese Looking for Work; Hours and Pay Slashed for Kia Factory Workers in Yancheng amid Sharp Decline in Sales."[36] A price also was paid in South Korean public opinion, with favorable views of China falling from 61 percent in 2015 to 34 percent in 2017.

A diplomatic agreement was reached in October 2017 with both sides compromising. The THAAD missile defense system stayed. South Korea refused to remove it but did acknowledge China's security concerns and affirmed that THAAD was aimed only at North Korea. It also agreed to not allow the US to add more THAAD systems, or connect the existing one to Japanese air defense systems. China reiterated those concerns but dropped its initial demand for THAAD removal. "Both sides shared the view that the strengthening of exchange and cooperation between Korea and China serves their common interests and agreed to expeditiously bring exchange and cooperation in all areas back on a normal development track," was the statement issued by the South Korean Foreign Ministry.[37]

Case Assessment

China's failure to compel South Korea to remove the THAAD missile system despite imposing substantial economic costs fits the balance of interests analysis. Keeping THAAD both as added security against the North Korean threat and affirming its alliance with the US were higher value objectives for South Korea than the limited threat THAAD posed was for China. Neither, though, did South Korea want to do excessive damage to relations with China. The diplomatic agreement reached included enough of a South Korean apology and concessions on any future missile defense systems for China to also claim a degree of success. China valued the trade and had incurred costs from the sanctions. This was a negotiated settlement, not a win for either side.

Australia: "Anti-Chinese" Domestic Politics, 2019–2021

While an American ally, Australia has also developed numerous areas of interaction and cooperation with China.[38] In 2015 they signed a bilateral free trade agreement. China grew to be Australia's largest trade partner, as of 2018–2019 taking in about 40 percent of all Australian exports. Recently tensions have increased over a number of issues, particularly Australian concerns about Chinese interference in its domestic politics. Added on to this was China's protests over Australia's April 2020 call for an international investigation of China's handling of the COVID-19 outbreak.

WHY Did China Impose Sanctions?

In 2017, Australian intelligence issued a report documenting Chinese efforts to intervene in Australian domestic politics as "a threat to [Australia's] sovereignty, the integrity of [its] national institutions, and the exercise of our citizens' rights."[39] Specifics included a member of parliament whose positions on various issues were so pro-China that he was forced to resign, a Chinese billionaire resident in Australia making major political donations with funds traced back to the United Front Work Department of the Chinese Communist Party, strings tied to Chinese funding of some university research institutes and programs, and Beijing's efforts to monitor Chinese nationals in Australia. With bipartisan support the Australian parliament passed tighter restrictions on foreign interference in domestic politics, which while cast in broad terms were directed particularly at China. These concerns were a main basis for Australia becoming one of the first countries to ban the Chinese company Huawei from developing its 5G wireless network (Chapter 5 case study).

China rejected the charges, deeming them anti-China propaganda and imposing an initial set of sanctions. When on top of these controversies, Australian prime minister Scott Morrison called for an international investigation of COVID-19 origins, Beijing accused Canberra of "poisoning relations" and stepped up the sanctions. "China is angry," a Chinese government official said. "If you make China the enemy, China will be the enemy."[40]

WHAT Types of Sanctions Were Imposed?

Beijing claimed not to be outright boycotting Australian barley, but it just so happened that it was then discovered that Australia was breaking WTO rules with unfair subsidies and thus, to be "fair" to other barley exporters, a 73.6 percent anti-dumping duty was imposed. So too with $126 billion of Australian wine allegedly being subsidized, and amounting to about one-third of Australian wine exports. Other products sanctioned included beef, timber, lobster, and coal.[41] "If the mood is going from bad to worse," China's ambassador to Australia commented with a characteristic nationalist-consumer cue, "maybe the ordinary people will say 'why should we drink Australian wine? Eat Australian beef?'"[42] Restrictions were also imposed on Chinese students studying in Australia, who constituted 27 percent of all foreign students and accounted for $27 billion in tuition and other spending.[43] Some tourism restrictions also were imposed, although the numbers were not as high as for South Korea or Taiwan.

Demonstrating its own domestic constraints, China did not sanction iron ore. While iron ore was Australia's number one export to China, it comprised 60 percent of China's supply of this vital industrial resource. Nor did Australian wool get restricted. China buys 75 percent of Australian wool exports, but that supply was much needed for textile manufacturers.

WHO Were the Key Actors?

Sender: China
Target: Australia
Third parties: Alternative trade partners for both.

HOW Did the Sanctions Play Out?

Coming amid Australia's first recession in many years, the sanctions did have economic bite. Two main reasons explain why it wasn't greater. One was the availability of alternative trade partners to which Australia diverted much trade. The 15 billion AUD (Australian dollars) drop in coal exports to China was mostly offset by increased coal exports to other countries. Barley, copper, seafood, and timber exports had similar patterns; the gains with other trade partners were even greater than the losses to China. According to Australian government estimates, sanctioned sectors lost about $4 billion in exports to China but that was offset with $3.3 billion in increased exports to alternative trade partners—a net loss of 0.25 percent of total national exports.[44]

China's domestic constraints exempting products like iron ore and wool were the other factor. In the first half of 2021, Australian iron ore exports to China still amounted to $53 billion. "So long as China wants to keep making 55% of the world's steel, it will have to keep buying about 68% of the world's seaborne iron ore," as an industry analyst put it. "China cannot ignore the nation [Australia] that supplies 60% of that exported ore."[45] Concern also rose over the coal sanctions when in December 2020 China suffered its worst power blackout in a decade, in part because of coal shortages.[46]

Case Assessment

For all that China rejects other countries interference in its domestic affairs, this is a case of its doing just that. Unlike Taiwan with its ambiguous international status, these sanctions were against a fully sovereign country. Thus, just as the balance of interests at stake has favored China when it has been the target of domestic political change sanctions, Australia had the greater stakes in this case and thus the incentives to resist. The Australian public was outraged by the interference in their political affairs. Those holding unfavorable views of China increased from 32 percent in 2017 to 57 percent in 2019.

In terms of secondary signaling objectives, the message China intended to send—"making an example of the country that's setting an example for pushing back," as a leading Australian strategist put it—was not the one received by other countries.[47] China damaged its reputation as a reliable trading partner. Along with other of its assertive regional actions, this fed into greater security cooperation among Australia, Japan, and India as well as a new major security agreement with the US and the UK (given the acronym AUKUS). This has not and likely will not go so far as an anti-China alliance. Disputes notwithstanding, all these countries highly value their relations with China. The negative consequences for China thus are limited, but nevertheless are there.

Hong Kong Democratization Protests, 2019–2020: NBA Case

In 1984, after over 100 years as a British colony, the process began for Hong Kong to be returned to China as of 1997. "One country, two systems" were the agreed treaty terms. Hong Kong was to maintain a degree of autonomy and democracy for fifty years until 2047, when it would fully become part of China. The 1997 arrangement has had tensions and flare-ups, but none so severe as those that began in March 2019, when massive pro-democracy protests challenged a new Beijing-imposed law making political dissenters more subject to extradition. By June as many as 2 million people had taken to the streets. Beijing and allies such as Hong Kong chief executive Carrie Lam made some compromises but overall became even more repressive. Among the companies and organizations expressing support for the pro-democracy dissenters—and targeted with cued sanctions—was the National Basketball Association (NBA).

WHY Did China Impose Sanctions on the NBA?

"Fight for Freedom, Stand with Hong Kong," tweeted Daryl Morey, general manager of the Houston Rockets on October 4, 2019. Amid all the other pro-demonstrator tweets, this was not particularly provocative. But coming from the general manager of the former team of Yao Ming, the biggest Chinese star ever in the NBA (both in achievements as a player and in being 7'6" tall) and now head of the Chinese Basketball Association (CBA), it touched a nerve. With 640 million Chinese watching NBA games and billions of dollars in China-NBA business deals, Beijing saw an opportunity.

WHAT Types of Sanctions Were Imposed?

Initial measures were targeted at the Houston Rockets. Yao Ming's CBA suspended all cooperation with the Rockets. China Central Television (CCTV) and the Chinese Internet company Tencent suspended all broadcasting and live-streaming of Rockets games. Rockets merchandise was removed from the commercial site Taobao. Chinese companies such as the shoe retailer Li Ning and the Shanghai Development Bank Card Center dropped sponsorships, costing the Rockets about $25 million. Then the full NBA was hit. CCTV announced that it would "immediately investigate all cooperation and exchanges involving the NBA." All eleven official NBA China sponsors suspended ties with the league. Player endorsement deals were canceled, scheduled media and fan events as well. Official sources cued up a social media firestorm.

Big money was involved. NBA China had doubled in value over the prior decade to $4 billion, yielding over $130 million for every NBA team franchise. The NBA-Tencent partnership had just been renewed in July 2019 to the tune of $1.5 billion. The 21 million Chinese fans who tuned in to the prior 2018 NBA finals was greater than the 18 million Americans. All told, the Chinese market amounted to about 10 percent of total NBA revenue.[48]

WHO Were the Key Actors?

Sender: China
Target: NBA, many international companies as well[49]
Third parties: China is not a market for which the NBA could substitute.

HOW Did the Sanctions Play Out?

Soon after Morey's tweet, NBA commissioner Adam Silver issued a statement widely seen as distancing from Morey:

We recognize that the views expressed by Houston
Rockets general manager Daryl Morey have deeply of-
fended many of our friends and fans in China, which is
regrettable. While Daryl has made it clear that his tweet
does not represent the Rockets or the NBA, the values
of the league support individuals' educating themselves and sharing their views on matters important to
them. We have great respect for the history and culture
of China and hope that sports and the NBA can be used
as a unifying force to bridge cultural divides and bring
people together.[50]

Rockets' owner Tilman Fertitta was blunter, tweeting that
Morey "does NOT speak for" the Rockets and that we the
team "are NOT a political organization." Morey deleted his
tweet and apologized: "I did not intend my tweet to cause any
offense to Rockets fans and friends of mine in China. I was
merely voicing one thought, based on one interpretation, of
one complicated event. I have had a lot of opportunity since
that tweet to hear and consider other perspectives."[51] Rockets
star player James Harden chimed in, "We apologize. You
know, we love China. We love playing there. . . . They show
us the most important love." LeBron James, the NBA's most
prominent player, criticized Morey as "misinformed or not really educated on the situation."[52] Joe Tsai, owner of the New
Jersey Nets born in Taiwan and cofounder of the other Chinese
Internet giant Alibaba, took to Facebook calling Morey's tweet
"damaging" and slamming the Hong Kong protests as a "sep-
aratist movement" fighting for a "third-rail issue."[53]

Back in the US, NBA Commissioner Silver was pummeled
by both Democrats and Republicans. A human rights
issue such as this should be prioritized over profits, then-
Democratic presidential primary candidates Julian Castro and
Beto O'Rourke proclaimed. The NBA "is throwing the GM of
the @Houston Rockets under the bus to please the Communist

Chinese Govt. Disgusting," tweeted Senator Marco Rubio (R-Florida). Democratic-Socialist Rep. Alexandria Ocasio-Cortez (D-New York) and archconservative Republican Senator Ted Cruz (R-Texas) issued a joint letter stating, "We are deeply concerned that individuals associated with the league may now engage in self-censorship that is inconsistent with American and the league's stated values." Conservative columnist Megan McArdle called them "spineless weaklings."[54]

Silver issued a second statement responding to but not fully conceding to American critics. While "over the last three decades the NBA has developed a great affinity for the people of China," this was not about "growing our business." There was no intention of "regulating what players, employees and team owners say or will not say on these issues." Our countries have "different political systems . . . different viewpoints over different issues. It is not the role of the NBA to adjudicate those differences." The guiding belief is in sports as "a unifying force that focuses on what we have in common as human beings rather than our differences."[55] China didn't see any need for balance. CCTV put out an official statement saying: "We voice our strong dissatisfaction and opposition to Adam Silver offering as an excuse the right to freedom of expression. We believe that no comments challenging national sovereignty and social stability fall within the scope of freedom of expression." Commissioner Silver reacted by calling CCTV's actions "unfortunate," and went further: "If that's the consequences of us adhering to our values, we still feel it's critically important we adhere to those values."[56]

Both sides made efforts to thaw the relationship. When a January 2020 helicopter crash tragically killed Kobe Bryant, among the most popular NBA stars in China, the Chinese ambassador to the US posted a tribute to him on Twitter. In February the NBA donated $1.4 million to help China fight the COVID-19 pandemic. Tencent started streaming some games of teams other than the Rockets. But it wasn't until October 9, 2020—a year and five days after the Morey tweet—that CCTV again televised an NBA game, this being the fifth and next to last game of the NBA finals. The CCTV spokesman noted the "holiday blessings" the NBA had conveyed for China's recent National Day and Mid-Autumn Festival, and "the good will continuously expressed by the N.B.A. for some time. Especially since the beginning of this year, the N.B.A. has made active efforts in supporting the Chinese people in fighting against the novel coronavirus epidemic."[57]

That good will, though, only went so far. Tencent carried games on the Internet including the Houston Rockets, for whom Daryl Morey no longer worked, but excluding the Philadelphia 76ers, the team for which Morey was now a top executive.[58] CCTV temporarily lifted the blackout for the March 2021 All-Star Game and the remainder of that season and playoffs. But in October 2021 when Enes Kanter, a Turkish American NBA veteran now playing for the Boston Celtics under his newly adopted legal name Enes Freedom, wore shoes emblazoned with "Free Tibet," Celtics games got blacked out and Chinese social media swarmed back at him. It wasn't until March 2022 that CCTV resumed broadcasting all NBA games.

Case Assessment

The NBA's initial responses were a bit of a jumble. Commissioner Silver later lamented that he may have initially tried "too hard to be a diplomat." Player and owner responses were largely that Silver had been too critical of China, politicians liberal and conservative alike that he had not been critical enough. Lost revenue was reportedly over $200 million.[59] All this made it difficult for the NBA to find midcourt. It eventually did. It backed Kanter's stand. And in January 2022 when Chamath Palihapitiya, part owner of the Golden State Warriors, dismissed concerns about the Uyghurs—"Nobody cares about what's happening to the Uyghurs, OK?"—the full team ownership, coach, and players swiftly issued a counterstatement.[60] Overall, while China did get some concessions, these were more limited than it wanted and at a cost of self-inflicting more reputational damage.

Summary: How Successful Have China's Sanctions Been?

China continues to say one thing and do another. "The position of the Chinese government," a top official stated in criticizing US-led sanctions against Russia for its 2022 invasion of Ukraine, "is that we believe that sanctions have never been a fundamental and effective way to solve problems, and China always opposes any illegal unilateral sanctions."[61] Yet in case after case, it has imposed its own unilateral sanctions. The cases in our chapter are by no means the only ones. The Australian think tank study cited earlier identifies nineteen cases between 2010 and 2020, half of which were imposed since 2018.[62] There have been a number of cases since then, for example, sanctions imposed in December 2021 against Lithuania for allowing Taiwan to open a trade promotion office in its capital Vilnius and not requiring it to use the province name Taipei.[63]

China's use of sanctions for coercing domestic political change in other countries has been little more successful than domestic political change sanctions targeted at it. China's sanctions imposed economic costs on Taiwan, but the pro-independence candidate won the presidency in 2016, and was re-elected four years later. That President Tsai Ing-wen has not pushed too hard in the pro-independence direction is much less a function of sanctions than the threat of Chinese military action and constraints imposed by the US. Neither has Australia wavered much from domestic policies deemed justified for the integrity of its own political system, with alternative trade partners offsetting much of the sanctions economic impact.

Chinese sanctions seeking foreign policy change have had some but only some success. France tempered its pro-Tibet stances but did not reverse them. Norway stood by Liu Xiaobo's 2010 Nobel Peace Prize but kept the Dalai Lama's 2014 visit to lower-level official meetings and worked out a compromise joint diplomatic statement with Beijing. South Korea pledged not to deploy further major missile defense systems but stood by the THAAD deployment. Broader secondary deterrent and signaling objectives also have been mixed: deterring heads of state willing to meet with the Dalai Lama on the one hand, but in the Australia case feeding into greater counter-China regional security cooperation on the other. Audrye Wong poses this distinction as some success with "transactional short-term objectives" but much less with "long-term strategic influence."[64] Or as columnist Fareed Zakaria more colorfully puts it, overuse of sanctions has been one of China's "own goals, leading countries to adopt the very policies Beijing has long tried to stop."[65]

As tight as its autocratic political control is, China has had its own domestic constraints on its use of sanctions. The boycott of H&M in the Uyghurs case also hurt over 600 Chinese factory suppliers, and amid the fired-up nationalist outrage drew some internal critical attention to the issue. The Norway, South Korea, and Australia cases all had limits on sanctions scope based on the needs of the Chinese economy.

Cued sanctions targeted at international businesses and organizations have been pretty successful. All the talk of decoupling and onshoring notwithstanding, close to 1.5 billion consumers is a market that can't be ignored. Whereas in 2009, China's $1.8 trillion retail goods market was less than half the American one, a decade later its $6 billion value exceeds the $5.5 trillion American one. Take Apple, which has about 20 percent of its worldwide sales in China, and General Motors, whose ambitious goal of all electric cars by 2035 projects as many sales in China as in the US. The concessions—indeed apologies—by Swedish retailer H&M and American semiconductor manufacturer Intel on the Uyghurs issue were hardly exceptions. China's capacity for its own weaponization of interdependence is quite substantial.

Export embargoes and foreign aid may start to be used more as Chinese industry and technology move up the value chain and as the

Belt and Road Initiative (BRI) extends investment and aid to more and more countries. There has been great concern in the US and Europe that these will bring China added leverage, "an extension of China's rising power," as a Council on Foreign Relations study put it.[66] Yet there are signs that China already is running into similar constraints as the US and other embargoers and aid donors have. For example, a study by the AidData research lab surveying 141 countries found wide acknowledgment of China's greater role as an aid provider but widespread negative views of it as a "development partner."[67]

SOVIET UNION/RUSSIA

ENERGY PIPELINES AND OTHER SANCTIONS

Chapter 5 included US sanctions cases targeted at the Soviet Union/Russia. Here we look at three questions related to Russia as sender state:

- How successful has the Soviet Union/Russia been in its use of sanctions?
- What have been the key issues with Soviet/Russian energy pipelines to Western Europe?
- Summary: How has the Soviet Union/Russia fared as a sanctions sender state?

How Successful Has the Soviet Union/Russia Been in Its Use of Sanctions?

The Hufbauer-Schott-Elliott study (data through 2000) identifies only twelve cases of Soviet/Russian sanctions, amounting to 5.9 percent of their data set. This compares to the Chapter 5 US total of 140 (68.6%), the Chapter 6 China total of nineteen cases just between 2010 and 2020, and the Chapter 8 EU total of forty-eight (1994–2019).

Here we examine three sets of cases: 1948–1955 Soviet sanctions against Yugoslavia as a Cold War example; Russian 1990s sanctions against newly independent countries formerly part of the Soviet Union; and countersanctions against the US,

EU, and other Western sanctions in the 2014 and 2022 Ukraine crises.

Soviet Sanctions against Yugoslavia, 1948–1955

Yugoslavia was among the Eastern European countries that became communist after World War II. Josip Broz Tito, long a member of the Communist Party and leader of the resistance struggle against Nazi Germany, became president. As an ardent nationalist, Tito was opposed to domination by the Soviet Union. Soviet leader Josef Stalin was intent on establishing control over Yugoslavia no less than over other Eastern European countries.

WHY Did the Soviet Union Impose Sanctions against Yugoslavia?

Tito refused, as one scholar put it, "to become an obedient satellite to the Soviet Union."[1] The Soviet expectation was that given its dominant trade position—almost 95 percent of Yugoslav imports came from and 56 percent of exports went to the Soviet Union or Eastern Europe—Tito either would be brought down or forced to comply.

WHAT Types of Sanctions Were Imposed?

Stalin's initial sanctions were partial ones, stalling negotiations for a new bilateral trade pact in December 1947 and withdrawing Soviet technical advisors three months later. A new trade agreement did get signed, but for less than 15 percent of prior trade levels because of, as the official TASS news agency put it, "the hostile policy of the Yugoslav government towards the Soviet Union."[2] Even this level of trade didn't last long, shifting in 1949 to comprehensive sanctions by the full Soviet bloc.

WHO Were the Key Actors?

Sender: Soviet Union
Target: Yugoslavia
Third parties: US, UK, other Western countries

HOW Did the Sanctions Play Out?

Sanctions hit hard. Yugoslav exports fell 33 percent, imports 26 percent, gross national income 11 percent. Unemployment was 29 percent higher than pre-sanctions. Soviet bloc military forces massed along the Yugoslav border. Radio broadcasts from Eastern Europe called for Tito's overthrow.[3]

But political influence did not follow. Tito was "idolized by his closest associates in a way that was unique in Communist parties, whose leaders for the most part were creatures of Moscow." Even with military threat on top of economic hardship, the Yugoslav people were willing to "'endure the pressure' for the sake of independence."[4] Whatever the ethnic tensions among the groups agglomerated into one nation-state, they had a shared resistance to being dominated by the Soviet Union.

Initially there was little receptivity in the West to Tito's plight. Tito had been locked in a territorial dispute with Italy, aided communist rebels in Greece, and nationalized American and European property. But with concurrent events like the Berlin blockade, the communist coup in Czechoslovakia, and the Korean War intensifying the Cold War, the strategic benefits from becoming Tito's alternative trade partner became increasingly evident. In December 1948, Britain signed a $120 million trade agreement. Early the next year the US liberalized export controls and later that year provided $20 million in economic assistance. In November 1950, Congress approved the Yugoslavia Emergency Relief Act providing another $50 million in aid. In 1952 the US and the UK provided more aid as well as a $500 million loan. By 1954, NATO nations accounted for 79 percent of Yugoslav imports and 71 percent of exports, compared to 39 percent and 30 percent respectively back in 1948.

Case Assessment

While the West's alternative trade did not fully offset the economic costs, it did reduce Yugoslav vulnerability sufficiently to make noncompliance viable. When Stalin's death in March 1953 opened the way for some rapprochement, a Yugoslav trade official welcomed Soviet and Eastern European markets "almost limitless possibilities for absorbing many Yugoslav products which cannot always be placed in the market of Western Europe."[5] In June 1956 new Soviet leader Nikita Khrushchev welcomed Tito to Moscow, proclaiming "the entire Soviet people greet you."[6] Among other things Khrushchev agreed to cancel $90 million in Yugoslav debt. When political relations again soured, Khrushchev sought to bring renewed economic pressure. But alternative trade partners were again available in the West, and more than earlier from at least some Eastern European countries. Soviet sanctions clearly failed.[7]

Russia and the Commonwealth of Independent States, 1990s

What had been the Union of Soviet Socialist Republics (USSR) collapsed as former Soviet republics became independent countries in the early 1990s.[8] In an effort to maintain some degree of influence, Russia created the Commonwealth of Independent States (CIS) with many of these former republics/now independent countries as members. As stated in the decree on "The Establishment of the Strategic Course of the Russian Federation with Member States of the CIS," the Russian government was "firmly guided by the principle of intolerance of damage to Russia's interests."[9] Economic sanctions were one of the measures used to pressure against policies Moscow deemed damaging its interests. Four such cases were sanctions against Kazakhstan, Turkmenistan, Latvia, and Ukraine.

WHY Did Russia Impose Sanctions against These Countries?

Russian sanctions against Kazakhstan were over five issues: returning to Russia the nuclear weapons based there as part of the Soviet arsenal; maintaining Russian access to some military and space exploration bases; Russian stakes in joint ventures in Kazakh's large oil and gas reserves; agreement not to allow Western control over energy or other strategic mineral deposits; autonomy for ethnic Russians in northern Kazakhstan.

Three of these issues also arose with Turkmenistan: protection of Russian minorities, military base access, and Russian stakes in oil and gas reserves.

The issue of ethnic Russian minorities bore especially on Latvia, where they constituted about 35 percent of the population. Along with fellow Baltic countries Lithuania and Estonia, Latvia had refused to join the CIS. It still had an early-warning radar site key to the Russian defensive early warning system. Here the energy issue was access to pipelines and port facilities.

Ukraine also had Soviet arsenal nuclear weapons to be relocated to Russia or disbanded. Control of the Black Sea Fleet and access to the port of Sevastopol were other major military issues. Control of the energy industry and pipelines running through Ukraine to Western Europe, and asset and debt disputes, were the main economic issues. All of these were within the "special place in the Russian consciousness" that history and culture give Ukraine.[10]

WHAT Types of Sanctions Were Imposed?

Some sanctions were the same across cases, some different.

Kazakhstan: oil pipeline transit fees and quotas, purchase cuts of Kazakh natural gas, payments for coal and other Kazakh products withheld, military and space specialists withdrawn from bases being disputed.

Turkmenistan: food supplies, energy industry equipment, cuts in overall bilateral trade.

Latvia: reduced oil supplies, natural gas purchase subsidy cuts and hard currency payment required, agricultural exports to Russia subjected to highest tariff category.

Ukraine: numerous energy sanctions including taking subsidies away from gas prices and letting them rise to world price levels, embargoing nuclear energy plant fuel, halting oil supplies for major refineries, cutting electricity supplies, higher tariffs and other taxes on Ukrainian exports to Russia.

WHO Were the Key Actors?

Sender: Russia
Targets: Kazakhstan, Turkmenistan, Latvia, Ukraine; third-party deterrence message to other former Soviet states
Third Parties: US, IMF also in Ukraine case

HOW Did the Sanctions Play Put?

Turkmenistan made the most concessions. While it had the least trade dependence on Russia (17% of its total trade), it had the weakest economy. Sanctions like food supply cuts hit sensitive vulnerabilities: "no meat, there's no flour, and there hasn't been milk for a long time," its foreign minister acknowledged.[11] As the first country to sign the CIS treaty, it wanted to continue overall good relations with Russia. In summer 1992 it signed a defense agreement putting some Turkmen forces under Russian command and air defense units under Russian control. In late 1993 it granted ethnic Russians dual citizenship. In 1995 it set up a joint energy venture under Russian control. In 1996 it signed a strategic partnership agreement with Russia. The two countries "don't have a single disputed or vague issue," President Saparmurat Niyazov declared in 1996.[12]

Kazakhstan also wanted overall good relations with Russia. It had been the last of the Soviet republics to declare its independence. It made significant concessions, although given the value it had to Moscow it got some Russian compromises as well. Russia had American support for consolidating all former Soviet nuclear weapons in Russia as a better path to arms control and nonproliferation than having what would have been three new nuclear weapons states (Belarus as well as Kazakhstan and Ukraine). With less historical tensions with Russia than Latvia and Ukraine, Kazakhstan felt less threatened by concessions on military bases. It had more trade at stake than the others, with Russia accounting for 63 percent of its total trade. But while constrained from going too far in energy and mineral deals with Western companies, President Nursultan Nazarbayev worked the commercial triangle both to get Russia to compromise and to strengthen his negotiating position with those Western companies on which he still had room to make deals. Nazarbayev risked domestic opposition if he went too far on Russian minority rights, so he granted some greater rights though not local autonomy or dual citizenship. He also went ahead and made Kazakh the official state language.

In posing its May 1990 declaration as a "restoration" of independence, Latvia was referencing Stalin's 1940 forced annexation. The high percentage of ethnic Russians reflected intentional Soviet policies over decades to alter the ethnic balance. The Latvian legislature passed a law restricting citizenship to individuals and families resident before the 1940 annexation. "Militant nationalism," Russian president Boris Yeltsin objected, singling out Russians living in Latvia as the most oppressed in any former Soviet country.[13] But when oil supplies were cut, Latvia seized control of the pipeline and shut it down totally, leaving Russia with $70 million of unfulfilled contracts. Latvia did agree to grant residency permits to the 70,000 Russian military officers and their families, but not full citizenship. The military base issue also resulted in compromise, Russia getting some access but also having to fulfill its commitment to withdraw all permanently stationed troops. On energy issues Gazprom did eventually get a stake, but only about one-third.

With high indebtedness to Russia and high energy dependence (89% of crude oil imports and 56% of natural gas imports), Ukraine's bilateral economic position appeared to make it vulnerable. Russian sanctions hit pretty hard, with costs estimated at over $1.5 billion. But Ukrainian distrust of Russia—for its loss of independence back in 1918, the 1930s famine under Stalin's forced collectivization, the 1986 Chernobyl nuclear energy plant disaster—was the flip side of Russian angst about Ukraine. It took America getting Russia to commit to respecting Ukrainian independence and territorial integrity as well as $1 billion in Russian subsidies for nuclear reactor fuel to get Kiev to agree to nuclear weapons divestment. It agreed to some—but only some—sharing of the Black Sea Fleet and Sevastopol port. On energy issues, it had the counterstrategy of offsetting Russian natural gas cuts by siphoning off gas intended for Western Europe in pipelines traversing Ukraine, at one point cutting that supply by 10 percent, with Russia contractually forced to pay almost $5 million in fines to its Western European clients. On the debt dispute it was helped by the IMF linking Russia's own aid package to Russian willingness to reschedule Ukrainian debt. Russian sanctions thus overall "bore little fruit."[14]

Case Assessment

Based just on economic dependence, Ukraine should have made the most concessions, Turkmenistan the least. Daniel Drezner explains this discrepancy stressing differential "conflict expectations," arguing that target states with a history of conflicts with sender states fear showing weaknesses that could further embolden the sender in future relations and thus have greater political will to resists sanctions compliance. Ukraine and Latvia had substantial conflict expectations with Russia and thus did not comply, whereas Turkmenistan and Kazakhstan did not have comparable insecurities and did comply. This pattern is similar to studies showing US sanctions against Western allies as more successful than those against adversaries (e.g., the Chapter 4 1956 Suez Crisis case study).

Russian Ukraine Crisis Countersanctions against the US, EU, and Other Western Countries, 2014 and 2022

The Chapter 5 case study was of US sanctions against Russia over its initial 2014 intervention in Ukraine and annexation of Crimea and 2022 invasion. Chapter 8 has some discussion of European Union sanctions over Ukraine. The focus here is on Russian 2014 and 2022 countersanctions against the US, EU, and other Western countries.

WHY Did Russia Impose Sanctions against the West?

"On Retaliation Measures (Countermeasures) for Unfriendly Actions by the United States of America and/or Other Foreign States": this was the title of the June 2018 law passed by the Russian Duma. Putin had already imposed some sanctions back in March 2014 when the West first imposed theirs. The legislative backing it provided, while not as significant as in a democracy, was still important in broadening Putin's power to take further steps. The 2022 countersanctions were imposed even more quickly.

WHAT Types of Sanctions Were Imposed?

The initial US 2014 sanctions included visa bans on eleven top Russian officials, including the deputy prime minister and speaker of the Federal Council. Putin retaliated in kind, banning visas for top US officials including House Speaker John Boehner, Senate Majority Leader Harry Reid, and Senator John McCain. In 2015 in a similar tit-for-tat for EU bans on Russian officials, Russia banned eighty-nine EU political figures and other officials.

The main trade sanctions were on food imports from the US, EU, and other Western countries. The EU had been providing about 40 percent of total Russian food imports. The US had less food market share overall, although it was higher in some products, such as 40 percent of Russian poultry imports.[15]

The 2022 countersanctions were of three main types. Two involved Russian energy exports, requiring payments be made in rubles and cutting natural gas supplies to countries that refused to pay in rubles, initially Poland and Bulgaria. The other was the threat to expropriate property and holdings of international companies that had pulled out of or cut back their business in Russia.

WHO Were the Key Actors?

Sender: Russia

Target: US, EU, other Western countries

Third parties: Some alternative trade partner shifting by both sides

HOW Did the Sanctions Play Out?

The countersanctions actually reinforced the 2010 Food Security Doctrine seeking greater self-sufficiency.[16] Along with government subsidies, it facilitated import substitution. With food imports dropping from 35 percent in 2013 to only 20 percent in 2018, domestic production of grain, chicken, pork, cheese, and other agricultural products increased. Trade with alternative partners such as Brazil (beef, pork), Chile (fish), Belarus (pork, fish), and China (pork, fish) helped meet remaining import needs. Prices did go up, though, hitting Russian consumers with, for example, cheese going up 23 percent, milk 36 percent, and vegetable oil 65 percent. One study calculated the negative effect at an annual hit of 4,400 rubles per person.[17]

Given that EU food exports to Russia had been worth about $15 billion and American ones only about $1.2 billion, the EU was in a more potentially vulnerable position. Yet overall EU exports of these goods actually increased, redirected to alternative markets.[18]

In 2022 European companies importing Russian natural gas were caught between the rubles payment requirement and EU warnings that these would be in violation of the financial sanctions. Initial reports were of some companies making the rubles payments, others not. Companies also were preparing to fight any expropriations.

Case Assessment

Putin's claim that Western sanctions only imposed $50 billion on the Russian economy and the EU lost $240 billion was more self-serving than accurate.[19] Russia had some offsets but did incur costs. The US and EU experience was largely the same. The bottom line: just as the US-led sanctions didn't change Russian policy, the Russian countersanctions didn't change American or European policy. Meanwhile, the sanctions and countersanctions cycle continued into 2021 with new rounds spurred by further issues, and then even more intensely amid the 2022 Ukraine war.[20]

What Have Been the Key Issues with Soviet/Russian Energy Pipelines to Western Europe?

Soviet/Russian oil and gas pipelines to Western Europe have repeatedly raised issues of whether energy dependence would give Moscow leverage to threaten or impose sanctions. We look at three cases: the early 1960s Friendship oil pipeline, the early 1980s West Siberia natural gas pipeline, and the recent Nord Stream 2 gas pipeline.[21] In all three cases the US tried to block the pipelines by imposing sanctions and other pressure against European countries and companies involved in building it in order to head off the prospect of the Soviets/Russians gaining economic coercive power of their own. In the 1960s and 1980s cases it did not succeed, in 2022 it did.

WHY Has Each of These Soviet/Russian Pipelines Engendered Controversy?

Endowed with rich oil and gas reserves, by the early 1960s the Soviets had increased oil exports to Western Europe about 400 percent. A 1962 State Department memo stressed a number of reasons why the Soviet "Oil Pipeline of Friendship" threatened US interests, including that it would "facilitate and improve relative military, strategic and economic strength of [the] USSR . . . and permit Soviets to intensify oil offensive" in Western Europe.[22] Italy was of particular concern to the Kennedy administration, Soviet oil already having a 22 percent share of its oil imports. Secretary of State Dean Rusk deemed stopping this growth the number one issue in US-Italy relations. While West Germany also was importing substantial volumes of Soviet oil, its role as the main supplier of the specialized wide-diameter steel pipe needed to build the pipeline (68% of Soviet wide-diameter steel pipe imports, 1958–1962) was of even greater concern. With Cold War tensions running high (1961 Berlin crisis, 1962 Cuban missile crisis), the overall containment strategy seemed at risk of being undermined by economic dependencies that could give the Soviets leverage over key US allies.

Cold War tensions in the early 1980s were higher than any time since the 1962 Cuban missile crisis. Tougher policies toward the Soviet Union were a key factor in Ronald Reagan's November 1980 presidential victory. Reagan saw 1970s détente as a failure and proof positive that efforts to cooperate including through trade were futile. "Why shouldn't the Western world quarantine the Soviet Union," one of his stump speeches went, "until they decide to behave like a civilized nation?" Energy trade was of particular concern. The 1970s OPEC oil crises caused Europe to turn increasingly to Soviet natural gas. West German imports were up from 7.5 percent of total natural gas consumption to 18.2 percent, Italy's from 10.3 percent to 24.8 percent, and France's from minuscule amounts to 13.9 percent. The new proposed West Siberian Natural Gas Pipeline (WSNGP) was projected to increase imports to over 30 percent by 1990. It was to be built with pipe and other parts and technology from European industries mired in the worst recession since the 1930s. A top Reagan official testified to Congress on the threat posed:

> First, it will generate substantial hard currency earnings for the Soviet Union that will finance a number of Soviet developments inimical to our interests. . . . Second, the revenues available to the Soviets will help to forge an economic link with Europe that will inevitably increase Moscow's influence among our allies. . . . Third, we believe that Europe will incur a dangerous vulnerability to the interruption of supplies of natural gas from the Soviet Union.[23]

An element of regime change was also part of the calculus, that without trade with the West "the Soviet leadership would be forced to choose between its military-industrial priorities and the preservation of a tightly controlled political system. . . . Thus, the West helps preserve the Soviet Union as a totalitarian dictatorship."[24]

Construction began in 2018 on the $11 billion Nord Stream 2 as another Russia-to-Western Europe natural gas pipeline, this one routed under the Baltic Sea (paralleling the existing Nord Stream 1) to a port in Germany and from there also to a number of European countries. With Russian gas already accounting for about 40 percent of overall EU gas imports and 55 percent for Germany, even before the 2022 Ukraine invasion Nord Stream 2 raised the issue of Russian leverage from gas dependence. Concerns also were raised about Ukraine losing the $3 billion in annual transit fees from the current pipeline running through its territory and being left more vulnerable to Russian shutdowns of its gas supply. Until the war started, Germany and some others resisted sanctioning Nord Stream 2. Once Russia launched the war, Germany agreed to block Nord Stream 2 from starting operations.

WHAT Sanctions Were Imposed?

In 1963 the US persuaded NATO to pass a resolution calling on member nations to keep Soviet oil imports to a 10 percent market share. It was, though, only a nonbinding resolution, and Italy voted against it. France and Britain supported the US, with concern about Soviet oil competing for markets with their own global oil companies a factor. The US shifted to a compensatory economic inducement strategy, getting major American oil companies whose own interests would be hurt by Soviets gaining larger world oil market shares to make deals with the state-owned Italian energy company Ente Nazionale Idrocarburi (ENI) providing guaranteed and discounted oil supplies. With West Germany, the emphasis was on American security guarantees on which West Germany and West Berlin were especially dependent.

The December 1979 Soviet invasion of Afghanistan and December 1981 imposition of martial law in Poland prompted numerous sanctions on which Europe and the US agreed. These included certain dual-use technologies with commercial and potential military applications, including robotics and telecommunications. But the allies resisted sanctions on natural gas imports and on products and technologies for WSNGP construction and operation. The most the Reagan administration could muster at a January 1982 NATO foreign ministers meeting was a statement that "the Allies will reflect on longer-term East-West economic relations, particularly energy," but any such reflection was left as "each of the allies will act in accordance with its own situation and laws." Leader-to-leader pressure at the Versailles summit a few months later also didn't get much more than agreement "to pursue a prudent and diversified economic approach to the USSR and Eastern Europe."[25] Within weeks the Reagan administration countered with secondary sanctions against European companies that were subsidiaries of American companies or were using technologies licensed or parts originating from the

US. The main target were the turbine-powered compressors for which the Soviets lacked domestic production capacity. Threatened penalties for violations included $100,000 fines, prison sentences for offending company executives, and loss of trading privileges with the US.

Nord Stream 2 sanctions have been one of the few issues in recent years to have bipartisan support in Congress. Since few American companies were involved, these have been mostly secondary sanctions targeted at European as well as Russian companies and individuals involved in Nord Stream 2 construction. When the Trump administration was lax in using this authority, two Republican senators wrote their own letter threatening a European company "if you were to attempt to finish the pipeline in the next 30 days, you would devastate your shareholders' value and destroy the future viability of your company." The company pulled out.[26] Just before leaving office, Trump did impose sanctions on the company owning the Russian pipe-laying vessel *Fortuna*. In May 2021, while stating "unwavering" opposition to Nord Stream 2, Secretary of State Antony Blinken cited keeping relations positive with allies for waiving sanctions against a European company.[27] Senator Ted Cruz (R-Texas) started labeling it the "Putin-Biden" pipeline and used Senate procedures to block Biden State Department appointments, including many that had nothing to do with Russia, Europe, or Nord Stream 2.

EU countries were split, some opposing Nord Stream 2 and others supporting, and with the EU Parliament voting in January 2021 to halt construction but the EU Commission continuing support. By the time the Ukraine war started in February 2022, Nord Stream construction was largely completed. Once the war started, sanctions were imposed to at least delay turning it on.

WHO Were the Key Players?

The roles can be looked at two ways. For the actual sanctions employed, the US was the sender, various European countries and companies the targets, and the Soviet Union/Russia the third party trying to induce the targets not to comply.

But the reason for these sanctions was the concern that the energy trade would position the Soviet Union/Russia as prospective sender with the Europeans the targets, and the US as the third party pressuring and inducing the Europeans away from the pipelines.

HOW Did the Sanctions Play Out?

In the Friendship oil pipeline case, Italy at first pushed back against American pressure but a combination of internal Italian political developments and the economic compensatory inducement package facilitated agreement. Italian imports of Soviet oil, growing every year since 1957, started falling in 1964. By 1964, the Soviet oil market share was down to that 10 percent figure. With West Germany the economic interests at stake were harder to offset. West German pipe manufacturers had increased and modernized production capacity based on expected further growth of the Soviet market. Other West German exporters were lured by the "dangling of East-West trade plums."[28] But as then Foreign Minister Gerhard Schroeder (same name but different person than the 1998–2005 German Chancellor who also later went on the payroll of the Russian natural gas monopoly Gazprom) put it, "My heart is completely with the iron and steel industry, with full employment and the full utilization of our capacity. . . . But I must choose between the interests of our foreign policy and the interests of our economy."[29] The remaining steel pipe contracts were canceled. Mannesmann, the largest contractor, lost over $25 million. Hoesch had to cut its welding capacity by two-thirds. Phoenix-Rheinrohr had to shut down an entire plant. West German exports to the Soviet Union fell by 25 percent, and would not again reach 1962 levels until 1968. But *Westpolitik* and the alliance with the US were reaffirmed.

The WSNGP pipeline split the alliance. French foreign minister Claude Cheysson spoke of a "progressive divorce" because "we no longer speak the same language." West German chancellor Helmut Schmidt angrily pledged, "The pipeline will be built." Even Conservative British prime minister Margaret Thatcher argued that "the question is whether one very powerful nation can prevent existing contracts from being fulfilled." The European Community (EC) formally protested this "unacceptable interference" in its sovereign affairs: "Whatever the effects on the Soviet Union, the effects on European Community interest of the United States' measures . . . are unquestionably and seriously damaging."[30] German, French, Italian, and British companies not only delivered on existing pipeline contracts but also signed new ones worth billions of dollars. The early 1980s recession was not a propitious time to expect European companies to forgo contracts or European governments to add to unemployment rates already close to 10 percent (14% in Britain). European governments thus were willing to risk the tough penalties the Reagan administration threatened. On the gas import side, the economic compensatory package intended to lead all of Western Europe away from Soviet gas the way Italy had been led away from Soviet oil two decades earlier was inadequate. What did kick in, though, were market conditions. The 32 percent decline in world oil prices (1980–1983) made gas relatively more expensive than originally calculated. Recessionary economic growth rates also slowed energy consumption. The net effect of such market changes was that Western European gas demand fell 8 percent, with projected growth rates of no more than 2 percent annually. Contracts for Soviet gas thus were negotiated downward, but still with smaller decreases than gas from other sources, and with the leverage now with the Western European consumer nations at lower prices.

Europe was more divided on Nord Stream 2 than on the earlier pipelines. Baltic and East European countries that had been under Soviet control during the Cold War were strongly opposed. Denmark had environmental concerns. France proposed retaliating against Nord Stream 2 for Russian imprisonment of dissident Alexei Navalny. Germany was the main proponent, although within its own politics the Green Party was critical, citing both environmental concerns and human rights linkages. American secondary sanctions played on these divisions. The December 2019 letter cited above from two Republican senators got the threatened company to pull out. Russia did feel the pressure. It changed the routing to meet Danish environment concerns. It accepted a Swedish court arbitration decision awarding $3 billion to Ukraine in a related gas transit deal. While delayed and with added costs, Nord Stream 2 was built. The Ukraine war, though, stopped the final permitting and commencement of operations.

Case Assessment

All three cases demonstrated divergent American and European interests on energy trade. Europe lacks the oil and gas resources the US has. The Soviet Union/Russia has those reserves, is geographically proximate, and with a need for European pipeline-related manufacturing capacity and advanced technology. All three cases also showed Europe to be less concerned about foreign policy vulnerabilities and more inclined to see foreign policy opportunities in energy trade with Russia. The 2022 Russian invasion of Ukraine did change that.

American capacity to provide economic compensation and draw on alliance leadership prestige provided the leverage needed for European compliance in the early 1960s Friendship oil pipeline case. Soviet oil continued to flow but at rates that didn't raise diplomatic-strategic concerns. The State Department estimated 278,400 tons of pipe were blocked by the embargo. Sweden provided some substitute pipe in keeping with its official policy of neutrality, but only 61,000 tons. The Soviets built two new pipe mills, but they fell short of production goals. Nevertheless the Friendship oil pipeline was eventually completed. And as European interest in improving relations with the Soviet Union increased, European-Soviet trade grew much faster than US-Soviet trade. A State Department report acknowledged that the "combination of circumstances" that had endowed the US with "leverage to influence their [the allies'] policies . . . are now drastically changed and our leverage in this field greatly diminished."[31]

By the early 1980s, Soviet vulnerability to energy sanctions seemed to be there. Oil and gas exports had increased from 18.3 percent of their hard currency earnings in 1970 to 62.3 percent in 1980. Plummeting world oil prices and their own stagnant production were squeezing at the same time that broader economic problems were increasing demand for machinery and equipment imports. But American and Western European interests diverged both economically and strategically. Western Europe's industrial recession made WSNGP equipment contracts that much more valuable. Why should they forgo these when the Reagan administration not only had lifted the Carter grain embargo but had offered the Soviets additional grain imports? The 1970s OPEC oil embargo and continued Middle East instability made dependence on Persian Gulf oil the main European energy security concern, for which Soviet gas provided some import diversification. There also was strategic disagreement with Reagan's overall hawkishness. That the allies did agree to sanction more militarily relevant technologies showed they were differentiators, not "appeasers." While a diplomatic face was put on the November 1982 US-European agreement—"substantial agreement on a plan of action"—it was with more American conceding than leveraging, and only after quite a bit of intra-alliance sanctions crossfire.[32]

Nord Stream 2 had more reasons for European opposition or at least leeriness than did the earlier pipelines. Those Central and Eastern European countries formerly dominated by Moscow were now part of the EU (some also of NATO).

Putin's increasing repressiveness disaffected European human rights activists. Environmental concerns pushed against greater natural gas consumption whatever the source. Still, until the Ukraine war Europe saw its interests as overall better served by participating in rather than blocking Nord Stream 2.

The war, though, showed that with Russian natural gas having reached about 40 percent of EU and 55 percent of German gas consumption, energy interdependence had become energy dependence. True, with about half of its federal budget and about one-third of its GDP coming from energy exports, Russia still needed the revenues. But for such a strategic resource as natural gas, allowing any country let alone one like Russia to have such large market shares brings vulnerability.[33] While being reluctant to fully sanction Russian natural gas, European countries used conservation, fuel switching, and alternative suppliers to start reducing their reliance on Russian gas. Germany, for example, brought Russian gas down to 35 percent within the first few months of the war. Whether this actually leads to full severing of the EU-Russian energy trade relationship or a rebalancing remains to be seen.

Summary: How Has the Soviet Union/Russia Fared as a Sanctions Sender State?

While plenty of other modes of coercion have been employed, the Soviet Union/Russia has used sanctions much less than other major powers. This speaks to the limited global attractiveness of Soviet/Russian non-military goods and technology—other than oil and natural gas.

The Yugoslav sanctions case exemplifies the crucial role of third parties as alternative trade partners and geopolitical protectors. This was the same dynamic in reverse as the Soviet role for Cuba against American sanctions, and back in Chapter 4 for Sparta with against Athens' Megaran Decree sanctions.

The 1990s CIS sanctions showed that Russia still maintained coercive leverage over some former Soviet republics, but not all. Those whose interests and sense of nationhood militated against too much domination from Moscow were more resistant to sanctions and more able to bargain some concessions (Latvia and Ukraine compared to Turkmenistan and Kazakhstan). This, though, may have been a function of the less assertive Russia of the 1990s. In October 2021, Putin cut gas off to Moldova where a pro-Western president had been elected the previous year.[34]

Energy trade with the Soviet Union/Russia has repeatedly been a source of European-American tensions. The 2022 Ukraine war brought some consensus, but only some, and with uncertainty about how the issue will play out in the future. In the early 1960s case, US ability to economically compensate Italy and invoke its security protection of Germany package leveraged some reductions in the pipeline deals. In the early 1980s case, American secondary sanctions set off intra-alliance cross-firing and the US did more conceding than leveraging. The 2022 Ukraine war revealed the extent to which Europe had become riskily dependent on Russian oil and gas, and how those revenues provided some offset to the other costs being imposed on the Russian economy. European-American consensus on energy sanctions thus was stronger than ever before, although more on oil and coal than natural gas. While it's pretty certain that postwar European-Russian energy trade will not go back up to pre-war levels, whether it stays at low wartime levels or finds levels that balance economic interests and geopolitical risks remains to be seen.

8

UNITED NATIONS AND EUROPEAN UNION

MULTILATERAL AND REGIONAL SANCTIONS

Chapter VII of the UN Charter—Action with Respect to Threats to the Peace, Breaches of the Peace, and Acts of Aggression—includes a number of provisions authorizing multilateral economic sanctions. If the Security Council determines under Article 39 the "existence of any threat to the peace, breach of the peace, or act of aggression," under Article 41 it can authorize "complete or partial interruption of economic relations." Under Article 42 it can enforce these through "such action as by air, sea or land forces as may be necessary." And under Article 25 "members of the United Nations agree to accept and carry out the decisions of the Security Council."

In Chapter 4 we discussed the 1935–1936 League of Nations sanctions against Mussolini's Italy for the invasion of Ethiopia and the UN 1966–1979 sanctions against Rhodesia and 1962–1994 sanctions against South Africa. This chapter focuses on the period since 1990. Four main questions are addressed:

- How often and for what objectives has the UN imposed sanctions?
- What sanctions has it principally used?
- How successful have UN sanctions been?
- What are some major cases?

In the second part of the chapter, both as an example of the role regional organizations play and for its importance in its own right, we focus on the European Union (EU). While other regional organizations such as the African Union (AU) and the Organization of American States (OAS) also have imposed sanctions, none has done so as frequently as the EU. For example, between 1980 and 2014 the EU accounted for 36 percent of the world's non-UN sanctions, making it the second-most active user after the US.[1] In addition, France's UN Security Council permanent memberships (Britain's too pre-Brexit, and closely coordinating since) have positioned the EU to play a more influential geopolitical role than other regional organizations.

Three sets of EU sanctions questions:

- Why does the EU impose sanctions? What types of sanctions? How effective?
- How is sanctions policy made within the EU?
- What has been the mix of US-EU sanctions cooperation and conflict? Some case examples?

The chapter concludes with a section drawing out policy implications for both the UN and EU.

UN and Multilateral Sanctions

How Often and for What Objectives Has the UN Imposed Sanctions?

The UN has imposed sanctions against:

(a) thirty-seven different countries (fourteen current as of this writing);
(b) terrorist organizations and non-state combatants such as the Taliban, Al Qaeda, and ISIL/Da'esh;
(c) thousands of targeted individuals and entities put on the UN Security Council Consolidated List.[2]

This case-counting, though, manifests some of the methodological issues raised back in Chapter 2. One is varying case counts across different databases: for example, looking just at the years for which they overlap, the EUSANCT database has forty-nine cases that HSE (Hufbauer-Schott-Elliott) and TIES (Threats and Imposition of Sanctions) do not. Another is whether different sets of sanctions imposed over time against the same target count as a single case, as "episodes" within the same case, or as different cases. The Targeted Sanctions Consortium (TSC) differentiates among sixty-three episodes in its twenty-three cases: for example, they split the 1997–2010 Sierra Leone sanctions into five episodes. When sanctions are lifted and then reimposed against the same country primarily for different reasons, they are counted as separate cases: for example, the Former Republic of Yugoslavia as two cases, one during the Croatia and Bosnia wars (1991–1996) and another in the Kosovo war (1998–2001). There also is variation on including sanctions threats that don't then get imposed: for example, sanctions threats against Syria in the 2005 UN investigation into the assassination of Lebanese prime minister Rafik Hariri that achieved enough cooperation for sanctions to not be imposed.[3]

As to objectives pursued, two main lines of analysis are taken. One is in terms of particular primary policy change objectives: nonproliferation, counterterrorism, democracy support, good governance (human rights, judicial processes), and ending armed conflict (ceasefires, peacebuilding, civilian protection, humanitarian relief). While most sanctions are geared to more than one objective, ending or at least ameliorating armed conflict has been the principal one.[4] The other differentiation is in secondary signaling terms: coerce a target to change its policies or constrain its capacity to pursue such policies by imposing costs and limiting capabilities, as well as signaling as stigmatization of the target as a norm offender and/or seeking to deter comparable action by other global actors.[5] Here, too, most cases have mixed objectives, often seeking to coerce immediate policy change and signal normative condemnation while also constraining and deterring future such action.[6]

What Sanctions Has the UN Principally Used?

In some cases UN sanctions have been comprehensive in scope. The Iraq sanctions were comprehensive from the start, imposed within days of its August 1990 invasion of Kuwait. The sanctions against the Former Republic of Yugoslavia started out in September 1991 as an arms embargo, but by May 1992 were made comprehensive, covering all trade as well as sports and cultural exchanges, scientific and technical cooperation, and travel bans for key officials. During their first year, the 1993–1994 Haiti sanctions were sectoral (arms, petroleum, financial assets) but then were ratcheted up to comprehensive. The severe humanitarian impact in these cases—"sanctions of mass destruction" in the Iraq case, "criminalizing consequences" in Serbia, *anbago* (embargo) transmuted to *anba gwo* ("under the heels of the rich and powerful") in Haitian Creole—prompted a shift to more targeted and allegedly "smart" sanctions.[7]

Arms embargoes, some mandatory and others advisory, have been the most frequently used sectoral sanctions.[8] Some have been geared to nonproliferation of nuclear and other weapons of mass destruction, others to conventional and small arms flowing into violent conflicts. Commodities sanctions also have been used, a main example being the Kimberley Process sanctions seeking to cut off "blood diamonds" from international commerce.[9] Financial sanctions such as assets freezes and limits on banking services, investments, and sovereign wealth funds have been used both generally and targeted at key individuals and organizations; for example, the counterterrorism sanctions against al Qaeda and ISIL/Da'esh include 260 individuals and 89 entities.

How Successful Have UN Sanctions Been?

As noted in Chapter 3, many studies point to multilateralism as a key factor for sanctions effectiveness. Yet the data show that UN sanctions have not had significantly greater success than country-initiated ones.[10] As with country-based sanctions, UN sanctions show some variation within the overall success rate based on principal objectives pursued. Among primary policy change objectives, good governance and democracy support have been the most achievable, counterterrorism and ending armed conflict less so, and nonproliferation the least. Among secondary objectives, signaling and constraining have been more successful than coercing. Arms embargoes, the most widely used UN sanction, have had little success; indeed, in cases such as Somalia, Yugoslavia, and Sudan (Darfur) they backfired with "perverse political effects that exacerbated the conflicts they were aimed at stopping."[11]

In some conflicts the UN gets caught in cross-pulls between sanctions and mediation efforts. On the one hand, sanctions threats can create incentives for peace negotiations. Their se-lective imposition against non-cooperating parties can raise the costs of continuing the conflict. Promising to lift sanctions in return for cooperation can provide the reciprocity needed for agreement. The threat to selectively reimpose sanctions can help ensure compliance. On the other hand, selective sanctions can exclude from the peace process parties whose agreement is ultimately needed. They also can feed into claims that the UN is not staying impartial and neutral. In these and other ways sanctions can, as one study put it, "close the space for mediation."[12]

Implementation and enforcement are another main UN sanctions problem.[13] Panels of Experts and Sanctions Monitoring Committees are set up for each set of sanctions. These are supposed to be independent experts recruited by the UN Secretariat. In some cases these have added important ca-pacity, as for example in uncovering Iranian weapons being supplied to the Shia Houthi rebels in the Yemen civil war. In other cases, though, Security Council member countries have sought to manipulate the panels and committees for their own interests. George Lopez, a sanctions scholar in his own right who served in 2010–2011 on the North Korea sanctions panel, recounted how "our young Chinese colleague was always bleary-eyed and tired because after a hard day of work on the panel, he was back on the phone at night with the Chinese authorities getting instructions." Similarly, Russia sought to stack sanctions panels for Mali, South Sudan, Central African Republic, and other African countries with Russian nationals to shield its own sanctions-busting.[14]

What Are Some Major Cases of UN Sanctions?

Iraq 1990s

The sanctions imposed following the August 1990 Iraqi invasion of Kuwait and continuing into the 2003 Iraq war were "the most comprehensive economic measures ever devised by the UN."[15] There's been lots of debate over their success/failure, and reasons why.

WHY Did the UN Impose Sanctions on Iraq?

On August 2, 1990, Iraq invaded Kuwait. That same day the UN Security Council passed Resolution (UNSCR) 660 demanding that Iraq withdraw. On August 6, UNSCR 661was passed imposing sanctions. The next day President George H. W. Bush launched Operation Desert Shield, with the US leading an international military coalition seeking to deter Iraq from possibly invading Saudi Arabia and to prepare for forcing Iraqi forces out of Kuwait. On November 29, the Security Council passed a resolution authorizing military action if Iraq did not meet a January 16, 1991, deadline. When it did not, despite much international opposition including from UN secretary-general Kofi Annan, Operation Desert Storm was launched as a US-led thirty-five-nation military operation, what came to be known as the Gulf War. By February 28, Iraq had retreated from Kuwait.

While immediate military victory was achieved, concerns remained about ongoing threats from Iraq, including development of weapons of mass destruction (WMD) and ballistic missiles. On April 3 the Security Council passed Resolution 687 extending sanctions until all WMD programs had been eliminated and with verification provisions requiring Iraq to admit UN nonproliferation inspectors. The UN Special Commission on Iraq (UNSCOM) was established for this purpose, working with the International Atomic Energy Agency (IAEA).

The US also had aspirations of regime change. "Sanctions will be there until the end of time, or as long as [Saddam] lasts," President Bill Clinton remarked in 1997. "Regime change in Iraq is the only certain means of removing a great danger to our nation," President George W. Bush declared in October 2002 in the wake of 9/11. Regime change, though, was not part of the UN resolutions.[16]

WHAT Types of Sanctions Were Imposed?

Sanctions were comprehensive, with only some medical and humanitarian exemptions. They included an oil boycott, arms embargo, suspension of international flights, freeze of Iraqi government financial assets held outside the country, and a prohibition on financial transactions. A naval blockade shut down much maritime shipping. Pipelines through Turkey were capped.

The sanctions on top of the war damage left the Iraqi people in severe humanitarian crisis. A March 1991 UN report raised alarm of "imminent catastrophe, which could include epidemic and famine."[17] The "oil-for-food" program was created, allowing for some export of Iraqi oil with revenues intended to be confined to financing food and other humanitarian relief.

WHO Were the Key Actors?

Sender: UN. The US and some other countries also had additional sanctions.

Target: Iraq

Third parties: Various sanction busters

HOW Did the Sanctions Play Out?

On top of the damage caused by the war, the sanctions had rapid and substantial economic impact. Within months, oil exports, which accounted for 60 percent of Iraqi GDP and 85 percent of its foreign exchange earnings, were down more than 90 percent. The UN Population Fund documented maternal mortality more than doubling, while UNICEF found 4,500 children under age five dying every month from hunger and disease. Some 25 percent of young adults were malnourished.[18] The combination of concessions made to Baghdad giving it greater political control over food distribution and oil revenues, corruption from various players, and UN bureaucracy severely hampered the oil for food program. Even with the US-led multinational Maritime Inspection Force, there also was plenty of other sanctions busting.[19] One study put illegal revenues at over $10 billion.[20] The discrediting of sanctions fed into the debate about going to war in 2003.

While harassed and obstructed by Saddam, UNSCOM and IAEA inspections did proceed for a number of years. In November 1998, Saddam kicked the inspectors out. The UN condemned the action as a flagrant violation of Security Council resolutions. The following month the US launched air strikes at military sites including ones suspected of hiding WMD programs. In September 2002, with the Bush administration threatening war, inspectors were readmitted (renamed UNMOVIC, UN Monitoring, Verification and Inspection Commission). Despite the four-plus-year interlude and Bush administration claims, UNMOVIC found "no indication of resumed nuclear activities . . . nor any indication of

nuclear-related prohibited activities at any inspected sites."
A British intelligence report provided its own confirming analysis that as long as sanctions were maintained, "Iraq would
not be able to produce a nuclear weapon."[21] The Bush administration nevertheless launched the war with WMD as a main
claim. Even with full run of the country as an occupying force,
it failed to find any significant WMD.

Case Assessment

Were the initial UNSCR 661 sanctions working well enough,
along with the Desert Storm deployment and other measures, to
have gotten Iraq to withdraw from Kuwait without the Desert
Storm military action? They did have substantial economic
impact. And they demonstrated broad multilateral support.
But as in other cases of sanctions against invasions (1935–1936
Mussolini Ethiopia, 1980 Soviet Union–Afghanistan, 2014 and
2022 Russia-Ukraine), the extensiveness of the objective was
disproportionate to even multilateral sanctions as a limited
instrument.

As to the post–Gulf War sanctions, some success was
achieved for military containment. Iraqi foreign minister Tariq
Aziz was strikingly frank in telling UN inspectors that "the only
reason Iraq was cooperating with UNSCOM was that it wanted
to be reintegrated into the international community. Chief
among the benefits was the lifting of the economic sanctions."[22]

Overall, Iraq acquired an estimated $47 billion less in arms
than it otherwise would have. Even with some sanctions
busting, the Iraqi army was left with "decaying, obsolete,
or obsolescent major weapons."[23] The fact that war was not
avoided was less the result that sanctions didn't work than the
Bush administration's determination to go to war, regardless.

Armed Conflicts

Dealing with armed conflicts—ceasing hostilities, negotiating
peace agreements, enforcing peace agreements, supporting

broader peace building—has been the most frequent UN sanctions objective. We focus on two major cases: Liberia (1992–2016) and Côte d'Ivoire (Ivory Coast, 2004–2016).

WHY Did the UN Impose Sanctions on Liberia/Côte d'Ivoire?

The UN imposed five rounds of sanctions against Liberia. The first round (November 1992–March 2001) was part of the effort to bring the civil war that had begun in 1989 to an end. Given the uncertain stability of the peace agreement reached in 1993, sanctions were maintained and UNOMIL (UN Observation Mission in Liberia) was deployed. Elections were held in 1997 only to have Charles Taylor, among the late twentieth century's most brutal and murderous leaders, manage to get elected president. Taylor's heinous rule not only plunged Liberia back into mass killings, it also exacerbated civil war in neighboring Sierra Leone. The UN both upgraded UNOMIL to UNMIL (UN Military Mission in Liberia) and imposed sanctions rounds two (March 2001–May 2003), three (May–December 2003) and four (December 2003–June 2006). Taylor was forced to flee. He eventually was captured and tried for and convicted of war crimes. In 2006, Ellen Johnson Sirleaf was elected president, the first female ever elected head of state in Africa. The UN lifted sanctions against the government but, seeking to support peacebuilding and promote good governance, imposed a fifth round (June 2006) targeted at rebel groups. These were kept in place until 2016.

From Côte d'Ivoire independence in 1961 until his 1993 death, President Félix Houphouët-Boigny maintained one-party rule. The years following his death were marked by extensive political instability. The 2000 election of Laurent Gbagbo ended the military regime, only to have Gbagbo rule so brutally as to spur ethnic conflict and civil war. After a 2003 peace agreement quickly fell apart, the UN deployed the peacekeeping force UNOCI (UN Operation in Côte d'Ivoire) and imposed the first of five rounds of sanctions. International pressure got Gbagbo to allow elections in 2010. Former prime minister Alassane Ouattara won. Gbagbo refused to recognize the results and fomented even greater violence. The UN Security Council passed a resolution recognizing Ouattara as the winner and calling for Gbagbo's arrest. In April 2011, UNOCI along with France's Operation Licorne captured Gbagbo. Later that year he was sent to the International Criminal Court (ICC) charged with crimes against humanity. In 2016 the UN lifted sanctions. In 2017 it ended UNOCI.

WHAT Types of Sanctions Were Imposed?

The initial Liberian sanctions were an arms embargo against all parties to the conflict. Round two expanded to diamonds exports ("blood diamonds"), a travel ban, and diplomatic measures. Round three added a timber export ban, round four a financial assets freeze against the Taylor regime and supporters. With Johnson Sirleaf now in control of the government, round five lifted the arms embargo and diamond and timber export bans while keeping sanctions against insurgent individuals and groups.

The Côte d'Ivoire sanctions started with an arms embargo, travel ban, and assets freeze. Round three added a diamonds export ban. Round five, which followed Ouattara becoming president, lifted sanctions against the government while tightening them against Gbagbo supporters and other insurgents.

WHO Were the Key Actors?

> Senders: UN, and other sanctions from the US, EU, African Union, Economic Community of West African States (ECOWAS)
>
> Targets: Liberia/Côte d'Ivoire
>
> Third Parties: No countries officially, but various sanctions busters

HOW Did the Sanctions Play Out?

Despite the arms embargo, parties to the Liberian conflict had little trouble acquiring weapons. The death toll went over 150,000. Close to a million refugees fled to neighboring countries. Only in the early 2000s when sanctions were toughened and made more targeted and UNMIL was deployed did progress start to be made.

In the Côte d'Ivoire case, Gbagbo managed to play on anti-foreigner sentiment to reinforce his authoritarian rule. Pressure was still sufficient to get him to agree to elections in 2011, and for these to be free enough for Ouattara to win. Gbagbo's attempt to nullify the elections was the push the UN needed to strengthen the sanctions and to give UNOCI a more robust peace enforcement mission supported by the French forces. The country was considered sufficiently stable for sanctions to be lifted in 2016.

Case Assessments

While acknowledging the broad economic costs and civilian pain sanctions had, the Liberia sanctions have been assessed as more effective than not. The first round, largely an arms embargo against all parties, was ineffective on all three counts of coercing, constraining, and signaling. Ensuing rounds adding blood diamonds and timber and targeting all the sanctions more at the insurgents while de-restricting the Johnson Sirleaf government were more effective. While UN peacekeepers, international war crimes tribunals, World Bank, and other financial aid also played key roles, the finding of the Liberian Sanctions Committee Panel of Experts that "sanctions helped to stabilize the situation" seems warranted.[24]

The Côte d'Ivoire sanctions come out largely ineffective. The first two rounds were ineffective across the board. Later rounds had some effectiveness but not enough to come out on balance as a success. And when in 2020 Ouattara opted for a third presidential term despite the constitutional two-term limit, much of the opposition boycotted the election. He won with 95 percent of the vote.

European Union Sanctions

Why Does the EU Impose Sanctions? What Types of Sanctions? How Effective?

Until the 1980s the European Community (EC) did not adopt sanctions of its own, leaving them to the individual governments.[25] The first major collective sanctions were against the Soviet Union for its invasion of Afghanistan. When the Yugoslav wars erupted in 1991, the EC imposed an arms embargo before the UN or US. Since 1994 when the Maastricht Treaty transformed the EC into the EU with greater authority for common foreign policy actions, the EU has imposed sanctions against close to sixty countries, some of which like UN sanctions have had numerous episodes of sanctions being increased. Four of its sanctions sets—chemical weapons, cyber-crime, human rights, and terrorism—encompass more than one country.[26] Its 2022 sanctions against Russia over Ukraine were the most far-reaching it had ever imposed. The EU Sanctions Map available online provides a good way of keeping up with sanctions that get lifted, revised, and added to.[27]

EU sanctions have overlapped with UN ones more than two-thirds of the time. In some instances the EU has acted before the UN: Sudan, Democratic Republic of Congo, Ethiopia/Eritrea, the Former Yugoslavia. Some EU sanctions have gone further than UN ones: for example, Iran and North Korea, although less extensive than US ones. Some have been maintained after the UN has lifted its—for example, Libya and Former Yugoslavia. Many of the EU sanctions that have not overlapped with UN ones have been against former colonies within the framework of the African, Caribbean, and Pacific Group of States (ACP)-EU Development Partnership Agreement. Some of these have been paired with sanctions from the African Union and other relevant regional organizations.

Democracy promotion has been the most frequent EU sanctions objective. Conflict management, post-conflict stabilization, signaling support for international law and norms, nonproliferation, and terrorism have been other recurring ones.[28] Travel bans and asset freezes are the most common types of sanctions. Arms embargoes also are used, as are trade, financial, and diplomatic sanctions.[29] In some instances so many sanctions have been piled one on the other that while official EU doctrine stresses targeted sanctions, they have ended up de facto comprehensive.[30]

While there are case-specific assessments of EU sanctions success/failure, there is as yet no systematic study of overall patterns.[31] The case-specific ones are much debated with similar assessment dilemmas, as seen with other sanctions senders reflecting the measurement challenges laid out in Chapter 2.

How Is Sanctions Policy Made within the EU?

Unanimity of the twenty-seven member states represented by their heads of state or government is required for sanctions to be imposed (abstentions do not count against unanimity).[32] The 2004 Basic Principles on the Use of Restrictive Measures (Sanctions) and 2018 Guidelines on Implementation and Evaluation of Restrictive Measures (Sanctions), along with the overarching Common Foreign and Security Policy, establish the basic parameters all EU sanctions are supposed to comport with. The Political and Security Committee, comprising member states' ambassadors, considers any such proposals as may other working groups. Once the Council approves new sanctions, the European External Action Service and the European Commission work with the Council to create legal texts and to work with member states on implementation guided by an EU "Best Practices" document. Working with member state embassies and intelligence services in relevant countries, the European Commission's Directorate General for Economic and Financial Affairs and the Council's Sanctions Committee identify and add individuals and entities to the EU's targeted Consolidated List. Targeted individuals and entities can use the Court of Justice of the EU to appeal sanctions, in some cases having done so successfully.

None of this precludes individual governments from imposing sanctions when the EU does not or adding more to what EU does: for example, in August 2020 a month before the EU acted, Lithuania, Latvia, and Estonia imposed their own sanctions on Belarusian president Aleksandr Lukashenko. Nor should the collective process be interpreted as equal voice for all members: Berlin and Paris often dominate (London did too until Brexit).

What Has Been the Mix of US-EU Sanctions Cooperation and Conflict? Some Case Examples?

As close allies and fellow democracies, the US and Europe often cooperate on sanctions. Yet as we've seen in such cases as Iran (Chapter 5) and the 1960s and 1980s Soviet energy pipelines (Chapter 7), sanctions can be a highly contentious intra-alliance issue. Six main points can be made based on these and other cases about the EU-US mix of cooperation and conflict.

First, when the EU has taken the lead on sanctions, it has been on cases within Europe. Its July 1991 arms embargo against Yugoslavia preceded both UN and American sanctions. The EU sanctioned Belarus in 2004, the US not until 2006. The incentive to take the lead responding to the May 2021 hijacking arrest of the Belarusian dissident journalist was even stronger given that it was against a European airline (Ryanair) and the geographic advantage to be tapped of banning Belarusian flights over EU airspace and access to EU airports.

Second, Europe has been most likely to cooperate with US-initiated sanctions when the sanctions respond to a shared security threat. This pattern comes through in all the Chapter 7 Soviet/Russian energy pipeline cases: strong cooperation on Cold War controls on militarily relevant exports but differences over the Friendship oil pipeline, cooperation on Afghanistan invasion sanctions but not on the West Siberian natural gas pipeline, and initial resistance to Nord Stream 2 pipeline sanctions but cooperation once Russia invaded Ukraine. Iran sanctions have had a similar pattern, with Europe being mostly resistant to US-pushed sanctions until the 2005 revelations about Iran's nuclear program raised the sense of security threat.

Third, even when sanctions have been imposed, Europe has tended to favor combining with active diplomacy. West German *Ostpolitik* in the 1960s and other European initiatives for East-West détente preceded the 1972 Nixon-Kissinger one. On Iran, scholar Brendan Taylor stresses "a bargain of sorts that was struck between the US and the EU, wherein the latter would be willing to support the use of sanctions should Iran fail to cease with its illicit nuclear activities, provided that Washington became more amenable to the offering of incentives as part of the international effort to avoid such an outcome."[33] This was why Europe was supportive of the Obama sanctions-and-diplomacy strategy but resistant to Trump's maximum pressure. The EU also has been more flexible than the US in a number of cases on lifting sanctions.[34]

Fourth, while Europe also uses sanctions for democracy promotion and human rights protection, it has not followed the American lead in pursuing regime change. On Cuba, European sanctions were always more limited than American ones. They also were more actively combined with diplomacy on human rights issues, as for example in 2010 when Spain and the Catholic Church negotiated the release of some political prisoners.[35] Similarly, with Venezuela the EU has imposed sanctions but has distanced itself from US efforts to overthrow the Maduro government.

Fifth, the structure of European economies make for divergent economic interests when it comes to international trade representing a much higher percentage of GDP for Europe (47% for Germany, 32% for France) than for the US (26%).

Sixth, the extraterritoriality issue has been a recurring source of tension. American extension of its own nationally determined sanctions through secondary sanctions seeking to supersede Europe's own policy processes has been disputed as a matter of international law, has grated as a matter of principle, and has angered as an abuse of power. This has come up repeatedly on Soviet Union/Russia sanctions as well as those on Iran and others.

Summary: What Are Some Key Policy Points for Multilateral Sanctions?

This chapter shows both the advantages of multilateralism for sanctions success, and also the limits.

The main advantages of UN sanctions are their normative legitimacy, international legal status, and lessening of alternative trade partners. Even with its flaws, the UN still carries more normative legitimacy globally than any other actor. Naming and shaming an offender is more effective when done by the full international community than if just by individual nation or coalition of nations. When UN sanctions are mandatory, all member countries are legally required to comply. These make it more difficult for sanctions target states to find alternative trade partners and geopolitical protection.

Yet as various studies show, the UN sanctions success rate is not as high as multilateral theory would project. Some of this is attributable to similar dilemmas as with country-based sanctions such as the disproportionality of sanctions as a limited instrument pursuing extensive objectives. Some manifest intra-UN institutional capacity problems of Security Council politics, circumscribed authority, resource limits, and bureaucracy. Initiatives such as the Geneva International Sanctions Network are working with the UN on these and related institutional capacity issues.[36]

The EU has become an increasingly important player in sanctions strategy. As the third-largest economy in the world and with its global foreign policy role, the EU is a key sanctions player. It has been using sanctions more frequently. The average number of annual sanctions cases was about five for the 1990s, twelve for the 2000s, and twenty-two for the 2010s, with numerous high-profile cases (e.g., Belarus, China, Russia, Myanmar) so far in the 2020s. The evidence thus far points to similar patterns of success and failure, as with US, UN, and other sanctions senders.[37]

EU-US relations on sanctions are a mix of cooperation and conflict. Cooperation was particularly strong on the 2022 Russia Ukraine and the Obama Iran sanctions. The Russia Ukraine case had a major shared security threat. The Obama Iran sanctions integrated sanctions with serious diplomacy. In other cases, though, divergent economic interests and differences on overall foreign policy strategy have made for intra-alliance tensions. Secondary sanctions imposing claims of extraterritoriality have been and continue to be particularly controversial.

CONCLUSION

SANCTIONS THEORY, SANCTIONS POLICY

Why do sanctions get used?
How to measure success?
What key factors affect success?

The 2022 sanctions against Russia over its invasion of Ukraine made these questions even more crucial. The sanctions were sweeping in scope. They had wide global support. They involved a brutal war with genuine risks of nuclear escalation. Understanding the why, how, and what of sanctions took on even more importance than ever.

This book has sought to blend a scholarly perspective and policy strategizing. No claim is made to a single parsimonious theory or off-the-shelf action plan. Sanctions are too complex for that (as, frankly, is most international relations and foreign policy). In closing, we take stock of what the book contributes in both these regards to "what everyone needs to know."

A Weapon of Choice

Sanctions are here to stay. The objectives for which the Biden administration uses them differ somewhat from the Trump administration, but the frequency of use by one American administration after another continues. The EU has its own long and growing list. For all its critique of Western sanctions as imperialistic, China has been wielding its own at an increasing rate. Russia has repeatedly imposed sanctions against former Soviet republics as well as retaliatory ones against the US and the EU. The UN currently has fourteen countries as well as three terrorist organizations on its sanctions list, plus offenders under the Kimberley Process regulating conflict minerals. And these are just the sanctions senders focused on in this book. There are plenty of others, on which further research and analysis is encouraged. Who imposes them against whom and for what objectives is subject to politics and events, but sanctions as a weapon of choice will remain a central feature of twenty-first-century international affairs.

Sanctions Theory and the Question of Success

The sanctions don't work/yes they do debate pervades the sanctions literature. Scholars differ over what constitutes a case, which metrics to measure success with, and how to take ethical considerations into account. The need is less for some singular consensus than being explicit about conceptual definitions and methodological approaches and staying self-conscious of possible selection effects on empirical validity, theoretical generalizability, and policy implications.

The six metrics delineated in Chapter 2 help break out of the success/failure dichotomy. Some success is inherent in sanctions having economic impact, but there is no one-to-one relationship showing the greater the economic impact, the more likely policy compliance. Degrees of success are to be recognized but with caveats of relative prioritization of objectives and a strategic interaction, not declaratory approach to signaling. Success on any of these measures needs to be net-assessed against various combinations of costs incurred (backfiring, misfiring, cross-firing, shooting in the foot). Relativity to alternative options needs to be considered without defaulting to sanctions based more on other options' negatives than sanctions' own projected efficacy. Timeframes for success can't be cut short on the one hand or left open-ended on the other. Both false positive credit-claiming when other elements of the overall strategy warrant it, and false negative blame-attribution when sanctions did their job but other policies did not, are to be avoided. Even if all these check out, ethical issues remain if the sanctions bring high civilian pain.

I especially wrestle with putting all these considerations together when it comes to human rights and atrocities. How could the US not impose sanctions on the Myanmar military amid its brutal February 2021 coup? Or against Serbia for the 1990s ethnic cleansing perpetrated against Bosnian Muslims? Or China for atrocities against the Uyghurs? Shouldn't brutalizers be made to pay a price? Don't internal opponents deserve to know that the international community stands with them? Isn't there soft power value to affirming principles?

Rarely, though, have such sanctions brought about substantial policy change. In some instances, they have been net negative, backfiring and making the problems even worse, and misfiring in hitting the populace more than the regime. In such instances the gains from taking a stand have to be weighed against the ramifications of doing so, manifesting the ethical dilemma of right intentions but possibly wrong consequences.

And what about whether to lift sanctions already in place against an offending regime for humanitarian reasons? Like Afghanistan after the Taliban victory in 2021: The Taliban were killing and arresting anyone at all deemed an opponent. They were again repressing women. They held American prisoners. They still had links to international terrorist groups. The sanctions against them while they were out of power—US,

UN, EU, World Bank, International Monetary Fund—now applied to the whole Afghan government. Yet as the winter of 2021–2022 set in, 9 million people were facing starvation. "The current humanitarian crisis," wrote David Miliband, president of the International Rescue Committee, in January 2022, "could kill far more Afghans than the past 20 years of war."[1] Should sanctions be lifted or at least reduced so as to provide relief to the Afghan people? Or would that teach the Taliban the wrong lesson that they can rule as brutally as they want and still get international support?

As to key factors determining success (Chapter 3), in case after case we saw how deceptive initial stocktaking of the sender–target economic power differential could be. Targets often have had counterstrategies for offsetting senders' initial economic power advantage. Third parties also come into the mix as alternative trade partners. Even when sanctions still had substantial economic impact, they did not regularly bring policy compliance.

Closing that economic impact-policy compliance gap depends heavily on the sanctions having reciprocity and proportionality. Given that sanctions, like other forms of coercive diplomacy, are a strategy for influencing not denying the target's choices, there must be terms of exchange based on a shared belief that if you do x, I will do y. The diplomatic crafting must be both firm enough that the target does not think it can get the benefits without having to reciprocate, and assured enough that the target can be confident that the reciprocal measures will follow. Proportionality of limited objectives being more achievable than extensive ones holds across both primary and secondary objectives, and the various subtypes of each. It has an ends-means logic, the scope of objectives being proportional to the coercively limited means that even comprehensive sanctions are. And it is more likely to avoid interests asymmetry in which the target has more to lose than the sender to gain.

Sanctions Policy

The policy analysis and recommendations made for different sanction senders in their respective chapters flow from this metrics-key factors framework.

The US long has been and continues to be the principal wielder of sanctions, turning to them as "the go-to solution for nearly every foreign policy problem," as Dan Drezner put it in a 2021 article—but with more go-to than solution.[2] American sanctions have been more effective in imposing economic costs than converting that impact to policy change. To the extent that policy change has been coerced, it has largely followed the pattern of limited objectives being more achievable than extensive ones.

The two Iran cases, success for the Obama sanctions and failure for the Trump ones, bring out the importance of reciprocity and proportionality. Obama's strategy had both, lifting sanctions in exchange for Iran agreeing to nuclear nonproliferation and keeping the objective to nonproliferation, not the wider agenda. Trump's maximum pressure had neither, upping demands for Iranian concessions with little reciprocation. With North Korea the reciprocity formula has been more elusive, in part because the regime's view of nuclear weapons as essential for its survival makes giving them up a much more disproportionate action.

Domestic political change sanctions against authoritarian regimes for which such reforms can be survival-threatening are classic interest asymmetries. While symbolic action credit can be claimed for standing up for principles, actual impact on the very people in whose name the sanctions are imposed often risks being net negative. Soviet Jewry emigration increased as part of the early 1970s détente but when the 1974 Jackson-Vanik sanctions made this an American demand, the numbers dropped. The leaked Tiananmen Papers show those sanctions to have fed into the Chinese regime's efforts for even more resilient authoritarianism. The Venezuelan sanctions' role in the humanitarian crisis can be acknowledged without taking Maduro off the hook. The same is true for the more than sixty years of sanctions against Cuba. Meanwhile the limited sanctions imposed on Saudi Arabia for the heinous murder of journalist Jamal Khashoggi, covering some of the Saudi officials involved but not Crown Prince Mohamed bin Salman even though he ordered the killing, provide plenty of basis for questioning American claims of principles.

In neither the Soviet 1980 Afghanistan nor Russian 2014 Ukraine invasion cases did sanctions or other measures coerce military withdrawals. The 2022 Russian war against Ukraine posed an especially formidable challenge. The Biden administration was clear and explicit in pre-invasion sanctions threats. But sanctions deterrence failed: Russia still invaded. This experience reinforces other cases on the importance whenever sanctions are used for signaling to get past declaratory face value and assess prospects for success as a matter of strategic interaction. While policymakers may not know for sure how others perceive American signaling at that policy moment, it cannot be assumed that message sent is message received.

The sanctions imposed once Russia invaded Ukraine had unprecedented scope and breadth. Even with some offset by Russian counterstrategies and alternative trade from India, China, and some others, the economic costs have been considerable. Yet thus far (May 2022) the economic impact–policy compliance gap has not been closed. If Russia does end up ending the war on terms acceptable to Ukraine and the international community, sanctions will warrant some credit, but the main credit will go to the military strategy. Had the Ukrainian forces not been so skilled and courageous and the United States and Europe not provided such massive military aid, no sanctions would have stopped Putin from conquest.

Even if this case ends relatively successfully, it will be more exception than precedent. Had Putin intervened more like he did in 2014, with small numbers of forces and less brutality, such a broad global sanctioning coalition would have been unlikely. Nor would there have been so much self-sanctioning by companies and organizations. Indeed, at the same time that a number of companies were ending and cutting back on their Russia business, they were trying to get around the Uyghurs sanctions against China.

As to China, its own frequent use of sanctions doesn't leave much basis anymore for opposing US and European sanctions as inherently imperialistic and violating sovereignty. Just as China resists sanctions targeting it for domestic political change, it has been finding its domestic political change targets also resistant (albeit less brutally). The sanctions imposed economic costs on Taiwan, but the pro-independence candidate won the presidency in 2016 and was re-elected four years later. Outraged by the interference in their political affairs, the percentage of the Australian public holding unfavorable views of China almost doubled, while alternative trade partners offset much of the sanctions economic impact.

China has had some success with sanctions seeking limited foreign policy change. South Korea did not block THAAD deployment but did limit future ones. Norway did not block Liu Xiaobao's Nobel Peace Prize but offered sufficient diplomatic apology for a rapprochement; French president Sarkozy went ahead with his meeting with the Dalai Lama, but other heads of state were deterred from doing so. On the other hand, coming along with other power-wielding actions in the Indo-Pacific region, the sanctions against South Korea and Australia antagonized more than deterred.

Cued sanctions targeted at Western companies, weaponizing the interdependence of its strong consumer market and inexpensive labor force numbering 1.5 billion, have been a signature Chinese strategy. Swedish retailer H&M and American semiconductor company Intel dampened their criticisms of Chinese treatment of the Uyghurs, the NBA its calling out of Chinese repression in Hong Kong. Numerous airlines and hotels tailored their website listings of Taiwan as a destination but not a country. Calls to boycott the 2022 Beijing Olympics got little international corporate support. While there is some talk of decoupling from China, it would take a Ukraine-like major magnitude crisis for the incentives for doing business in China to change that significantly.

As Chinese industry and technology move up the value chain and as the Belt and Road Initiative extends investment and aid to more and more countries, questions are being raised as to whether China will also gain export embargo and foreign aid conditionality leverage. While there are some cases in which such gains have been made, there also are signs of China running into similar constraints as the US and other embargoers and aid donors have faced from target state counterstrategies and alternative partners.

It says a lot about the Russian economy's limited appeal that Moscow has used sanctions less than other major powers. It mostly used them against Soviet-era satellites and within the Russia-dominated Commonwealth of Independent States, and even there with mixed success. Oil and natural gas are its most attractive exports, particularly to Western Europe, as seen in the three energy pipeline cases. The issue in all three was whether energy dependence would give Moscow leverage to threaten or impose sanctions or if the mutuality of this trade, accounting for large shares of Russian hard currency earnings and government budget revenues, would balance out. In the 1960s case, US pressure got Europeans to reduce their Soviet oil imports and cut their steel pipe exports, but the pipeline still was completed. In the 1980s case, Europe largely resisted US pressure. In neither case did the Soviets get significant foreign policy leverage from the pipelines. By the time of Russia's invasion of Ukraine, Europe had increased its Russian natural gas imports so much as to have become overly dependent. While the Nord Stream 2 pipeline was sanctioned and there was talk of eliminating all Russian gas imports, more likely is a rebalanced energy portfolio with less but still some Russian gas, even perhaps down the road an operating Nord Stream 2.

Data and cases showing the limited success of UN sanctions are a bit unsettling given the importance so often given to multilateralism. These do not negate the advantages working through the UN does have, particularly the normative legitimacy and potentially getting the major powers to work together. Such analysis can be a useful push for some hardheaded strategizing about what it takes to make multilateral sanctions effective, as with the work done by the Geneva International Sanctions Network and others.

The objectives EU sanctions seek and the challenges they often face are akin to those of the US and UN. If serious efforts now get made for greater overall foreign policy "strategic autonomy," it will be interesting to see whether the EU takes the lead more in who gets sanctioned and whether the cooperation-tension mix on issues such as US secondary sanctions tilts more in the latter direction.

* * *

All told, sanctions will continue to pose puzzles for scholars and challenges for policymakers. While no claim is made to having provided everything everyone needs to know, hopefully this book provides a helpful chunk.

APPENDIX

2022 RUSSIA-UKRAINE WAR SANCTIONS

Timeline (key policies and events through May 2022)

Nov 2021–Jan 2022 US warns of a likely invasion; The US and its allies engage in diplomatic efforts, threaten sanctions.

Jan 25, 2022 US warns Russia it is prepared to inflict "massive consequences that were not considered in 2014."

Feb 21 Putin recognizes the sovereignty of two breakaway regions in Ukraine, orders Russian troops to the regions; US sanctions the regions, EU adopts sanctions.

Feb 22 US imposes sanctions on Russian-owned financial institutions. UK imposes first set of sanctions. Germany halts the certification of the Nord Stream 2 pipeline.

Feb 23 Australia imposes first set of sanctions. The EU adopts first import/export sanctions.

Feb 24: Russia initiates massive invasion of Ukraine.

Feb 24 Japan, Canada, and Iceland adopt first set of sanctions; UK, Australia bolster sanctions; US sanctions twenty-four Belarusian individuals and entities and Russian financial institutions.

Feb 25 Taiwan adopts first set of sanctions. EU, US, Japan continue to bolster sanctions. US sanctions Vladimir Putin and Minister of Foreign Affairs Sergey Lavrov among other Russian leaders.

Feb 26 UNSC resolution calling for Russia's withdrawal from Ukraine: Eleven countries support, three abstain (China, India, United Arab Emirates) but Russia vetoes.

Feb 27–28 US sanctions semiconductors and other high-tech products and technologies with defense sector as well as commercial applications. EU, UK, Canada, Japan, Australia, New Zealand announce plans to impose similar sanctions. South Korea and Taiwan, both major semiconductor producers, also comply.

Feb 28 US, EU and Australia sanction the Central Bank of Russia. Norway sovereign wealth fund plans to divest from Russia. Switzerland, South Korea adopt first set of sanctions.

Mar 1 Japan strengthens sanctions. Brazil and Mexico announce they will not impose sanctions.

Mar 2 The UN General Assembly adopts a resolution calling for Russia to end its aggression in Ukraine by 141–5 with 35 abstentions. Liechtenstein adopts first set of sanctions.

Mar 4 Switzerland bans transactions with Russian central bank, adopts EU measures on Russia's access to SWIFT; Argentina announces it will not impose sanctions.

Mar 5 Singapore adopts its first set of sanctions.

Mar 8 Japan and Australia strengthen sanctions. The US bans imports of Russian oil, liquefied natural gas, and coal.

Mar 9 Indonesia says it will not sanction Russia. UK says it will stop importing Russian oil. EU sanctions Belarus. New Zealand imposes first independent sanctions on Russia.

Mar 10 Australia bans Russian oil and coal imports. EU, UK, and Canada strengthen sanctions.

Mar 11 US, EU, UK, Canada, France, Germany, Italy, and Japan announce eliminating Russia's WTO membership benefits and its borrowing privileges at the World Bank and IMF.

Mar 12 Bahamas ban financial institutions from conducting business with Russian entities sanctioned by Western countries.

Mar 13 Turkey announces it will not sanction Russia. Australia strengthens sanctions.

Mar 15 EU and UK implement sanctions in accordance with the March 11 statement; New Zealand, South Korea, Iceland, Australia join G7's WTO stance on Russia.

Mar 16 The US, Australia, Canada, Germany, France, Italy, Japan, the UK, and the EU create the Russian Elites, Proxies, and Oligarchs (REPO) multilateral task force.

Mar 17 Australia and the UK strengthen sanctions. South Africa announces it will not sanction Russia.

Mar 24 G7 and EU leaders agree to take steps to crack down on sanction evasion. Norway adopts EU sanctions. US, UK, Australia, and Canada strengthen sanctions.

Mar 25 Japan implements sanctions announced in March 11 statement. Switzerland adopts almost all EU sanctions.

Apr 4 Australia strengthens export sanctions, New Zealand sanctions more Russian oligarchs.

Apr 6 US sanctions Putin's daughters; G7 and EU announce plans to document war crimes in Bucha and impose additional sanctions in response; UK plans to end coal/oil imports by 2022.

Apr 7 US Congress votes to suspend all normal trade relations with Russia.

Apr 8 Japan increases sanctions, freezing more Russian bank assets and boycotting more imports.

Apr 8 EU bans Russian coal imports and implements additional targeted sanctions including Putin's two daughters.

Apr 13 Switzerland adopts EU sanctions package from April 8; UK strengthens financial sanctions, bans imports of iron and steel.

Apr 14 Australia adds 14 Russian state-owned entities to sanctions list, UK expands its sanctions.

Apr 19 New Zealand sanctions Russian banks, UK targets Moscow Stock Exchange.

Apr 21 US, Australia, UK, Japan, and Canada expand sanctions.

Apr 29 Biden proposes seizing and selling Russian oligarchs' assets for Ukrainian humanitarian and reconstruction aid.

May 3 EU begins process of imposing a phased-in ban Russian oil and adds other sanctions.

May 2-3, 16-17 Australia and New Zealand impose additional financial and other sanctions.

May 3, 4, 8, 18 UK imposes additional sanctions.

May 18 Finland and Sweden apply for NATO membership.

May 24 US Treasury starts blocking Russia from paying American bondholders to push towards default.

Individually Targeted Sanctions (examples)

Financial asset freezes, travel bans, superyacht seizures and other measures; imposed by varying combinations of US, UK, EU, Switzerland, Canada, Japan, Australia, New Zealand; two main categories of targets:

Oligarchs

Igor Sechin: CEO of Rosneft (one of the largest publicly traded oil companies in the world) and his son, Ivan Igorevich Sechin

Andrey Kostin: Chairman of VTB bank (Russian state-owned bank)

Alexey Miller: CEO of Gazprom (largest publicly traded natural gas company in the world and the largest company in Russia in terms of revenue)

Nikolai Tokarev: president of the Russia state-owned pipeline company Transneft

Russian Officials

Vladimir Putin: President of Russia

Katerina Tikhonova and Maria Vorontsoa, daughters

Mikhail Mishustin: Prime Minister of Russia

Sergei Lavrov: Minister of Foreign Affairs and member of
    Russian Security Council
Sergei Shoigu, Minister of Defense

Private Sector Self-Sanctions

Massive international public pressure and reputational
concerns prompted close to 1000 companies—American,
European, many others—to self-sanction, limiting and in
some instances fully ending business in and with Russia beyond what required by their governments' policies. Some
examples:

Air Travel

Airbus (Europe)   British Air (UK)
Aircraft Leasing (Ireland)   Korea Air (South Korea)
Air France (France)   Lufthansa (Germany)
American Airlines (US)   United (US)
Boeing   (US)

Automotive

Ford (US)   Porsche (Germany)
General Motors (US)   Renault (France)
Hyundai (South Korea)   Subaru (Japan)
Jaguar (UK)   Toyota (Japan)

Consumer Goods

Amazon (US)   Ikea (Sweden)
ASOS (UK)   Marks and Spencer (UK)
Carlsberg (Denmark)   Paulig (Finland)
Coca-Cola (US)   Puma (Germany)

Financial and Consulting

American Express (US)   Commerzbank (Germany)
Aon (UK)   Credit Agricole (France)

Bank Polski (Poland)   McKinsey (US)
Citi (US)

Food, Hospitality, and Entertainment

Accor (France)   Netflix (US)
Disney (US)   Nintendo (Japan)
Hilton (US)   Starbucks (US)
McDonald's (US)

Information Technology

Apple (US)   Intel (US)
Atlassian (Australia)   Leika (Germany)
Canon (Japan)   Nokia (Finland)
Ericsson (Sweden)   Samsung (South Korea)
IBM (US)

Oil and Gas

British Petroleum (UK)   Equinor (Norway)
ENEOS (Japan)   ExxonMobil (US)
ENI (Italy)   Shell (Netherlands)

Shipping

CMA CGM (France)   Maersk (Denmark)
Hapag-Lloyd (Germany)   Yang Ming (Taiwan)

Energy Sector

Pre-Ukraine war:

- Russia the world's third largest oil producer and second largest natural gas producer.
- Oil and natural gas export earnings provided about half of Russian federal budget and about one-third of its GDP.
- Russia-European Union:

- About 50% of all Russian oil exports go to EU, constituting about 25% EU oil imports.
- About 35% of all Russian natural gas exports go to EU, constituting about 40% EU natural gas consumption, 55% for Germany
- About 45% of EU coal imports came from Russia, but for climate change reasons coal only accounting for about 13% of EU electricity generation
- China is the world's largest importer of oil and natural gas. Russia has been its second largest oil supplier and third largest natural gas supplier.

Principal energy sector sanctions:

- Germany halted the license approval process of Nord Stream 2, a pipeline from Russia to Germany, which would double the flow of Russian gas to Germany.
- EU banned Russian coal imports.
- US, UK, and Australia banned Russian oil imports; EU began process of doing so.
- No EU sanctions on Russian natural gas, although some cutbacks (fuel switching, conservation, other suppliers of liquefied natural gas).
- India and China among the major importers of Russian oil and natural gas that have not sanctioned.
- Saudi Arabia and United Arab Emirates among the major oil producers that refused to increase production to help limit rising oil prices.
- Some Russian sanction-busting re-routing "destination unknown" oil shipments.

Non-Economic Sanctions

Sports

FIFA (World Football/Soccer) International Skating Union
Formula One International Tennis Federation
  International Cat Federation Paralympics
International Boxing Federation UEFA Champions League
International Chess Federation Wimbledon Tennis
International Ice Hockey Federation

Cultural

Cannes Film Festival Metropolitan Opera (New York)
Eurovision Montreal Symphony Orchestra
Individual artists and performers Munich Philharmonic
    Orchestra

Economic Impact on Russia

- GDP effect: 4.7% growth 2021; 2022 projections 10%–15% contraction (April)
- Value of the ruble: 84 rubles/USD before invasion; by early March depreciated to 154 rubles/USD; by mid-April Russian Central Bank policies reduced but did not eliminate decline.
- Inflation: 16.7% annual rate (April), projections potentially much higher Debt.
- International debt: risk of defaulting, would be first default on foreign currency debt since the 1917 Russian revolution.
- Unemployment: projected to exceed 9% for first time in a decade. In mid-April Moscow Mayor projected 200,000 jobs at risk in the city.
- Semiconductor and other parts and technology embargoes constraining military equipment resupply for losses incurred in the war.

Global Economic Impact (of the war as well as the sanctions)

- Global GDP growth projections fell from 4.4% to 3.6% (International Monetary Fund, April), 3.6% to 2.6% (UN)
  - Ukraine projection 45% GDP decline
  - Eurozone growth only 0.2%, 2022 1st quarter
  - Poor and developing countries hardest hit including food shortages: e.g., wheat for which Russia and Ukraine supplied closer to 50% of imports for a number of Arab and African countries.
- World oil prices, about $96/barrel pre-war went as high as $139/barrel (highest in 14 years), leveled off to $103/barrel by late April.
- Contributed to rising inflation in US, Europe and most other countries.
- Other commodities hit by high inflation and major supply change disruptions include coal, steel, aluminum, nickel, and palladium.

NOTES

Introduction

1 Natasha Bertrand, "US Sanctions on Russia Would Impose 'Severe and Overwhelming Costs,' Officials Say," CNN, January 8, 2022, https://www.cnn.com/2022/01/08/politics/biden-russia-ukraine-potential-economic-sanctions/index.html

2 U.S. Department of the Treasury, "Active Sanctions Programs," https://home.treasury.gov/policy-issues/financial-sanctions/sanctions-programs-and-country-information (accessed December 21, 2021).

3 European Union, "EU Sanctions Map," https://www.sanctionsmap.eu/#/main; Government of the United Kingdom, "The UK Sanctions List," https://www.gov.uk/government/publications/the-uk-sanctions-list; Government of Canada, "Current Sanctions Imposed by Canada," https://www.international.gc.ca/world-monde/international_relations-relations_internationales/sanctions/current-actuelles.aspx?lang=eng (all accessed December 21, 2021).

4 Thomas J. Biersteker, Sue E. Eckert, and Marcos Tourinho, eds., *Targeted Sanctions: The Impact and Effectiveness of UN Action* (Cambridge: Cambridge University Press, 2016); Thomas J. Biersteker, Sue E. Eckert, Marcos Tourinho, and Zuzana Hudáková, "UN Targeted Sanctions Datasets (1991–2013)," *Journal of Peace Research* 55:3 (2018); Sue E. Eckert, "Assessing the Effectiveness of UN Targeted Sanctions," Memo prepared for Workshop on the Deterring and Signaling Effects of Sanctions, Bridging the Gap and Center for a New American Security,

January 31–February 1, 2019. On UN sanctions see also David Cortright and George A. Lopez, *The Sanctions Decade: Assessing UN Strategies in the 1990s* (Boulder, CO: Lynne Rienner Publishers, 2000); Patrick M. Weber and Gerald Schneider, "Post–Cold War Sanctioning by the EU, the UN and the US: Introducing the EUSANCT Data Set," *Conflict Management and Peace Science* (2020), https://journals.sagepub.com/doi/10.1177/0738894220948729; and "EUSANCT Data Set Case Summaries," University of Konstanz: Unpublished Working Paper; German Institute of Global Affairs (GIGA) Sanctions Data Set (2020), https://data.gesis.org/sharing/#!Detail/10.7802/1346.

5   Gary Clyde Hufbauer, Jeffrey J. Schott, and Kimberly Ann Elliott (hereafter HSE), *Economic Sanctions Reconsidered*, 2nd ed. (Washington, DC: Peterson Institute for International Economics, 1990); T. Clifton Morgan and Navin Bapat with Valentin Krustev and Yoshiara Kobayashi, "Threats and Imposition of Sanctions Data Base" (TIES), University of North Carolina–Chapel Hill, http://sanctions.web.unc.edu; T. Clifton Morgan, Navin Bapat, and Yoshiharu Kobayashi, "The Threat and Imposition of Economic Sanctions 1945–2005: Updating the TIES Dataset," *Conflict Management and Peace Science* 31:5 (2014): 541–558.

6   The Global Sanctions Data Base (GSDB) spanning the period 1950–2019 and with further updates to follow is one such effort. Its data, though, have yet to be much assessed by other scholars; Aleksandra Kirilaka, Gabriel Felbermayr, Constantinos Syropoulos, Erdal Yalcin, and Yoto V. Yotov, "The Global Sanctions Data Base: An Update That Includes the Years of the Trump Presidency," Drexel School of Economic Working Paper 2021–10, https://drive.google.com/file/d/1ERc5uNcTumu8gyjO hzDtRNIWgkpk03T8/view.

7   HSE, *Economic Sanctions Reconsidered*; Morgan et al., "Threats and Imposition of Sanctions Data Base" (TIES), and "Threat and Imposition of Economic Sanctions 1945–2005"; Robert A. Pape, "Why Economic Sanctions Do Not Work," *International Security* 22:2 (Fall 1997): 90–136.

8   Thomas Weiss, David Cortright, George A. Lopez, and Larry Minear, *Political Gain and Civilian Pain* (Lanham, MD: Rowman & Littlefield, 1997); John Mueller and Karl Mueller, "Sanctions of Mass Destruction," *Foreign Affairs* 78:3 (May–June 1999): 43–53;

Erica Moret, "Humanitarian Impacts of Economic Sanctions on Iran and Syria," *European Security* 24:1 (2015): 120–140.

9 David A. Baldwin, *Economic Statecraft* (Princeton, NJ: Princeton University Press, 1985), 4, 144. See also Daniel W. Drezner, "The Hidden Hand of Economic Coercion," *International Organization* 57:3 (2003): 643–659.

Chapter 1

1 Albert O. Hirschman, *National Power and the Structure of Foreign Trade* (Berkeley: University of California Press, 1980). Among others, Hirschman castigates Machiavelli for "the complete failure . . . to perceive any connection between economics and politics"; xv; Baldwin, *Economic Statecraft*; Henry Farrell and Abraham L. Newman, "Weaponized Interdependence: How Global Economic Networks Shape State Coercion," *International Security* 44:1 (Summer 2019): 42–79.

2 For a sense of the commonalities as well as differences in how economic sanctions are defined, see HSE, *Economic Sanctions Reconsidered*, 3; Jean-Marc F. Blanchard and Norrin M. Ripsman, *Economic Statecraft and Foreign Policy: Sanctions, Incentives and Target State Calculations* (London: Routledge, 2013), 5; Drezner, "Hidden Hand of Economic Coercion," 643; David Lektzian and Mark Souva, "The Economic Peace between Democracies: Economic Sanctions and Domestic Institutions," *Journal of Peace Research* 40:6 (2003): 642; Bryan Early and Menevis Cilizoglu, "Economic Sanctions in Flux: Enduring Challenges, New Policies, and Defining the Future Research Agenda," *International Studies Perspectives* 21:4 (2020): 2.

3 The TIES data set is one that includes economic objectives such as tariff and other trade disputes.

4 Cited in David L. Gordon and Royden Dangerfield, *The Hidden Weapon: The Story of Economic Warfare* (New York: Harper and Brothers, 1947), 16. This book is a fascinating account of American economic warfare against Nazi Germany written by the former chiefs of the Blockade Division, Foreign Economic Administration, State Department. For an account of the history and economics of economic warfare, see Yuan-li Wu, *Economic Warfare* (New York: Prentice-Hall, 1952).

5 "Arms Embargoes," Stockholm International Peace Research Institute (SIPRI), https://www.sipri.org/databases/embargoes. Unilateral US arms embargoes are not included in the SIPRI data.

6   U.S. Department of the Treasury, "Specially Designated Nationals and Blocked Persons List (SDN) Human Readable Lists," accessed June 16, 2021, https://home.treasury.gov/policy-issues/financial-sanctions/specially-designated-nationals-and-blocked-persons-list-sdn-human-readable-lists. See also European Union, "Overview of Sanctions and Related Tools," accessed April 9, 2022, https://ec.europa.eu/info/business-economy-euro/banking-and-finance/international-relations/restrictive-measures-sanctions/what-are-restrictive-measures-sanctions.

7   HSE, *Economic Sanctions Reconsidered*; Morgan et al., "Threats and Imposition of Sanctions Data Base" (TIES), and "Threat and Imposition of Economic Sanctions 1945–2005: Updating the TIES Dataset."

8   Michael Mastanduno, *Economic Containment: CoCom and the Politics of East-West Trade* (Ithaca, NY: Cornell University Press, 1992).

9   Hirschman, *National Power and the Structure of Foreign Trade*, 29.

10 Morgan, Bapat, and Krustev, "Threat and Imposition of Economic Sanctions," Appendix, 106; HSE, *Economic Sanctions Reconsidered*, 52–53; Biersketer et al., *Targeted Sanctions: Impact and Effectiveness of UN Action*; Francesco Giumelli, *Coercing, Constraining, Signalling: Explaining UN and EU Sanctions after the Cold War* (University of Essex: European Consortium for Political Research Press, 2011). For some other authors' versions of objectives see my "Economic Sanctions and Post–Cold War Conflicts: Challenges for Theory and Policy," in *International Conflict Resolution after the Cold War*, ed. Paul C. Stern and Daniel Druckman, National Research Council (Washington, DC: National Academy Press, 2000), 172, note 12.

11 Brendan Taylor, *Sanctions as Grand Strategy* (London: International Institute for Strategic Studies, 2010). On showing resolve see Joshua D. Kertzer, *Resolve in International Politics* (Princeton, NJ: Princeton University Press, 2016); Jonathan Mercer, *Reputation and International Politics* (Ithaca, NY: Cornell University Press, 1996); Danielle L. Lupton, *Reputation for Resolve: How Leaders Signal Determination in International Politics* (Ithaca, NY: Cornell University Press, 2020); Robert Jervis, *Perception and Misperception in International Politics* (Princeton, NJ; Oxford: Princeton University Press, 1979).

12 Peter Rowland, *David Lloyd George* (New York: Macmillan, 1975), 723.

13 Taehee Whang, "Playing to the Home Crowd? Symbolic Use of Economic Sanctions in the United States," *International Studies Quarterly* 55 (2011): 787–801.

14 Jessica L. Weeks, "Autocratic Audience Costs: Regime Type and Signaling Resolve," *International Organization* 62 (Winter 2008): 35–64.

15 Harry Strack, *Sanctions: The Case of Rhodesia* (Syracuse, NY: Syracuse University Press, 1978), 86, 90; Donald L. Losman, *International Economic Sanctions: The Cases of Cuba, Israel, and Rhodesia* (Albuquerque: University of New Mexico Press, 1979), 102; R. B. Sutcliffe, "The Political Economy of Rhodesian Sanctions," *Journal of Commonwealth Political Studies* 7:2 (July 1969): 113–125. On vulnerability of states that lack the capacity to substitute imports with domestic production, see William Akoto, Timothy M. Peterson, and Cameron G. Thies, "Trade Composition and Acquiescence to Sanction Threats," *Political Research Quarterly* 73:3 (September 2020): 526–539.

16 "Iran's Flourishing Stock Market Reflects Its Resilient Economy," *The Economist*, March 12, 2022, https://www.economist.com/finance-and-economics/2022/03/12/irans-flourishing-stockmarket-reflects-its-resilient-economy.

17 The classical philosopher Jean Bodin, cited in Edward L. Morse, *Modernization and the Transformation of International Relations* (New York: Free Press, 1976), 32. Ignoring nationalist defiance to resist despite economic costs being borne amounts to "naïve theories of economic warfare"; Johan Galtung, "On the Effects of International Economic Sanctions, with Examples from the Case of Rhodesia," *World Politics* 19:3 (April 1967): 389.

18 Cited in Miroslav Nincic, *The Logic of Positive Engagement* (Ithaca, NY: Cornell University Press, 2011), 24.

19 Jentleson and Whytock, "Who Won Libya?"

20 Larry Diamond, *Promoting Democracy in the 1990s: Actors and Instruments, Issues and Imperatives* (Washington, DC: Carnegie Commission on Preventing Deadly Conflict, 1995), 55.

21 The classical philosopher Jean Bodin, cited in Edward L. Morse, *Modernization and the Transformation of International Relations* (New York: Free Press, 1976), 32. Ignoring nationalist defiance to resist despite economic costs being borne amounts to "naïve

theories of economic warfare"; Johan Galtung, "On the Effects of
International Economic Sanctions, with Examples from the Case
of Rhodesia," *World Politics* 19:3 (April 1967): 389.

22 Bryan R. Early, *Busted Sanctions: Explaining Why Economic
Sanctions Fail* (Stanford, CA: Stanford University Press,
2015), and "Hunting Whales to Promote Sanctions
Compliance: Understanding OFAC's Sanctions Implementation
Strategy and Future Challenges," Memo prepared for the
Bridging the Gap—Center for a New American Security
Workshop on Economic Sanctions, February 2019.

23 International Consortium of Investigative Journalists, "The
Pandora Papers," https://www.icij.org/investigations/
pandora-papers/; Environmental Investigation Agency,
"Sanctions-Busting Italian Timber Traders Defy EU Law to
Import Myanmar Teak, Aiding the Military Junta," November
25, 2021, https://eia-international.org/news/sanction-busting-
italian-timber-traders-defy-eu-law-to-import-myanmar-teak-
aiding-the-military-junta/; K. Oanh Ha, Lin Kyaw, and Jin
Wu, "Myanmar's Generals Run a Nearly Sanctions-Proof
Empire," *Bloomberg News*, May 10, 2021, https://www.
bloomberg.com/graphics/2021-myanmar-military-business/;
Katie McQue, "Smuggled Iranian Fuel and Secret Nighttime
Transfers: Seafarers Recount How It's Done," *Washington Post*,
January 3, 2022, https://www.washingtonpost.com/world/
middle_east/iran-oil-smugglng-sanctions/2022/01/02/97a
6bf90-5457-11ec-83d2-d9dab0e23b7e_story.html.

24 Anthony Faiola, "How Russian Oligarchs Are Finding Safe
Havens Outside the West," Washington Post, April 1, 2022,
https://www.washingtonpost.com/world/2022/04/01/
turkey-aue-dubai-russian-oligarchs-safe-haven/.

Chapter 2

1 The quote is from Peter Wallensteen, "Characteristics of
Economic Sanctions," *Journal of Peace Research* 5:3 (1968): 262.
Others making similar negative assessments: Henry Bienen and
Robert Gilpin, "the nearly unanimous conclusion of scholars
that sanctions seldom achieve their purposes and more likely
have severe counterproductive consequences"; Margaret Doxey,
that "In none of the cases analyzed in this study have economic
sanctions succeeded in producing the desired political result";

Rita and Howard Taubenfeld, that "in modern times at least, economic sanctions against a non-belligerent do not ever appear to have achieved the stated aims of the sanctionists"; these and others cited in Baldwin, *Economic Statecraft*, 55–57.

2 Pape, "Why Economic Sanctions Do Not Work," 92.

3 Baldwin, *Economic Statecraft*, 4, 144. Baldwin isn't ready to swing the pendulum too far to stating that sanctions always work, instead calling for "more qualification, more patience, more rigor and more caution" in generalizing about sanctions utility; 370.

4 Blackwill and Harris, *War by Other Means*, 200.

5 HSE and TIES cover all sanctions senders, with widely varying case counts (174, 1,412 respectively) only partially attributable to time period variation (1914–2000, 1945–2005); HSE, *Economic Sanctions Reconsidered*, and Morgan et al., "Threats and Imposition of Sanctions Data Base." Data sets focusing just on the US, EU, and UN also show case count variation: EUSANCT (1989–2015, 326 cases) and GIGA (1990–2010, 290 cases); Patrick M. Weber and Gerald Schneider, "Post–Cold War Sanctioning by the EU, the UN and the US: Introducing the EUSANCT Data Set," *Conflict Management and Peace Science* (2020), https://journals.sagepub.com/doi/10.1177/0738894220948729, and "EUSANCT Data Set Case Summaries" (2020), University of Konstanz: Unpublished Working Paper; German Institute of Global Affairs (GIGA) Sanctions Data Set, https://data.gesis.org/sharing/#!Detail/10.7802/1346.

The Targeted Sanctions Consortium (UN sanctions 1991–2014) tabulates sixty-three different "episodes" within twenty-three sets of sanctions; Biersteker, Eckert, Tourinho, and Hudáková, "UN Targeted Sanctions Datasets (1991–2013)." EUSD, which is confined to EU during the period 1993–2019, has forty-eight cases; Francesco Giumelli, Fabian Hoffmann, and Anna Ksiazczakova, "The When, Where, What and Why of European Union Sanctions," *European Security* 30:1 (August 2020): 1–23. The Global Sanctions Data Base counts 1,101 cases for 1950–2019; Kirilata, Felbermayr, et al., "Global Sanctions Data Base," https://www.tandfonline.com/doi/full/10.1080/09662839.2020.1797685.

6 672 of the 1,412 TIES cases are those with economic objectives; Morgan, Bapat, and Krustev, "Threat and Imposition of Economic Sanctions, 1971–2000," 94.

7   Drezner, "Hidden Hand of Economic Coercion," 643–645. Drezner cites an e-mail exchange with Kimberly Ann Elliott in which she acknowledges "there are many [threat cases] that we have missed."

8   TIES' criteria that the threats "may or may not be specific," do not need to be full commitments, only that "sanctions are a possibility," and can be made "through verbal statements by government officials" have similar issues of measurement reliability and validity; Morgan, Bapat, and Kobayashi, "Threat and Imposition of Sanctions," 543

9   TSC differentiates sixty-three episodes within its twenty-three UN-mandated cases. EUSD also works with episodes, eighty-five in its forty-eight EU cases. TIES is more episode-based than HSE, with seventeen cases singly counted by HSE having a second TIES case, two a third TIES case, and two having four TIES cases. For example, HSE treats the 1973 OPEC oil embargo as one case, while TIES breaks it down into eight cases. Particularly striking is HSE treating as one case US economic pressure against various International Criminal Court (ICC) member countries to get them to sign agreements exempting US personnel from ICC prosecution, while TIES breaks these down to seventy-one separate country cases.

10 Jentleson and Whytock, "Who Won Libya?"

11 Nicholas L. Miller, "The Secret Success of Nonproliferation Sanctions," *International Organization* 68:4 (2014): 913–944.

12 Cited in Bruce W. Jentleson, *The Peacemakers: Leadership Lessons from 20th Century Statesmanship* (New York: W. W. Norton, 2018), 213.

13 US Government Accountability Office, *Economic Sanctions: Agencies Assess Impacts on Targets, and Studies Suggest Several Factors Contribute to Sanctions' Effectiveness*, GAO-20-145, October 2019, https://www.gao.gov/assets/710/701891.pdf.

14 Isabel Ivanescu and Andrew Greco make this argument with regard to Syria; "How Biden Can Manage the JCPOA's Consequences in Syria," *The National Interest*, March 1, 2021, https://nationalinterest.org/blog/middle-east-watch/how-biden-can-manage-jcpoa%E2%80%99s-consequences-syria-179025.

15 TIES cites 1962 US sanctions on Haiti, 1963 US on Dominican Republic, and 1970 Zimbabwe on Zambia (1970013001).

16 Notable efforts to better assess and define sanctions success include Dursun Peksen, "When Do Imposed Economic Sanctions Work? A Critical Review of the Sanctions Effectiveness Literature," *Defence and Peace Economics* 30:6 (2019): 635–647; and Amira Jadoon, Dursun Peksen, and Taehee Whang, "How Can We Improve Our Understanding of Sanctions Success?" *International Studies Perspectives* 21 (2020): 464–471.

17 HSE use an ordinal "success score" coding based on two measures, "the extent to which the policy objective sought by the sender state was achieved" and "the contribution made by the sanctions (as opposed to other factors, such as military action)." Each was coded 1 to 4. Policy results: 1 for failed outcome, 2 if unclear but possibly positive, 3 for partial success, and 4 for goals largely achieved. For sanctions contribution: 1 actually means the sanctions were counterproductive, 2 made little to no contribution, 3 made a substantial contribution, 4 were the decisive factor. If multiplying the two scores came to 9 or above, the case was deemed a success, below 9 a failure. TSC gradates the HSE scale to a 5-point one, with at least a 4 for attributing any success. The Global Sanctions Data Base bases success on official statements by sender states and institutions, with which I see serious problems of reliability and validity; Kirilata, Felbermayr, et al., "Global Sanctions Data Base."

18 Dursun Peksen, "Better or Worse? The Effect of Economic Sanctions on Human Rights," *Journal of Peace Research* 46:1 (2009): 59–77; Dursun Peksen and A. Cooper Drury, "Coercive or Corrosive: The Negative Impact of Economic Sanctions on Democracy," *International Interactions* 36:3 (2010): 240–264. See also Reed M. Wood, "'A Hand upon the Throat of the Nation': Economic Sanctions and State Repression, 1976–2001," *International Studies Quarterly* 52:3 (2008): 489–513; Susan H. Allen, "The Domestic Political Costs of Economic Sanctions," *Journal of Conflict Resolution* 52:6 (2008): 924–925.

19 Andrew Nathan, "The Consequences of Tiananmen," in *The Tiananmen Papers: The Chinese Leadership's Decision to Use Force against Their Own People—In Their Own Words*, comp. Zhang Lian and ed. Andrew Nathan and Perry Link, vii–xxiii (New York: Public Affairs, 2002).

20 Jerg Gutmann, Matthias Neuenkirch, and Florian Neumeier, "Sanctioned to Death? The Impact of Economic Sanctions on

Life Expectancy and the Gender Gap," *Journal of Development Studies* 57(2021): 1; Dominic Parker, Jeremy Foltz, and David Elsea, "Unintended Consequences of Sanctions for Human Rights: Conflict Minerals and Infant Mortality," *Journal of Law and Economics* 59:4 (2016): 731–774; Allen and Lektzian, "Economic Sanctions: A Blunt Instrument?"; Thomas Weiss, David Cortright, George A. Lopez, and Larry Minear, *Political Gain and Civilian Pain* (Lanham, MD: Rowman & Littlefield, 1997).

21 Pranshu Verma and Vivian Yee, "Trump's Syria Sanctions 'Cannot Solve the Problem,' Critics Say," *New York Times*, August 4, 2020, https://www.nytimes.com/2020/08/04/world/ middleeast/trump-assad-syria-sanctions.html. All too often, "Besieging an oppressive regime," as journalist Peter Beinart puts it, "usually harms not the oppressor but the oppressed"; "America's Other Forever War," *New York Times*, February 15, 2021, https://www.nytimes.com/2021/02/15/opinion/ us-sanctions.html.

22 In his work on broader Cold War sanctions, Michael Mastanduno brings out how while supportive of overall containment goals, "allied governments chafed under what they viewed as the extraterritorial and coercive imposition of U.S. economic power"; "Hegemony and Fear: The National Security Determinants of Weaponized Interdependence," in *The Uses and Abuses of Weaponized Interdependence*, ed. Daniel W. Drezner, Henry Farrell, and Abraham L. Newman (Washington, DC: Brookings Institution, 2021), 74.

23 Cited in Baldwin, *Economic Statecraft*, 107.

24 "In an effort to destroy . . . English sea power . . ., Napoleon deprived the manufacturers in his own lands of all their raw materials"; William M. Sloane, "The Continental System of Napoleon," *Political Science Quarterly* 13:2 (1898): 230.

25 William Mauldin, "U.S. Weighs Limited Options to Punish China over Hong Kong; Major Steps against the Territory's Financial System Risk Hurting U.S., Western and Hong Kong Companies and Consumers," *Wall Street Journal*, July 12, 2020 https://www.wsj.com/articles/u-s-weighs-limited-options-to-pun ish-china-over-hong-kong-11594576800.

26 "Policymaking involves making decisions," as Baldwin rightly stresses, "and decision-making involves choosing among alternative courses of action. The advantages and disadvantages

of various policy options acquire significance primarily by comparison with the options"; *Economic Statecraft*, 15.

27   A point stressed by Alexander George in his work on coercive diplomacy; see, for example, his chapter "Coercive Diplomacy: Definitions and Characteristics," in George and Simons, *Limits of Coercive Diplomacy*.

28   Even taking into account negative effects persisting post-apartheid, Audie Klotz still sees sanctions as on balance a success, indeed one that "stands out historically"; Klotz, "Making Sanctions Work: Comparative Lessons," in *How Sanctions Work: Lessons from South Africa*, ed. Neta C. Crawford and Audie Klotz (New York: St. Martin's Press, 1999), 273. While not a sanctions case per se, the Conference on Security and Cooperation in Europe (CSCE) and Helsinki process established in the mid-1970s as part of Cold War détente shows similar timeframe assessment variability. Derided for many years as talk shops, by 1989–1990 CSCE and Helsinki were hailed by leaders like Czechoslovak dissident-turned-president Václav Havel as having kept them alive even if imprisoned; Nicolas Badalassi and Sarah B. Snyder, eds., *CSCE and the End of the Cold War: Diplomacy, Societies and Human Rights, 1972–1990* (New York: Berghahn Books, 2019).

29   George Lopez and David Cortright, "Containing Iraq: Sanctions Worked," *Foreign Affairs* 83:4 (July–August 2004): 90–103.

30   TIES codes for diplomatic actions such as these as well as economic and other incentives. HSE include companion policies such as covert action, quasi-military action, and regular military action. All the TSC UN multilateral cases included one or more of twelve other policy instruments (e.g., threats of and use of force, legal processes such as the International Criminal Court, diplomatic negotiations).

31   John Mueller and Karl Mueller, "Sanctions of Mass Destruction," *Foreign Affairs* 78:3 (May–June 1999): 43–53. See also Moret, "Humanitarian Impacts of Economic Sanctions on Iran and Syria."

32   Jentleson, "Economic Sanctions and Post–Cold War Conflicts," in Stern and Druckman, *International Conflict Resolution after the Cold War*, 147.

33   Human Rights Watch, *Maximum Pressure: US Economic Sanctions Harm Iranians' Right to Health*, by Tara Sepehri Far (2019),

https://www.hrw.org/report/2019/10/29/maximum-pressure/
us-economic-sanctions-harm-iranians-right-health; Korea
Peace Now, *The Human Costs and Gendered Impact of Sanctions on
North Korea* (2019), https://koreapeacenow.org/wp-content/
uploads/2019/10/human-costs-and-gendered-impact-of-
sanctions-on-north-korea.pdf.

34 Jentleson, "Economic Sanctions and Post–Cold War
Conflicts," 148.

35 Danny Makki, Twitter Post, June 7, 2020, 4:45 AM, https://twitter.
com/dannymakkisyria/status/1269551089755586561.

36 BBC Global News Podcast, "The UN Says Afghanistan
Faces a Profound Humanitarian Crisis," December 14, 2021,
https://www.bbc.co.uk/programmes/p0bb0tml.

37 "Still unjust, just in different ways" is how Bryan Early
and Marcus Schulzke assess targeted sanctions' adverse
consequences comparable to traditional ones; Bryan R. Early
and Marcus Schulzke, "Still Unjust, Just in Different Ways: How
Targeted Sanctions Fall Short of Just War Theory's Principles,"
International Studies Review 21 (2019): 57–80.

38 Cited in Idriss Jazairy, "Unilateral Economic Sanctions,
International Law and Human Rights," *Ethics and International
Affairs* 33:3 (Fall 2019): 294.

39 As Joy Gordon puts it, banks, oil companies, shippers, and
others deem it "safer to simply withdraw altogether from
doing business with a sanctioned country, even if their business
does not directly engage any blacklisted entity. The result is
that the country's access to banking, shipping, fuel, and goods
is diminished far beyond the parameters of the sanctions";
Gordon, "The Not So Targeted Instrument of Assets Freezes,"
Ethics and International Affairs 33:3 (Fall 2019): 310. See also
her 1999 article "A Peaceful, Silent, Deadly Remedy: The
Ethics of Economic Sanctions," *Ethics and International Affairs*
13:1 (1999): 123–142; Joseph Daher and Erica Moret,
*Invisible Sanctions: How Overcompliance Limits Humanitarian
Work on Syria* (Berlin: IMPACT Civil Society Research and
Development, 2020), https://impact-csrd.org/reports/
Invisible_Sanctions_IMPACT_EN.pdf.

40 See, for example, Emanuela Chiara-Girard, *Recommendations
for Reducing Tensions in the Interplay between Sanctions,
Counterterrorism Measures and Humanitarian Impact*, Chatham

House International Security Department and International Law
Programme, August 2017, https://www.chathamhouse.org/
sites/default/files/publications/research/CHHJ5596_NSAG_
iv_research_paper_1708_WEB.pdf.

41   Peksen, "Political Effectiveness, Negative Externalities and
Ethics of Economic Sanctions," 280; Gordon, "Not So Targeted
Instrument of Assets Freezes"; Jazairy, "Unilateral Economic
Sanctions, International Law and Human Rights."

Chapter 3

1   "Make no mistake," Daniel Drezner makes the point, "for
sanctions to lead to concessions, the sanctioning actor needs to
demonstrate the ability to impose costs on the target. . . . But costs
are not the only factor at play"; Drezner, "Economic Sanctions
Are about More Than Imposing Costs," *Washington Post*, April 18,
2018, https://www.washingtonpost.com/news/posteverything/
wp/2018/04/18/economic-sanctions-are-about-more-than-
imposing-costs/. HSE find economic costs "among the more
statistically significant and robust variables," but with some
cases with low success scores despite high economic impact
and with a great deal of variation based on such other factors
as regime type and policy objective; *Economic Sanctions
Reconsidered*, 161, 163–166. TIES find that "severe costs on target
states are positively and robustly related to sanctions success
at every stage in sanctions episodes," but so too are a range
of other factors including the role of international institutions
and whether the costs are borne heavily by the target regime
and its supporters; Navin Bapat, Tobias Heinrich, Yoshiharu
Kobayashi, and T. Clifton Morgan, "Determinants of Sanctions
Effectiveness: Sensitivity Analysis Using New Data," *International
Interactions* 39:1 (2013): 79–98; Morgan and Schwebach, "Fools
Suffer Gladly."

2   Dursun Peksen, "When Do Imposed Economic Sanctions Work?
A Critical Review of the Sanctions Effectiveness Literature,"
Defense and Peace Economics 30:6 (2019): 637.

3   "Diplomacy Sayings and Quotes," https://www.wiseoldsayings.
com/diplomacy-quotes/.

4   T. Clifton Morgan and Valerie L. Schwebach, "Fools Suffer
Gladly: The Use of Economic Sanctions in International Crises,"
International Studies Quarterly 41 (March 1997): 27–50. Paul

Bentall, "United Nations Targeted Sanctions and Other Policy Tools: Diplomacy, Legal, Use of Force," in Biersteker, Eckert, and Tourinho, *Targeted Sanctions*, 89–91. The 2022 Russia sanctions over the Ukraine war is a variant on this in which direct military force was not used but indirect military force was through weaponry and other military aid to the Ukrainian army and insurgency. To the extent that Russia is coerced to end the war on terms acceptable to Ukraine, the United States and the international community, sanctions will warrant some credit but the military strategy (Ukrainian resistance, US and NATO military assistance) will have been the main factor.

5　Todd S. Sechser, "A Bargaining Theory of Coercion," in *Coercion: The Power to Hurt in International Relations*, ed. Kelly M. Greenhill (New York: Oxford University Press, 2018), 55–76.

6　Rupal N. Mehta, "Manipulating State Behavior: How to Use Sanctions and Rewards to Get What You Want," *International Affairs Blog*, https://medium.com/international-affairs-blog/manipulating-state-behaviour-how-to-use-sanctions-and-rewards-to-get-what-you-want-7cadaef3b0fd. On the strategic logic beyond just sanctions, see Schelling, *Arms and Influence*; Robert J. Art and Patrick M. Cronin, eds., *The United States and Coercive Diplomacy* (Washington, DC: US Institute of Peace Press, 2003); Bruce W. Jentleson, "Coercive Diplomacy: Scope and Limits, Theory and Policy," in *The Routledge Handbook of Security Studies*, ed. Victor Mauer and Myriam Dunn Cavelty (London: Routledge, 2009), 404–414; Alexander L. George and Richard Smoke, *Deterrence in American Foreign Policy: Theory and Practice* (New York: Columbia University Press, 1974); Robert M. Axelrod, *The Evolution of Cooperation* (New York: Basic Books, 2006); Nincic, *Logic of Positive Engagement*; David A. Baldwin, "The Power of Positive Sanctions," *World Politics* 24:1 (October 1971): 19–38.

7　Cortright and Lopez, *Sanctions Decade*, 31.

8　Julia Grauvogel and Hana Attia, "Easier In Than Out: The Protracted Process of Ending Sanctions," German Institute of Global Affairs (GIGA), October 5, 2019, https://www.giga-hamburg.de/en/publications/11854089-easier-in-than-out-protracted-process-ending-sanctions/.

9   Stephan Haggard and Marcus Noland, *Hard Target: Sanctions, Inducement and the Case of North Korea* (Stanford, CA: Stanford University Press, 2017).

10 Alistair Smith, "International Crises and Domestic Politics," *American Political Science Review* 92:3 (1998): 623–638; Michael Tomz, "Domestic Audience Costs in International Relations: An Experimental Approach," *International Organization* 61:4 (2007): 821–840; Lektzian and Souva, "Economic Peace between Democracies"; Whang, "Playing to the Home Crowd?"; James D. Fearon, "Domestic Political Audiences and the Escalation of International Disputes," *American Political Science Review* 88:3 (1994): 577–592; Susan H. Allen, "Political Institutions and Constrained Response to Economic Sanctions," *Foreign Policy Analysis* 4:3 (2008): 255–274; Kim Richard Nossal, "Liberal Democratic Regimes, International Sanctions, and Global Governance," in *Globalization and Global Governance*, ed. Raimo Vayrrynen (Lanham, MD: Rowman and Littlefield, 1999), 302.

11 Weeks, "Autocratic Audience Costs"; Lektzian and Souva, "Institutional Theory of Sanctions Onset and Success"; Julia Grauvogel and Christian von Soest, "Claims to Legitimacy Count: Why Sanctions Fail to Instigate Democratization in Authoritarian Regimes," *European Journal of Political Research* 53:4 (2014): 635–653; Bryan R. Early and Dursun Peksen, "Shadow Economies and the Success of Economic Sanctions: Explaining Why Democratic Targets Are Disadvantaged," *Foreign Policy Analysis* 16:3 (July 2020): 353–372; HSE, *Economic Sanctions Reconsidered*, 166–167.

12 Miller, "Secret Success of Nonproliferation Sanctions," and *Stopping the Bomb.*

13 HSE, *Supplemental Case Histories*, 341

14 Richard N. Haass, "Sanctioning Madness," *Foreign Affairs*, November/December 1997, 80; Risa Brooks, "Sanctions and Regime Type: What Works, and When?" *Security Studies* 11:4 (2002): 1–50; Kirshner, "Microfoundations of Economic Sanctions."

15 Jentleson and Whytock, "Who 'Won' Libya?"; Lektzian and Souva, "Institutional Theory of Sanctions Onset and Success."

16 Morgan, Bapat, and Kobayashi report a 51–31 percent success rate advantage for multilateral sanctions compared to unilateral ones; "Threat and Imposition of Economic Sanctions," 550; HSE

find multilateralization especially important when the foreign policy goal is major rather than modest; *Economic Sanctions Reconsidered*, 161.

17 Lisa L. Martin, *Coercive Cooperation: Explaining Multilateral Economic Sanctions* (Princeton, NJ: Princeton University Press, 1992).

18 Anne Miers and T. Clifton Morgan, "Multilateral Sanctions and Foreign Policy Success: Can Too Many Cooks Spoil the Broth?" *International Interactions*, April–June 2002, 117–136; HSEO, *Economic Sanctions Reconsidered*, 172–175; Kaempfer and Lowenberg, "International Economic Sanctions: A Public Choice Approach"; Bryan R. Early and Robert Spice, "Economic Sanctions, International Institutions, and Sanctions Busters: When Does Institutionalized Cooperation Help Sanctioning Efforts?" *Foreign Policy Analysis* 11:3 (2015): 340.

19 Cortright and Lopez, *Sanctions Decade*; Biersteker, Eckert, and Tourinho, *Targeted Sanctions*, 205–207.

20 Thanks to Ida Sawyer of Human Rights Watch and a Wilson Center Fellow for sharing her work on the DRC case.

21 Early and Ciligozlu, "Consequences of Economic Sanctions," 459.

22 Dursun Peksen, "Better or Worse? The Effects of Economic Sanctions on Human Rights," *Journal of Peace Research* 46:1 (2009): 59.

23 Juan Zarate, *Treasury's War: The Unleashing of a New Era of Financial Warfare* (New York: Public Affairs, 2013); Blackwill and Harris, *War by Other Means*, 197; Elizabeth Rosenberg, Zachary K. Goldman, Daniel Drezner, and Julia Solomon-Strauss, *The New Tools of Economic Warfare: Effects and Effectiveness of Contemporary U.S. Financial Sanctions* (Washington, DC: Center for a New American Security, 2016); Farrell and Newman, "Weaponized Interdependence"; Thomas Oatley, "Weaponizing International Financial Interdependence," in Drezner, Farrell, and Newman, *Uses and Abuses of Weaponized Interdependence*.

24 Oatley, "Weaponizing International Financial Interdependence," 117; Julia Morse, "Blacklists, Market Enforcement and the Global Regime to Combat Terrorist Financing," *International Organization* 73:3 (Summer 2019): 511–545.

25 International Consortium of Investigative Journalists, *The Panama Papers*, https://www.icij.org/investigations/panama-papers/.

26 Gordon, "Not So Targeted Instrument of Assets Freezes," 310.

27 Matt Apuzzo and Jane Bradley, "Oligarchs Got Richer despite
    Sanctions. Will This Time Be Different?" *New York Times*, March
    16, 2022, https://www.nytimes.com/2022/03/16/world/
    europe/russia-oligarchs-sanctions-putin.html.

28 Pulitzer Prize-winning columnist Eugene Robinson makes this
    point quite powerfully: "What the Shocking Images of Ukraine's
    Dead Say about the Media—And Our Biases," *Washington
    Post*, March 14, 2022, https://www.washingtonpost.com/
    opinions/2022/03/14/victims-of-yemen-deserve-as-much-
    concern-as-family-killed-in-irpin-and-maternity-hospital-
    victims/.

29 Graham Bowley and Zachary Small, "US Study Finds Further
    Regulation of the Art Market Not Needed Now," *New York Times*,
    February 4, 2022, https://www.nytimes.com/2022/02/04/arts/
    design/art-market-regulation.html.

30 HSE have a 51 percent success for "modest policy changes"
    compared to 34 percent overall; *Economic Sanctions Reconsidered*,
    159. TIES get 27.2 percent for total or partial acquiescence
    but 37.5 percent for the more limited successes of negotiated
    settlements; Morgan, Bapat, and Kobayashi, "Threat and
    Imposition of Sanctions 1945–2005," 546; TSC has 27 percent
    effective for constraining and signaling but 10 percent for the
    more extensive objective of coercing; Biersteker, Eckert, and
    Tourinho, *Targeted Sanctions*, Appendix 2.

31 "The strength of the opponent's motivation not to comply is
    highly dependent on what is demanded of him"; George and
    Simons, *Limits of Coercive Diplomacy*, 281.

32 Lise Morje Howard, *Power in Peacekeeping*
    (Cambridge: Cambridge University Press, 2019), 87–89.

33 Arms Control Association, "The Wassenaar Arrangement at
    a Glance," February 2022, https://www.armscontrol.org/
    factsheets/wassenaar; Nuclear Suppliers Group,
    https://www.nuclearsuppliersgroup.org/en/.

34 Christian von Soehst and Michael Wahman, "The
    Underestimated Effect of Democratic Sanctions," *E-International
    Relations*, 2014, https://wcfia.harvard.edu/publications/
    underestimated-effect-democratic-sanctions-0.

35 Peksen, "Better or Worse?"

36 As Elizabeth Rosenberg and Jordan Tama argue, "Sanctions often
    have more potential to deter unwanted actions than to compel

policy reversals"; *Strengthening the Economic Arsenal: Bolstering the Deterrent and Signaling Effects of Sanctions*, Center for a New American Security, December 2019, https://www.cnas.org/publications/reports/strengthening-the-economic-arsenal, 2. See also Schelling, *Arms and Influence*, 70–71.

Chapter 4

1 My approach draws on the structured focused comparison methodology developed by Alexander George and colleagues. See Alexander L. George, "Case Studies and Theory Development," in *Diplomacy: New Approaches in Theory, History and Policy*, ed. Paul Gordon Lauren (New York, Free Press, 1979); Alexander George and Andrew Bennett, *Case Studies and Theory Development in the Social Sciences* (Cambridge, MA: MIT Press, 2005).

2 Donald Kagan, *The Outbreak of the Peloponnesian War* (Ithaca, NY: Cornell University Press, 1969), 265–266; Sir Alfred Zimmern, *Greek Commonwealth*, 5th ed. (Oxford: Clarendon Press, 1931), 426–427, quoted in Baldwin, *Economic Statecraft*, 152, 154.

3 Aristophanes, *The Acharnians*, lines 523–533; http://classics.mit.edu/Aristophanes/acharnians.html.

4 Henry Bienen and Robert Gilpin, "An Evaluation of the Use of Economic Sanctions to Promote Foreign Policy Objectives, with Special Reference to the Problem of Terrorism and the Promotion of Human Rights," a report prepared for the Boeing Corporation (April 2, 1979), cited in Baldwin, *Economic Statecraft*, 150.

5 Thucydides, *History of the Peloponnesian War*, 14, is quoted in Jonathan Kirshner, "Handle Him with Care: The Importance of Getting Thucydides Right," *Security Studies* 28:1 (2019).

6 Baldwin, *Economic Statecraft*, 154.

7 Eli F. Heckscher, *The Continental System: An Economic Interpretation* (Oxford: Clarendon Press, 1922), 88. See also William M. Sloane, "The Continental System of Napoleon," *Political Science Quarterly* 13:2 (1898): 213–231; Tor Egil Førland, "The History of Economic Warfare: International Law, Effectiveness, Strategies," *Journal of Peace Research* 30:2 (1993): 151–162; Daniel P. Ahn, "Economic Sanctions: Past, Present, and Future," *Georgetown Journal of International Affairs* 20 (2019): 126–132.

8 Heckscher, *The Continental System*, 367.

9   Carl von Clausewitz, *The Campaign of 1812 in Russia*,
     https://www.clausewitzstudies.org/readings/1812/Clausewitz-
     CampaignOf1812inRussia-EllesmereTranslation.pdf; 212. At the
     time, Clausewitz was a Prussian military officer who defected
     from the French army and joined Russian imperial headquarters.

10 Jesse Greenspan, "Why Napoleon's Invasion of Russia Was the
     Beginning of the End," September 14, 2020, https://www.history.
     com/news/napoleons-disastrous-invasion-of-russia.

11 Andrew Holt, "No More Hoares to Paris," *Review of International
     Studies* 37:3 (2011): 1383–1401; George Baer, "Sanctions and
     Security: The League of Nations and the Italian-Ethiopian War,
     1935–1936," *International Organization* 27:2 (1973): 165–179.

12 G. Bruce Strang, "'The Worst of All Worlds': Oil Sanctions and
     Italy's Invasion of Abyssinia, 1935–1936," *Diplomacy and Statecraft*
     19:2 (2008): 210–235; Perry Willson, "Empire, Gender, and the
     'Home Front' in Fascist Italy," *Women's History Review* 16:4
     (2007): 487–500; Cristiano Andrea Ristuccia, "The 1935 Sanctions
     against Italy: Would Coal and Oil Have Made a Difference?"
     European Review of Economic History 4:1 (2000): 85–110; Nicholas
     Mulder, *The Economic Weapon: The Rise of Sanctions as a Tool of
     Modern War* (New Haven: Yale University Press, 2022).

13 Robin Renwick, *Economic Sanctions* (Cambridge, MA: Harvard
     University Center for International Affairs, 1981), 48; Doxey,
     Economic Sanctions and International Enforcement, 5.

14 HSE, *Economic Sanctions Reconsidered*, 102.

15 Howard Taubenfeld and Rita Falk Taubenfeld, "The Economic
     Weapon: The League and the United Nations," *Proceedings of
     the American Society of International Law at Its Annual Meeting
     (1921–1969)* 58 (1964): 184–185

16 Baer, "Sanctions and Security," 178–179.

17 Ristuccia, "1935 Sanctions against Italy"; Willson, "Empire,
     Gender and the 'Home Front' in Fascist Italy," 489, 495.

18 HSE, *Economic Sanctions Reconsidered: Supplemental Case Histories*,
     2nd ed. (Washington, DC: Institute for International Economics,
     1990), 36.

19 Taubenfeld and Taubenfeld, "The 'Economic Weapon'"; Strang,
     "The Worst of All Worlds."

20 Baer, "Sanctions and Security," 177.

21 Frederick Hartman, *The Relations of Nations* (New York: Macmillan, 1973), 369; Mulder, *The Economic Weapon*, 222.

22 Jentleson, *The Peacemaker*, Chapter 4.

23 Sanctions also were imposed against France and Israel, but the British case is the most significant for our study.

24 William Hitchcock, *The Age of Eisenhower: America and the World in the 1950s* (New York: Simon & Schuster, 2018), 319.

25 Hitchcock, *The Age of Eisenhower*, 306; Robert R. Bowie, *International Crises and the Role of Law: Suez 1956* (London: Oxford University Press, 1956), 22, cited in HSE, *Economic Sanctions Reconsidered*, 156.

26 Jentleson, *Peacemakers*, 115.

27 Kunz, *Economic Diplomacy of the Suez Crisis*, 138.

28 Kunz, *Economic Diplomacy*, 130.

29 Bowie, *Suez 1956*, 64.

30 For detailed analyses of the Rhodesian case see Harry Strack, *Sanctions: The Case of Rhodesia* (Syracuse, NY: Syracuse University Press, 1978); Donald L. Losman, *International Economic Sanctions: The Cases of Cuba, Israel, and Rhodesia* (Albuquerque: University of New Mexico Press, 1979); Doxey, *Economic Sanctions and International Enforcement*.

31 "Mr. Wilson's Visit to Rhodesia," *Keesing's Record of World Events* 11 (December 1965): 21087, http://web.stanford.edu/group/tomzgroup/pmwiki/uploads/1804-1965-12-KS-a-RRW.pdf.

32 HSE, *Economic Sanctions Reconsidered*, 290.

33 Economic data derived from Losman, *International Economic Sanctions*, 89–91, 102, 107, 110, 115; Strack, *Sanctions: Rhodesia*, 86, 90, 117.

34 Memorandum from Secretary of State Henry Kissinger to CIA Director George Bush, "Present South African Attitudes on the Rhodesian Situation," August 31, 1976, https://www.cia.gov/library/readingroom/docs/LOC-HAK-91-6-31-0.pdf.

35 Strack, *Sanctions: Rhodesia*, 164.

36 See Baldwin, *Economic Statecraft*, 190.

37 Roy Licklider, *Political Power and the Arab Oil Weapon: The Experience of Five Industrial Nations* (Berkeley: University of California Press, 1988); Hanns Maull, "Oil and Influence: The Oil Weapon Examined," *The Adelphi Papers* 15:117 (1975): 1–2; Doxey, *Economic Sanctions and International Enforcement*.

38 Arab League resolution cited in HSE, *Economic Sanctions Reconsidered*, 341.

39 Walter Laqueur, *The Struggle for the Middle East: The Soviet Union and the Middle East, 1958–68* (London: Routledge & K. Paul, 1970), 127.

40 Bruce W. Jentleson, *Pipeline Politics: The Complex Political Economy of East-West Energy Trade* (Ithaca, NY: Cornell University Press, 1986), 138–139.

41 Maull, *Oil and Influence*, 33–34.

42 William B. Quandt, *Decade of Decisions: American Policy toward the Arab-Israeli Conflict, 1967–1976* (Berkeley: University of California Press, 1977), 267–268.

43 Audie Klotz, *Norms in International Relations: The Struggle against Apartheid* (Ithaca, NY: Cornell University Press, 1995); Crawford and Klotz, *How Sanctions Work*; Robert M. Price, *The Apartheid State in Crisis: Political Transformation in South Africa, 1975–1990* (New York: Oxford University Press, 1991).

44 Philip I. Levy, "Sanctions on South Africa: What Did They Do?," Yale Economic Growth Center Discussion Paper, February 1999, http://www.econ.yale.edu/growth_pdf/cdp796.pdf.

45 Bruce W. Jentleson, "American Diplomacy: Around the World and Along Pennsylvania Avenue," in *A Question of Balance: The President, Congress and Foreign Policy*, ed. Thomas E. Mann (Washington, DC: Brookings Institution Press, 1990), 157.

46 Crawford and Klotz, *How Sanctions Work*, 3.

Chapter 5

1 HSE, *Economic Sanctions Reconsidered*, Table 5.1, 127; TIES calculated based on Morgan, Bapat, and Kobayashi, "Threats and Imposition of Sanctions"; Daniel W. Drezner, "The United States of Sanctions: The Use and Abuse of Economic Coercion," *Foreign Affairs*, September/October 2021, https://www.foreignaffairs.com/articles/united-states/2021-08-24/united-states-sanctions; Robert Kahn, "Have Sanctions Become the Swiss Army Knife of U.S. Foreign Policy?," Council on Foreign Relations, July 24, 2017, https://www.cfr.org/blog/have-sanctions-become-swiss-army-knife-us-foreign-policy.

2 Reema Shocair Ali, "OFAC 2019 Year in Review," *JD Supra*, February 5, 2020, https://www.jdsupra.com/legalnews/ofac-2019-year-in-review-part-1-of-3-47987/; Sam Dorshimer and

Francis Shin, *Sanctions by the Numbers: 2020 Year in Review*, Center for a New American Security, January 14, 2021, https://www.cnas.org/publications/reports/sanctions-by-the-numbers-2020.

3 Hirschman, *National Power and Structure of Foreign Trade*, 13; Farrell and Newman, "Weaponized Interdependence," 45.

4 Bryan R. Early and Amira Jadoon, "Using the Carrot as the Stick: US Foreign Aid and the Effectiveness of Sanctions Threats," *Foreign Policy Analysis* 15:3 (July 2015): 350–369.

5 Jentleson, "Weaponized Interdependence, Dynamics of 21st Century Power and U.S. Grand Strategy," in *Uses and Abuses of Weaponized Interdependence*, ed. Drezner, Farrell, and Newman, 247; Blackwill and Harris, *War by Other Means.*

6 US Treasury Department, OFAC, *SDN List.* DC law firms specialize in helping companies navigate these regulations; there's even one that calls itself OFAC Law Group; "Contact Us," OFAC Law Group, https://ofaclawyer.net/contact-us/.

7 Blackwill and Harris, *War by Other Means*, 200.

8 HSE, *Economic Sanctions Reconsidered*, Table 5.1, 127. The TIES data were somewhat higher but with similar periodization: 1945–1969, 58 percent success; 1970–1989, 49 percent; Morgan, Bapat, and Kobayashi, "Threats and Imposition of Sanctions."

9 Drezner, "United States of Sanctions." The Global Sanctions Data Base (GSDB) does go up to 2010, but as noted earlier its basing success on official statements by sender states and institutions has serious problems of reliability and validity; Kirilata, Felbermayr, et al., "Global Sanctions Data Base."

10 As of this writing the 2022 Russia Ukraine case is still ongoing. To the extent that Russia is coerced to end the war on terms acceptable to Ukraine, the United States and the international community, sanctions will warrant some credit but the military strategy (Ukrainian resistance, US and NATO military assistance) will have been the main factor. More in the case study later in this chapter and the Appendix.

11 With a broader set of cases, HSE calculate about a 35 percent success rate for limited domestic political change.

12 Miller, "Secret Success of Nonproliferation Sanctions," and *Stopping the Bomb.*

13 Whang, "Playing to the Home Crowd?" In the 2022 Russia Ukraine case, while 64% of those polled supported increasing

sanctions even if they further increased inflation, only 42% approved and 47% disapproved of President Biden's overall handling of the Ukraine crisis; Ashley Parker, Emily Gustin, and Scott Clement, "Big Majority of Americans Back Sanctions on Russia, Aid to Ukraine, Poll Finds," *Washington Post*, May 2, 2022, https://www.washingtonpost.com/politics/2022/05/02/poll-ukraine-support-biden/

14   HSE, *Economic Sanctions Reconsidered*, 134–135. The 1983–2014 cases showed thirty-six of seventy-five opposed by the president but approved by Congress; Jordan Tama, "Forcing the President's Hand: How the US Congress Shapes Foreign Policy through Sanctions Legislation," *Foreign Policy Analysis* 16:3 (July 2020): 397–416.

15   Guillermo J. Grenier and Qing Lai, *2020 FIU Cuba Poll: How Cuban Americans in Miami View U.S. Policies toward Cuba* (Miami: Florida International University, 2020).

16   Bruce W. Jentleson, "Economic Sanctions and Post–Cold War Conflicts," in *International Conflict Resolution after the Cold War*, ed. Stern and Druckman, 138, *With Friends Like These: Reagan, Bush and Saddam, 1982–1990* (New York: W. W. Norton, 1994), 80–86. The 1980 grain embargo against the Soviet Union is another example. Farmers vented their anger at Jimmy Carter by voting overwhelmingly for Ronald Reagan. Once in office, notwithstanding his anti-Soviet hawkishness, Reagan quickly lifted the grain embargo. More on that in the case study below.

17   *Checklists of Foreign Countries Subject to Sanctions* (Thompson Coburn LLP, March 2020); US Department of State, Bureau of International Security and Nonproliferation, *Nonproliferation Sanctions*, updated April 20, 2021, https://www.state.gov/key-topics-bureau-of-international-security-and-nonproliferation/nonproliferation-sanctions/; "Primer on Agencies That Enforce US Sanctions: Department of the Treasury," *SanctionsAlert.com*, July 21, 2016, https://sanctionsalert.com/primer-on-agencies-that-enforce-us-sanctions-department-of-the-treasury/.

18   Ana Swanson, "The Agency at the Center of America's Tech Fight with China," *New York Times*, March 26, 2021, https://www.nytimes.com/2021/03/26/business/economy/commerce-department-technology-china.html?smid=em-share.

19   Crawford and Klotz, *How Sanctions Work*; Michael John Garcia and Todd Garvey, *State and Local Sanctions: Constitutional Issues*,

Congressional Research Service, February 20, 2013, RL 33948; John M. Kline, "Continuing Controversies over State and Local Foreign Policy Sanctions in the United States," *Publius* 29:2 (1999): 111–134, http://www.jstor.org/stable/3330894.

20 Meg Voorhes, "The U.S. Divestment Movement," in *How Sanctions Work*, ed. Crawford and Klotz, 130.

21 "United States v. Curtiss-Wright Export Corp (1936)," in *Foreign Relations and National Security Law: Cases, Materials and Simulations*, ed. Thomas M. Franck and Michael J. Glennon (St. Paul, MN: West Publishing, 1987), 33, 35.

22 Office of Governor Gavin Newsom, "Governor Newsom Calls for State Sanctions on Russia," March 1, 2022, https://www.gov.ca.gov/2022/03/01/governor-newsom-calls-for-state-sanctions-on-russia/.

23 William J. Burns, *The Back Channel: A Memoir of American Diplomacy and the Case for Renewal* (New York: Random House, 2019); Richard Nephew, *The Art of Sanctions: A View from the Field* (New York: Columbia University Press, 2017).

24 Congressional Research Service, *Iran Sanctions*, updated January 20, 2020, RS20871, 52–53, 66.

25 Nahal Toosi, "Trump Team Scours Intel Sent by Iranians as It Weighs New Sanctions," *Politico*, December 3, 2019, https://www.politico.com/news/2019/12/03/donald-trump-sanctions-iran-074961; Richard Goldberg, "Trump Has an Iran Strategy. This Is It," *New York Times*, January 24, 2020, https://www.nytimes.com/2020/01/24/opinion/trump-iran.html.

26 Gjoza, *Counting the Costs of Financial Warfare*, 14.

27 The United States Department of Justice, Office of Public Affairs, *BNP Paribas Sentenced for Conspiring to Violate the International Emergency Economic Powers Act and the Trading with the Enemy Act*, May 1, 2015, https://www.justice.gov/opa/pr/bnp-paribas-sentenced-conspiring-violate-international-emergency-economic-powers-act-and. This also included violations with Cuba and Sudan.

28 One Iranian diplomat responded to the first INSTEX transaction by saying that it was "too little, too late, but still good." Giorgio Cafiero and Maysam Behravesh, "U.S.-EU Tensions Set to Escalate over Iran's Coronavirus Crisis," Atlantic Council, April 29, 2020, https://www.atlanticcouncil.org/blogs/iransource/us-eu-tensions-set-to-escalate-over-irans-coronavirus-crisis/.

29 Gerard Araud, Twitter Post, August 20, 2020, 4:06 PM,
    https://twitter.com/GerardAraud/status/1296539217334603780.
30 Strobe Talbott and Maggie Tennis, "The Only Winner of the
    US-Iran Showdown Is Russia," Brookings
    Institution, January 9, 2020, https://www.brookings.edu/blog/
    order-from-chaos/2020/01/09/the-only-
    winner-of-the-us-iran-showdown-is-russia/.
31 "Maximum Pressure: U.S. Economic Sanctions Harm Iranians'
    Right to Health," Human Rights Watch, October 29, 2019,
    https://www.hrw.org/report/2019/10/29/maximum-
    pressure/us-economic-sanctions-harm-iranians-right-health;
    Congressional Research Service, "Iran Sanctions," RS20871,
    January 24, 2020, 68; Erin Cunningham, "As Coronavirus Cases
    Explode in Iran, U.S. Sanctions Hinder Its Access to Drugs
    and Medical Equipment," *Washington Post*, March 29, 2020,
    https://www.washingtonpost.com/world/middle_east/
    as-coronavirus-cases-explode-in-iran-us-sanctions-hinder-its-
    access-to-drugs-and-medical-equipment/2020/03/28/0656a196-
    6aba-11ea-b199-3a9799c54512_story.html.
32 Jentleson, "Weaponized Interdependence, Dynamics of 21st
    Century Power and U.S. Grand Strategy," in *Uses and Abuses of
    Weaponized Interdependence*, ed. Drezner, Farrell, and Newman,
    239–256.
33 Buttonwood, "Persian Lessons: Iran's Flourishing Stock Market
    Reflects Its Resilient Economy," *The Economist*, March 12,
    2022, 68.
34 A full list of sanctions against the Soviet Union and Russia would
    be a long one, for example, such other recent ones as those for
    Russian interference in the 2016 American presidential election,
    military intervention in Syria, and the nerve agent attack against
    former double-agent Sergei Skripal living in the UK. Chapter 7
    includes various Soviet/Russian energy pipeline sanctions
    including the recent Nord Stream 2 natural gas pipeline project.
35 Jackson-Vanik and the 1980 Afghanistan sanctions are drawn
    from Bruce W. Jentleson, *Pipeline Politics: The Complex Political
    Economy of East-West Energy Trade* (Ithaca, NY: Cornell University
    Press, 1986), 142–159.
36 On the 2022 Russia Ukraine sanctions see also the Appendix for
    greater detail.

37 Secretary of State Antony J. Blinken, *Imposing Sanctions on Russia for the Poisoning and Imprisonment of Aleksey Navalny*, March 2, 2021, https://www.state.gov/imposing-sanctions-on-russia-for-the-poisoning-and-imprisonment-of-aleksey-navalny/.

38 US Department of the Treasury, "Treasury Sanctions Russia with New Sweeping Sanctions Authority," April 15, 2021, https://home.treasury.gov/news/press-releases/jy0127.

39 European Union, "EU Restrictive Measures in Response to the Crisis in Ukraine," https://www.consilium.europa.eu/en/policies/sanctions/ukraine-crisis/.

40 Simon Carswell, "Irish Aircraft-Leasing Firms to Sever Agreements with Russian Airlines," *Irish Times*, March 4, 2022, https://www.irishtimes.com/business/transport-and-tourism/irish-aircraft-leasing-firms-to-sever-agreements-with-russian-airlines-1.4817878.

41 Andrew Roth, "Navalny Aides to Push for Sanctions against Putin-Linked Oligarchs," *Guardian*, March 5, 2021, https://www.theguardian.com/world/2021/mar/05/navalny-aides-to-push-for-sanctions-against-putin-linked-oligarchs.

42 Elliott Smith, "US Sanctions against Russia 'Mostly Symbolic' and Will Not Trouble Moscow, Economists Say," CNBC, April 16, 2021, https://www.cnbc.com/2021/04/16/economists-us-sanctions-mostly-symbolic-and-wont-trouble-russia.html.

43 For a view stressing the economic impact these sanctions had, see Nigel Gould-Davies, "Sanctions on Russia Are Working: Why It's Important to Keep Up the Pressure," *Foreign Affairs*, August 22, 2018, https://www.foreignaffairs.com/articles/russian-federation/2018-08-22/sanctions-russia-are-working, and "Russia, the West and Sanctions," *Survival* 62:1 (2020): 7–28.

44 Thomas Graham, "Let Russia Be Russia: The Case for a More Pragmatic Approach to Moscow," *Foreign Affairs* 98:6 (November/December 2019), https://www.foreignaffairs.com/articles/russia-fsu/2019-10-15/let-russia-be-russia. Indeed, Putin seized property from more liberal elites and gave it to his inner circle, offsetting losses sanctions had imposed; Gjoza, "Counting the Costs of Financial Warfare," 8.

45 Rachel Maddow, *Blowout: Corrupted Democracy, Rogue State Russia and the Richest Most Destructive Industry on Earth* (New York: Crown, 2019), 241–243, 338.

46 Anton Troianoksvki and Patricia Cohen, "Bleak Assessments of
    the Russian Economy Clash with Putin's Rosy Claims," April 18,
    2022, *New York Times*, https://www.nytimes.com/2022/04/18/
    world/europe/russian-economy-bleak-assessments.html.

47 Shruti Menon, "Ukraine Crisis: Why India Is Buying More
    Russian Oil," *BBC*, April 26, 2022, https://www.bbc.com/news/
    world-asia-india-60783874.

48 Editorial Board, "Can Sanctions Really Stop Putin?," *New York
    Times*, April 22, 2022, https://www.nytimes.com/2022/04/22/
    opinion/sanctions-russia-ukraine-war.html; senior
    administration official and President Biden quoted in Bruce
    W. Jentleson, "Biden Is Ready to Deploy Sanctions, But Will the
    Bite Live Up to the Bark?," *Washington Post*, January 25, 2022,
    https://www.washingtonpost.com/opinions/2022/01/25/
    biden-is-ready-deploy-sanctions-against-russia-will-bite-live-up-
    bark/.

49 Greg Miller and Spencer Woodman, "U.S. Hunt for Oligarchs'
    Huge Fortunes Faces Barriers Offhsore," *Washington Post*,
    April 11, 2022, https://www.washingtonpost.com/world/
    interactive/2022/russia-oligarchs-sanctions-pandora-
    papers/?itid=hp_special-topic-chain-2_4.

50 Jentleson, *Peacemakers*, 45.

51 President Biden later tried to backtrack on this. "I did not say
    that in fact the sanctions would deter him. Sanctions never
    deter," he claimed at a March 24 news conference. Official
    statements, though, were quite clear. "The purpose of those
    sanctions is to deter Russian aggression," Secretary of State
    Antony Blinken said in January; "the President believes that
    sanctions are intended to deter," national security adviser
    Jake Sullivan stated in February. The White House, "Remarks
    by President Biden in Press Conference," March 24, 2022,
    https://www.whitehouse.gov/briefing-room/speeches-
    remarks/2022/03/24/remarks-by-president-biden-in-press-
    conference-7/; State Department, "Secretary Antony J. Blinken
    with Dana Bash of CNN State of the Union," January 23, 2022,
    https://www.state.gov/secretary-antony-j-blinken-with-dana
    -bash-of-cnn-state-of-the-union-2/; the White House, "Press
    Briefing by Press Secretary Jen Psaki and National Security
    Advisor Jake Sullivan, February 11, 2022," https://www.
    whitehouse.gov/briefing-room/press-briefings/2022/02/11/

press-briefing-by-press-secretary-jen-psaki-and-national-security-advisor-jake-sullivan-february-11-2022/.

52 Anton Troianovski and Ivan Nechepurenko, "Russian Tycoon Criticized Putin's War: Retribution Was Swift," *New York Times*, May 1, 2022, https://www.nytimes.com/2022/05/01/world/europe/oligarch-putin-oleg-tinkov.html.

53 "Putin Says Western Sanctions Are Akin to Declaration of War," *Reuters,* March 5, 2022, https://www.reuters.com/world/europe/putin-says-western-sanctions-are-akin-declaration-war-2022-03-05/.

54 "The Consequences of Tiananmen," Andrew Nathan Talks to Maria Elena Viggiano, June 3, 2009, *Reset Dialogues on Civilizations*, https://www.resetdoc.org/story/the-consequences-of-tiananmen/.

55 "Tiananmen Square Protest Death Toll 'Was 10,000,'" BBC, December 23, 2017, https://www.bbc.com/news/world-asia-china-42465516.

56 C. J. Werleman, "'Death Is Everywhere': Millions More Uyghurs Missing," *Byline Times*, August 24, 2020, https://bylinetimes.com/2020/08/24/death-is-everywhere-millions-more-uyghurs-missing/.

57 David Skidmore and William Gates, "After Tiananmen: The Struggle over U.S. Policy toward China in the Bush Administration," *Presidential Studies Quarterly* 27:3 (1997): 514–539.

58 Andrew Nathan, "The Consequences of Tiananmen," in *The Tiananmen Papers: The Chinese Leadership's Decision to Use Force against Their Own People—In Their Own Words*, comp. Zhang Lian and ed. Andrew Nathan and Perry Link, vii–xxiii (New York: Public Affairs, 2002).

59 Lindsay Gorman and Matt Schrader, "U.S. Firms Are Helping Build China's Orwellian State," *Foreign Policy*, March 19, 2019, https://foreignpolicy.com/2019/03/19/962492-orwell-china-socialcredit-surveillance/.

60 Liza Lin, "Intel Erases Reference to China's Xinjiang after Social-Media Backlash," *Wall Street Journal*, January 10, 2022, https://www.wsj.com/articles/intel-erases-reference-to-chinas-xinjiang-after-social-media-backlash-11641808676.

61 Jane Perlez, "With Pressure and Persuasion, China Deflects Criticism of Its Camps for Muslims," *New York Times*, April 8,

2019, https://www.nytimes.com/2019/04/08/world/asia/china-muslims-camps.html.

62   Kuzzat Altay, "Why Erdogan Has Abandoned the Uyghurs," *Foreign Policy*, March 2, 2021, https://foreignpolicy.com/2021/03/02/why-erdogan-has-abandoned-the-uyghurs/.

63   BBC, "Tiananmen Square Protest Death Toll 'Was 10,000.'"

64   Adam Segal, "Huawei, 5G and Weaponized Interdependence," in *Uses and Abuses of Weaponized Interdependence*, ed. Drezner, Farrell, and Newman, 160.

65   Tim Higgins, "Apple Takes Smartphone Lead in China, Helping Drive Record Profit," *Wall Street Journal*, January 28, 2022, https://www.wsj.com/articles/apple-takes-smartphone-lead-in-china-helping-drive-record-profit-11643371201; Dan Strumpt, "Freed Huawei Finance Chief Meng Wanzhou Returns to Company Spotlight," *Wall Street Journal*, March 28, 2022, https://www.wsj.com/articles/freed-huawei-finance-chief-meng-wanzhou-returns-to-company-spotlight-11648470472; Susan Decker, "Huawei Ranks No. 5 in U.S. Patents in Sign of Chinese Growth," *Bloomberg News*, January 11, 2022, https://www.bloomberg.com/news/articles/2022-01-11/huawei-ranks-no-5-in-u-s-patents-in-sign-of-chinese-growth.

66   "China Sanctions US, Canadian Officials over Xinjiang," *Associated Press News*, March 27, 2021, https://apnews.com/article/hong-kong-china-8030f658c955d7572f3fa562b54bc302.

67   George Leopold, "U.S. Clings to Semiconductor Dominance as China Mounts Challenge," *EE Times*, July 10, 2020, https://www.eetimes.com/u-s-clings-to-semiconductor-dominance-as-china-mounts-challenge/.

68   The "logic of security" prevailing over "commercial logic," as Henry Farrell puts it; "Weaponized Interdependence and Networked Coercion: A Research Agenda," in *Uses and Abuses of Weaponized Interdependence*, ed. Drezner, Farrell, and Newman, 316.

69   Stephan Haggard and Marcus Noland, *Famine in North Korea* (New York: Columbia University Press, 2007), 86.

70   Hugh Griffiths et al., *Report of the Panel of Experts Established Pursuant to Resolution 1874 (2009)*, United Nations Security Council, March 5, 2018; "Q&A: North Korea, Sanctions, and Human Rights," Human Rights

Watch, March 30, 2018, www.hrw.org/news/2018/05/30/
qa-north-korea-sanctions-and-human-rights#.

71　Ed Caesar, "Rocket Men," *New Yorker*, April 26 and May 3, 2021,
46; Michelle Nichols, "Exclusive: U.N. Sanctions Experts Warn—
Stay Away from North Korea Cryptocurrency Conference,"
Reuters, January 15, 2020, https://www.reuters.com/article/
us-northkorea-sanctions-un-exclusive/exclusive-u-n-sanctions-
experts-warn-stay-away-from-north-korea-cryptocurrency-
conference-idUSKBN1ZE0I5; Katie Benner, "North Koreans
Accused of Laundering $2.5 Billion for Nuclear Program,"
New York Times, May 28, 2020, https://www.nytimes.
com/2020/05/28/us/politics/north-korea-money-laundering-
nuclear-weapons.html; BBC News, "North Korean Hackers Stole
$400 Million of Cryptocurrency in 2021, Report Says," January
14, 2022, https://www.bbc.com/news/business-59990477.

72　Kyoochul Kim, "Finding Loopholes in Sanctions: Effects of
Sanctions on North Korea's Refined Oil Prices," *KDI Journal
of Economic Policy* 42:4 (November 2020): 1–25; Kevin Gray,
"Sanctions on North Korea Are Counterproductive," *Just
Security*, November 26, 2019, https://www.justsecurity.
org/67473/sanctions-on-north-korea-are-counterproductive/.

73　Choe Sang-Hun, "North Korea Party Congress Opens with
Kim Jong-un Admitting Failures," *New York Times*, January 5,
2021, https://www.nytimes.com/2021/01/05/world/asia/
north-korea-kim-jong-un-party-congress.html.

74　Kolja Brockmann, "European Union Sanctions on North
Korea: Balancing Non-Proliferation with the Humanitarian
Impact," Stockholm International Peace Research Institute,
December 11, 2020, https://www.sipri.org/commentary/topical-
backgrounder/2020/european-union-sanctions-north-korea-
balancing-non-proliferation-humanitarian-impact.

75　Haggard and Noland, *Hard Target*, 228.

76　Matthew Smith, "Venezuela's Crude Oil Industry
May Never Recover," OilPrice.com, October 3, 2020,
https://oilprice.com/Energy/Crude-Oil/Venezuelas-Oil-
industry-May-Never-Recover.html; Oriana Van Praag,
"Understanding the Venezuelan Refugee Crisis," Wilson
Center, September 13, 2020, https://www.wilsoncenter.org/
article/understanding-the-venezuelan-refugee-crisis; Mark
Weisbrot and Jeffrey Sachs, "Economic Sanctions as Collective

Punishment: The Case of Venezuela," Center for Economic and Policy Research, April 2019, 2, https://cepr.net/images/stories/reports/venezuela-sanctions-2019-04.pdf.

77 Weisbrot and Sachs, "Economic Sanctions as Collective Punishment: Venezuela."

78 Congressional Research Service, "Venezuela: Background and U.S. Relations," R44841, March 31, 2021, https://fas.org/sgp/crs/row/R44841.pdf.

79 Ernesto Londoño and Nicholas Casey, "Trump Administration Discussed Coup Plans with Rebel Venezuelan Officers," *New York Times*, September 8, 2018, https://www.nytimes.com/2018/09/08/world/americas/donald-trump-venezuela-military-coup.html; Julie Turkewitz and Frances Robles, "An Incursion into Venezuela, Straight out of Hollywood," *New York Times*, May 7, 2020, https://www.nytimes.com/2020/05/07/world/americas/venezuela-failed-overthrow.html.

80 Francisco R. Rodriguez, "Biden Must Change Not Deepen Trump's Failed Venezuela Strategy," *Just Security*, January 5, 2022, https://www.justsecurity.org/79733/biden-must-change-not-deepen-trumps-failed-venezuela-strategy/.

81 Financial Action Task Force, "Consolidated FATF Strategy on Combatting Terrorist Financing," February 19, 2016, http://www.fatf-gafi.org/media/fatf/documents/reports/FATF-Terrorist-Financing-Strategy.pdf.

82 Julia Kagan, "Hawala," Investopedia, March 17, 2021, https://www.investopedia.com/terms/h/hawala.asp.

83 Farrell and Newman, "Weaponized Interdependence," 68–69. See Zarate, *Treasury's War*; and Julia C. Morse, "Blacklists, Market Enforcement and the Global Regime to Combat Terrorist Financing," *International Organization* 73:3 (Summer 2019): 511–545.

84 Morse, "Blacklists, Market Enforcement and the Global Regime to Combat Terrorist Financing," 511.

85 US Department of the Treasury, Office of Foreign Assets Control (OFAC), *Terrorist Assets Report: Twenty-seventh Annual Report to the Congress on Assets in the United States Relating to Terrorist Countries and Organizations Engaged in International Terrorism*, 2018, https://home.treasury.gov/system/files/126/tar2018.pdf.

86 Charlie Savage, "U.S. Seizes Bitcoin Said to Be Used to Finance Terrorist Groups," *New York Times*, August 13, 2020,

https://www.nytimes.com/2020/08/13/us/politics/bitcoin-terrorism.html; Pranshu Verma, "U.S. Imposes Sanctions on Qaeda Financier Who Trades in Gems," *New York Times*, October 19, 2020, https://www.nytimes.com/2020/10/19/us/politics/treasury-sanctions-qaeda-gems.html.

87 US Department of the Treasury, "Assistant Secretary for Terrorist Financing David S. Cohen Remarks on Terrorist Financing," January 28, 2010, https://www.treasury.gov/press-center/press-releases/Pages/tg515.aspx.

88 General Accountability Office, *Economic Sanctions*.

89 Mark Carney, "The Growing Challenges for Monetary Policy in the Current International Monetary and Financial Systems," Bank of England, August 23, 2019, https://www.bankofengland.co.uk/-/media/boe/files/speech/2019/the-growing-challenges-for-monetary-policy-speech-by-mark-carney.pdf.

90 US Department of the Treasury, *The Treasury 2021 Sanctions Review*, October 2021, https://home.treasury.gov/system/files/136/Treasury-2021-sanctions-review.pdf.

91 A number of other factors are also contributing to reduced dollar dominance; Enda Curran, "The U.S. Dollar's Dominance Is Stealthily Eroding," *Bloomberg News*, March 25, 2022, https://www.bloomberg.com/news/articles/2022-03-25/the-dollar-s-dominance-is-being-stealthily-eroded-imf-paper.

92 Elizabeth Rosenberg, Peter Harrell, and Ashley Feng, *A New Arsenal for Competition: Coercive Economic Measures in the U.S.-China Relationship*, Center for a New American Security, April 2020, 3. See also https://www.atlanticcouncil.org/blogs/new-atlanticist/the-rebirth-of-the-state-departments-office-of-sanctions-coordination-guidelines-for-success/.

93 US Treasury Department, *Treasury 2021 Sanctions Review*.

Chapter 6

1 James Reilly, "China's Unilateral Sanctions," *Washington Quarterly* 35:4 (Fall 2012): 121.

2 Elizabeth Rosenberg, Peter E. Harrell, and Ashley Feng, *A New Arsenal for Competition: Coercive Economic Measures in the U.S.-China Relationship* (Washington, DC: Center for a New American Security, April 2020), 24.

3 Kurt M. Campbell and Rush Doshi, "How America Can Shore Up Asian Order: A Strategy for Restoring Balance and

Legitimacy," *Foreign Affairs*, January 12, 2021, https://www.
foreignaffairs.com/articles/united-states/2021-01-12/how-ameri
ca-can-shore-asian-order.

4 Fergus Hanson, Emilia Currey, and Tracy Beattie, *The Chinese
Communist Party's Coercive Economic Diplomacy*, Australia
Strategic Policy Institute, Policy Brief Report No. 36/2020, 15.

5 In addition to sources already cited, others on China's use
of sanctions include William J. Norris, *Chinese Economic
Statecraft: Commercial Actors, Grand Strategy, and State Control*
(Ithaca, NY: Cornell University Press, 2016); Angela Poh,
*Sanctions with Chinese Characteristics: Rhetoric and Restraint in
China's Diplomacy* (Amsterdam: Amsterdam University Press,
2021); Ketian Zhang, "Cautious Bully: Reputation, Resolve and
Beijing's Use of Coercion in the South China Sea," *International
Security* 44:1 (Summer 2019): 117–159; Peter E. Harrell, Elizabeth
Rosenberg, and Edoardo Saravelle, *China's Use of Coercive
Economic Measures* (Washington, DC: Center for a New American
Security, June 2018).

6 Cited in Bruce W. Jentleson, "Refocusing U.S. Grand Strategy on
Pandemic and Environmental Mass Destruction," *Washington
Quarterly* 43:3 (Fall 2020): 8

7 The 2005 sanctions against Japanese goods retaliating for
Prime Minister Junichiro Koizumi's visit to the controversial
Yasukuni Shrine, dedicated to fallen Japanese including some
who committed atrocities during the World War II occupation of
China, was another domestic political change case.

8 Other limited foreign policy change cases include the 2010–2012
maritime dispute with Japan and the 2012–2016 maritime dispute
with the Philippines.

9 US Department of State, US Embassy in Georgia,
China's Houston Consulate a Center of Malign Activity,
August 12, 2020, https://ge.usembassy.gov/
chinas-houston-consulate-a-center-of-malign-activity.

10 Judith Alison Lee et al., *China's New Draft Export Control Law
and Its Implications for International Trade*, Gibson, Dunn &
Crutcher LLP, August 31, 2020, https://www.gibsondunn.com/
china-new-draft-export-control-law-and-its-implications-for-
international-trade/.

11 Cate Cadell and Tony Munroe, "China Imposes Sanctions on
28 Trump-Era Officials Including Pompeo," *Reuters*, January 20,

2021, https://www.reuters.com/article/us-usa-china-pompeo-blinken/china-imposes-sanctions-on-28-trump-era-officials-including-pompeo-idUSKBN29P14K.

12   Li Yuan, "China's Political Correctness: One Country, No Arguments," *New York Times*, October 11, 2019, https://www.nytimes.com/2019/10/11/business/china-hong-kong-education.html.

13   Tommy Hilfiger, Adidas, Nike, Converse, Calvin Klein, and other Western companies also were attacked. Raymond Zhong and Paul Mozur, "How China's Outrage Machine Kicked Up a Storm over H&M," *New York Times*, March 29, 2021, https://www.nytimes.com/2021/03/29/business/china-xinjiang-cotton-hm.html; Li Yuan, "As China Targets H&M and Nike, Local Brands See Their Chance," *New York Times*, April 6, 2021, https://www.nytimes.com/2021/04/06/business/china-xinjiang-boycott-heytea-nio.html; "Statement on H&M in China," H&M Group, March 31, 2021, https://hmgroup.com/news/statement_hm_china/.

14   Thomas P. Cavanna, "China's Belt and Road Initiative: Coercion Unbound?" in *Uses and Abuses of Weaponized Interdependence*, ed. Drezner, Farrell, and Newman, 221–235.

15   Draws on Reilly, "China's Unilateral Sanctions"; and Harrell, Rosenberg, and Saravelle, *China's Use of Coercive Economic Measures*.

16   "China Vows 'proper' Response to US Arms Sale to Taiwan," *Associated Press*, November 4, 2020, https://apnews.com/article/virus-outbreak-beijing-taiwan-china-ebf86031e75bdd0b4f4d341691a758ed; Bonnie Girard, "With New Offensive Weapons Package, Trump Administration Goes All-in for Taiwan," *The Diplomat*, October 30, 2020, https://thediplomat.com/2020/10/with-new-offensive-weapons-package-trump-administration-goes-all-in-for-taiwan/.

17   The Republic of China (Taiwan), Ministry of Foreign Affairs, *Cross-Strait Relations*, 2020, https://www.taiwan.gov.tw/content_6.php. The airlines worked out various compromises, some such as United and Delta listing the destination as just the city of Taipei, others like Air France and Lufthansa adopting "Taiwan, China" but still doing the business. Marriott also took on the Taiwan, China, listing. For Marriott, see Amy Webb, *The Big Nine: How the Tech Titans and Their Thinking Machines Could*

Warp Humanity (New York: Public Affairs, 2020), 73–74. The Gap apologized for a T-shirt that had a map of China without including Taiwan, 2018.

18 Ken Moritsugu and Elaine Kurtenbach, "Taiwan Sends Message of 'Peace, Parity, Democracy' to Beijing," *Christian Science Monitor*, January 12, 2020, https://www.csmonitor.com/World/Asia-Pacific/2020/0112/Taiwan-sends-message-of-peace-parity-democracy-to-Beijing.

19 Liu Zhen, "China 'Will Continue to Oppose Taiwan Independence' after Tsai Ing-wen's Election Victory," *South China Morning Post*, January 20, 2020, https://www.scmp.com/news/china/politics/article/3046757/china-will-continue-oppose-taiwan-independence-after-tsai-ing.

20 Kat Devlin and Christine Huang, "In Taiwan, Views of Mainland China Mostly Negative," *Pew Research Center*, May 12, 2020, https://www.pewresearch.org/global/2020/05/12/in-taiwan-views-of-mainland-china-mostly-negative/.

21 "Wrong Stance on Tibet Hinders Ties with China," *China Daily*, March 5, 2009, http://www.chinadaily.com.cn/china/2009-03/05/content_7538147.htm.

22 "China Lodges Strong Protest to France over Dalai Lama Meeting," *China Daily*, December 7, 2008, http://www.chinadaily.com.cn/china/2008-12/07/content_7279242.htm.

23 Nobel Media AB, *The Nobel Peace Prize for 2010*, May 10, 2021, https://www.nobelprize.org/prizes/peace/2010/press-release/.

24 Reilly, "China's Unilateral Sanctions," 126.

25 Harvard Bergo, "Norway Woos China by Refusing to Meet with Dalai Lama," *Global Risk Insights*, May 11, 2014, https://globalriskinsights.com/2014/05/norway-woos-china-by-refusing-to-meet-with-dalai-lama/.

26 Cited by Reilly, "China's Unilateral Sanctions," 127.

27 Ding Qingfen, "France Goes Back on China's Shopping List," *China Daily*, October 29, 2009, http://www.chinadaily.com.cn/china/2009-10/29/content_8865307.htm.

28 Trading Economics, "France Exports to China," updated May 2021, https://tradingeconomics.com/france/exports/china.

29 Luke Patey, "China Is an Economic Bully—and Weaker Than It Looks," *Foreign Policy*, January 4, 2021, https://foreignpolicy.com/2021/01/04/

china-is-an-economic-bully-and-weaker-than-it-looks/; Hanson, Currey, and Beattie, *Chinese Communist Party's Coercive Economic Diplomacy*, 18.

30 Bergo, "Norway Woos China by Refusing to Meet with Dalai Lama."

31 Sewell Chan, "Norway and China Restore Ties, 6 Years after Nobel Prize Dispute," *New York Times*, December 19, 2016, https://www.nytimes.com/2016/12/19/world/europe/china-norway-nobel-liu-xiaobo.html.

32 "Norway PM Solberg Accused of Being 'Relieved' at Death of Liu Xiaobo," *The Local*, July 15, 2017, https://www.thelocal.no/20170714/norway-pm-solberg-accused-of-being-relieved-at-death-of-liu-xiaobo.

33 Harrell, Rosenberg, and Saravelle, *China's Use of Coercive Economic Measures*, 43.

34 Wikipedia, "List of Overseas Visits by the 14th Dalai Lama outside India," updated April 16, 2021, https://en.wikipedia.org/wiki/List_of_overseas_visits_by_the_14th_Dalai_Lama_outside_India.

35 Ethan Meick and Nargiza Salidjanova, *China's Response to U.S.-South Korean Missile Defense System Deployment and Its Implications* (Washington, DC: U.S.-China Economic and Security Review Commission, 2017), https://www.uscc.gov/sites/default/files/Research/Report_China%27s%20Response%20to%20THAAD%20Deployment%20and%20its%20Implications.pdf; and Harrell, Rosenberg, and Saravelle, *China's Use of Coercive Economic Measures*.

36 Trefor Moss, "Beijing's Campaign against South Korean Goods Leaves Chinese Looking for Work," *Wall Street Journal*, August 23, 2017, https://www.wsj.com/articles/beijings-campaign-against-south-korean-goods-leaves-chinese-looking-for-work-1503480601/

37 Christine Kim and Ben Blanchard, "China, South Korea Agree to Mend Ties after THAAD standoff," *Reuters*, October 30, 2017, https://www.reuters.com/article/us-northkorea-missiles/china-south-korea-agree-to-mend-ties-after-thaad-standoff-idUSKBN1D003G.

38 Amy Searight, "Countering China's Influence Operations: Lessons from Australia," Center for Strategic and International Studies, May 8, 2020, https://www.csis.org/

analysis/countering-chinas-influence-operations-lessons-australia; Harrell, Rosenberg, and Saravelle, *China's Use of Coercive Economic Measures*; Hanson, Currey, and Beattie, *Chinese Communist Party's Coercive Economic Diplomacy*.

39 "ASIO Annual Report 2016–2017" (Australian Security and Intelligence Organisation, August 24, 2017), https://www.asio.gov.au/sites/default/files/Annual%20Report%20.pdf, 5.

40 Jonathan Kearsley, Eryk Bagshaw, and Anthony Galloway, "'If You Make China the Enemy China Will Be the Enemy': China's Fresh Threat to Australia," *Sydney Morning Herald*, November 18, 2020, https://www.smh.com.au/world/asia/if-you-make-china-the-enemy-china-will-be-the-enemy-beijing-s-fresh-threat-to-australia-20201118-p56fqs.html.

41 Kath Sullivan, "China's List of Sanctions and Tariffs on Australian Trade Is Growing. Here's What Has Been Hit So Far," ABC News, December 16, 2020 https://www.abc.net.au/news/2020-12-17/australian-trade-tension-sanctions-china-growing-commodities/12984218.

42 Shaimaa Khalil, "How Australia-China Relations Have Hit 'Lowest Ebb in Decades,'" BBC News, October 11, 2020, https://www.bbc.com/news/world-australia-54458638.

43 Liu Caiyu and Fan Anqi, "Australia Faces Blow in Losing Chinese Education Market," *Global Times*, September 23, 2020, https://www.globaltimes.cn/content/1201874.shtml.

44 Roland Rajah, "The Big Bark but Small Bite of China's Economic Coercion," *The Interpreter*, Lowy Institute, April 8, 2021, https://www.lowyinstitute.org/the-interpreter/big-bark-small-bite-chin a-s-trade-coercion; Jeffrey Wilson, "Australia Shows the World What Decoupling from China Looks Like," *ForeignPolicy.com*, November 9, 2021, https://foreignpolicy.com/2021/11/09/australia-china-decoupling-trade-sanctions-coronavirus-geopolitics/.

45 Peter Ker, "Why China Can't Grow without Australian Ore," *Australian Financial Review*, December 5, 2020, https://www.afr.com/companies/mining/why-china-can-t-grow-without-australian-iron-ore-20201204-p56knl.

46 Cissy Zhou and Wang Zixu, "China Suffers Worst Power Blackouts in a Decade, on Post-Coronavirus Export Boom, Coal Supply Shortage," *South China Morning Post*, December 23, 2020, https://www.scmp.

com/economy/china-economy/article/3115119/
china-suffers-worst-power-blackouts-decade-post-coronavirus.

47 Rory Medcalf, cited in Alex W. Palmer, "The Man behind China's
New Aggressive Voice," *New York Times*, July 7, 2021,
https://www.nytimes.com/2021/07/07/magazine/china-
diplomacy-twitter-zhao-lijian.html.

48 Victor Cha and Andy Lim, "Flagrant Foul: China's Predatory
Liberalism and the NBA," *Washington Quarterly* 42:4 (Winter
2020): 25.

49 For example, luxury clothing designers Coach, Givenchy, and
Versace were pressured to take off the market shirts that showed
Hong Kong as a separate country from China. Which they did.
"Versace reiterates that we love China deeply, and resolutely
respect China's territory and national sovereignty"; Elizabeth
Paton, "Versace, Givenchy and Coach Apologize to China after
T-Shirt Row," *New York Times*, August 12, 2019,
https://www.nytimes.com/2019/08/12/fashion/china-
donatella-versace-t-shirt.html.

50 Cindy Boren, "The NBA's China–Daryl Morey Backlash
Explained," *Washington Post*, October 7, 2019, https://www.
washingtonpost.com/sports/2019/10/07/nba-china-tweet-dary
l-morey/.

51 Boren, "NBA's China–Daryl Morey Backlash."

52 Sylvan Lane, "NBA Sparks Anger with Apology to China,"
The Hill, October 7, 2019, https://thehill.com/policy/
finance/464748-nba-sparks-anger-with-china-apology;
Ben Cohen, "LeBron James Says Tweet Supporting Hong
Kong Protests Was 'Misinformed,'" *Wall Street Journal*,
October 14, 2019, https://www.wsj.com/articles/
lebron-james-says-tweet-supporting-hong-kong-protests-was-mis
informed-11571107697.

53 Bari Weiss, "The World's Wokest Sports League Bows to
China," *New York Times*, October 7, 2019, https://www.nytimes.
com/2019/10/07/opinion/nba-china-hong-kong.html.

54 Marco Rubio. Twitter Post. October 7, 2019, 7:46 AM. https://
twitter.com/marcorubio/status/1181173981422014464; Scott
McDonald, "AOC, Ted Cruz Co-Sign Letter Blasting NBA
for Its Support of China Instead of 'American Values,'"
Newsweek, October 10, 2019, https://www.newsweek.com/
aoc-ted-cruz-co-sign-letter-blasting-nba-its-support-china-

instead-american-values-1464296; Megan McArdle, "These Spineless Weaklings Have Shamed Themselves and Their Country," *Washington Post*, October 11, 2019, https://www.washingtonpost.com/opinions/2019/10/11/maybe-woke-nbas-hypocrisy-china-has-awakened-us-consumers-about-their-own/.

55   National Basketball Association, *Adam Silver's Statement on NBA and China*, October 8, 2019, https://www.nba.com/news/adam-silver-statement-china-nba; https://thegrayzone.com/2019/11/04/nba-free-speech-cold-war-china/.

56   Sopan Deb, "Adam Silver Commits to Free Speech as Chinese Companies Cut Ties with N.B.A.," *New York Times*, October 8, 2019, https://www.nytimes.com/2019/10/08/sports/adam-silver-nba-china-hong-kong.html.

57   Sopan Deb, "Chinese State TV to Air N.B.A. for First Time since Hong Kong Rift," *New York Times*, October 9, 2020, https://www.nytimes.com/2020/10/09/sports/basketball/nba-china-cctv.html.

58   "2020–21 International Broadcast Information," National Basketball Association, http://global.nba.com/broadcaster-schedule/.

59   "CCTV Set to End NBA Blackout from March," Sportcal, February 21, 2021, https://www.sportcal.com/News/FeaturedNews/135968.

60   "Golden State Warriors Distance from Minority Owner after His Comments about Uyghurs," *ESPN.com*, January 18, 2022, https://www.espn.com/nba/story/_/id/33094233/golden-state-warriors-distance-minority-owner-comments-uyghurs.

61   Austin Ramzy, "China Criticizes Sanctions against Russia as Ineffective and Warns of Wider Damage," *New York Times*, February 23, 2022, https://www.nytimes.com/2022/02/23/world/europe/china-russia-ukraine-sanctions.html.

62   Hanson, Currey, and Beattie, *Chinese Communist Party's Coercive Economic Diplomacy*; Norris, *Chinese Economic Statecraft*; Poh, *Sanctions with Chinese Characteristics*; Harrell, Rosenberg, and Saravelle, *China's Use of Coercive Economic Measures*.

63   Andrew Higgins, "In an Uneven Fight with China, a Tiny Country's Brand Becomes Toxic," *New York Times*, February 21,

2022, https://www.nytimes.com/2022/02/21/world/europe/
china-lithuania-taiwan-trade.html.

64 Audrye Wong, "How Not to Win Allies and Influence
Geopolitics: China's Self-Defeating Economic Statecraft," *Foreign
Affairs* (May/June 2021), 52.

65 Fareed Zakaria, "Xi's China Can't Seem to Stop Scoring
Own Goals," *Washington Post*, May 27, 2021,
https://www.washingtonpost.com/opinions/2021/05/27/
xis-china-cant-seem-stop-scoring-own-goals/.

66 Andrew Chatzky and James McBride, "China's Massive
Belt and Road Initiative," Council on Foreign Relations,
January 28, 2020, https://www.cfr.org/backgrounder/
chinas-massive-belt-and-road-initiative#chapter-title-0-4.

67 Samantha Custer, Rodney Knight, Amber Hutchinson, and
Vera Choo, "Poll: China's Influence Is Not Inevitable," *Foreign
Policy*, July 15, 2021, https://foreignpolicy.com/2021/07/15/
poll-china-influence-abroad-foreign-aid/.

Chapter 7

1 Robert O. Freedman, *Economic Warfare in the Communist Bloc*
(New York: Praeger, 1970), 29.

2 Freedman, *Economic Warfare in the Communist Bloc*, 29.

3 Gary Clyde Hufbauer, Jeffrey J. Schott, and Kimberly Ann Elliott,
Economic Sanctions Reconsidered: Supplemental Case Histories, 2nd
ed. (Washington, DC: Institute for International Economics,
1990), 94–95.

4 Adam Ulam, *Expansion and Coexistence* (New York: Praeger, 1968),
462; Freedman, *Economic Warfare in the Communist Bloc*, 25

5 Cited in Freedman, *Economic Warfare in the Communist Bloc*, 5.

6 Cited in HSE, *Economic Sanctions Reconsidered*, 95.

7 HSE give this case the lowest score on their scale. HSE, *Economic
Sanctions Reconsidered*, 93–99.

8 This case draws principally on Daniel Drezner, "Allies,
Adversaries and Economic Coercion: Russian Foreign Economic
Policy since 1991," *Security Studies* 6:3 (Spring 1997): 65–111.

9 Cited in Drezner, "Allies, Adversaries and Economic
Coercion," 75.

10 Drezner, "Allies, Adversaries and Economic Coercion," 96.

11 Drezner, "Allies, Adversaries and Economic Coercion," 85.

12 Drezner, "Allies, Adversaries and Economic Coercion," 88.

13 Drezner, "Allies, Adversaries and Economic Coercion," 106.

14 Drezner, "Allies, Adversaries and Economic Coercion," 105.

15 Paulina Pospieszna, Joanna Skrzypczynska, and Beata Stepien, "Hitting Two Birds with One Stone: How Russian Countersanctions Intertwined Political and Economic Goals," *PS* 53:2 (April 2020): 243–246.

16 Pospieszna, Skrzypczynska, and Stepien, "Hitting Two Birds with One Stone."

17 "Putin's Counter-Sanctions Cost Russians $70 per Person Every Year," *Moscow Times*, October 29, 2019, https://www.themoscowtimes.com/2019/10/29/putins-counter-sanctions-cost-70-person-a67947.

18 Daniel Gros and Mattia Di Salvo, "Revisiting Sanctions on Russia and Countersanctions on the EU: The Economic Impact Three Years Later," *Commentary: Thinking Ahead for Europe*, July 13, 2017, http://aei.pitt.edu/88442/1/CEPS_Commentary_Sanctions_on_Russia__Gross_Di_Salvo.pdf.

19 "Moscow Extends Counter-Sanctions against US, EU and Allies through 2020," *Russia Times*, June 24, 2019, https://www.rt.com/business/462563-putin-extends-food-embargo/.

20 Henry Foy, "Russia Counters US Sanctions with Diplomat Expulsions," *Financial Times*, April 16, 2021, https://www.ft.com/content/f9aa0948-f535-4481-84c1-cd136a62e86e.

21 The early 1960s and early 1980s cases draw principally on my book, *Pipeline Politics: The Complex Political Economy of East-West Energy Trade* (Ithaca, NY: Cornell University Press, 1986).

22 Jentleson, *Pipeline Politics*, 97.

23 Assistant Secretary of Defense Richard N. Perle, cited in Jentleson, *Pipeline Politics*, 173.

24 Secretary of Defense Caspar W. Weinberger, cited in Jentleson, *Pipeline Politics*, 178.

25 Jentleson, *Pipeline Politics*, 192–194.

26 "Sens. Cruz, Johnson Put Companies Installing Putin's Pipeline on Formal Legal Notice," December 18, 2019, https://www.cruz.senate.gov/?p=press_release&id=4826.

27 Secretary of State Antony Blinken, "Nord Steam 2 and European Energy Security," May 19, 2021, https://www.state.gov/nord-stream-2-and-european-energy-security/.

28 Jentleson, *Pipeline Politics*; State Department cable cited on 115.

29 Jentleson, *Pipeline Politics*, 118.

30 Jentleson, *Pipeline Politics*, 195.
31 Jentleson, *Pipeline Politics*, 128.
32 Jentleson, *Pipeline Politics*, 197.
33 In a 2018 German war gaming of a major natural gas shortage "some hospitals, nursing homes and jails were forced to close; companies shut; livestock was left to die; hundreds of thousands of jobs vanished; rationing for households was imposed"; Javier Blas, "Putin's Gas Strategy Gives Germany Only Bad and Worse Choices," *Bloomberg News*, April 29,2022, https://www.bloomberg.com/opinion/articles/2022-04-29/on-russian-gas-germany-has-bad-options-or-worse-options.
34 Isabelle Khurshudyan, "How Russia Pushed Moldova's Pro-Western Government to the Brink of a Gas Crisis," *Washington Post*, October 30, 2021, https://www.washingtonpost.com/world/europe/moldova-russia-gas-shortage/2021/10/30/f50a5bfc-3598-11ec-9662-399cfa75efee_story.html.

Chapter 8

1 European Parliament, "EU Sanctions: A Key Foreign and Security Policy Instrument," May 2018, https://www.europarl.europa.eu/RegData/etudes/BRIE/2018/621870/EPRS_BRI(2018)621870_EN.pdf.
2 HSE, *Economic Sanctions Reconsidered*, Appendix 1-A, 20–25; Biersteker, Eckert, Tourinho, and Hudáková, "UN Targeted Sanctions Datasets (1991–2013)"; and Biersteker, Eckert, and Tourinho, *Targeted Sanctions: Impacts and Effectiveness of UN Action*; Eckert, "Assessing Effectiveness of UN Targeted Sanctions," Bridging the Gap—Center for a New American Security February 2019 Workshop memo; Weber and Schneider, "Introducing the EUSANCT Data Set" and "EUSANCT Data Set Case Summaries"; GIGA Sanctions Data Set, https://data.gesis.org/sharing/#!Detail/10.7802/1346.
3 "EUSANCT Data Set Case Summaries," case 2005022501.
4 Mapping onto the framework we've used in other chapters for country-based sanctions, nonproliferation categorizes as limiting military capabilities, counterterrorism as foreign policy restraint, democracy support and good governance as domestic political change, and armed conflict as a mix of all three.

5 Signaling can correspond to any of our secondary objectives of target deterrence, third-party deterrence, and principled symbolic action.

6 In the TSC study, impacting armed conflict was the objective in 60 percent of the episodes. Among secondary objectives, coercion was the most frequent (55.5%) followed by constraining (41.3%) and signaling (3.5%). Yet taking into account mixed strategies, coercion was the least frequently used (29%), with signaling at 36.6% and constraining 34.3%; Biersteker, Eckert, and Tourinho, *Targeted Sanctions*; Giumelli, *Coercing, Constraining and Signaling*.

7 Mueller and Mueller, "Sanctions of Mass Destruction"; Jentleson, "Economic Sanctions and Post–Cold War Conflicts"; Andreas, "Criminalizing Consequences of Sanctions."

8 Stockholm International Peace Research Institute (SIPRI), "Arms Embargoes," https://www.sipri.org/databases/embargoes.

9 The Kimberley Process was established in May 2000 by the UN General Assembly. The name comes from the city in the Republic of South Africa where the organizing meeting was held.

10 Biersteker, Eckert, and Tourinho, *Targeted Sanctions: Impacts and Effectiveness of UN Action*, 233–245 and Appendices 1 and 2; Cortright and Lopez, *Sanctions Decade*, 204.

11 Kimberly Ann Elliott, "The Impacts of United Nations Targeted Sanctions," in *Targeted Sanctions*, ed. Biersteker, Eckert, and Tourinho, 175, 185. Indeed, the most widely supported recent sanctions, those against Russia for its 2022 invasion of Ukraine, never had UN authorization. They even included countries like Switzerland, despite its long tradition of neutrality, and Singapore, which had never before imposed non-UN sanctions. And whereas most sanctions are opposed by major multinational companies, these were at least partially supported by oil companies like BP and Exxon/Mobil, auto companies like General Motors and Renault, retail giants like Nike and Adidas, entertainment companies like Disney, and numerous others. While this was an unusual case in the severity of the security threat posed and profundity of the principles violated, it does show that substantial multilateralism can be achieved without formal UN action.

12 Thomas Biersteker, Rebecca Brubaker, and David Lanz, *UN Sanctions and Mediation: Establishing Evidence to Inform Practice* (New York: United Nations University Centre for Policy

Research, 2019). See also *Compendium: High-Level Review of United Nations Sanctions* (Providence, RI: Watson Institute, Brown University, November 2015).

13 Bryan Early and Robert Spice argue that as a large institution the UN has more problems getting and sustaining the collective action needed for sanctions monitoring and enforcement than some regional organizations do; "Economic Sanctions, International Institutions and Sanctions Busters: When Does Institutionalized Cooperation Help Sanctions Busters?," *Foreign Policy Analysis* 11 (2015): 339–360.

14 Colum Lynch, "Sunset for UN Sanctions?," *ForeignPolicy.com*, October 14, 2021, https://foreignpolicy.com/2021/10/14/sanctions-united-nations-expert-panels-russia-china-africa-western-countries/.

15 This case draws principally on Cortright and Lopez, "Sanctions against Iraq," chap. 3 in *The Sanctions Decade*, quote is at 37; Jentleson, "Economic Sanctions and Post–Cold War Conflicts"; and George A. Lopez and David Cortright, "Containing Iraq: Sanctions Worked," *Foreign Affairs*, July/August 2004, https://www.foreignaffairs.com/articles/iraq/2004-07-01/containing-iraq-sanctions-worked.

16 Clinton cited in Cortright and Lopez, *Sanctions Decade: 1990s*, 56; Bush October 7, 2002, speech transcript in *The Guardian*, https://www.theguardian.com/world/2002/oct/07/usa.iraq.

17 Cortright and Lopez, *Sanctions Decade: 1990s*, 45.

18 Cortright and Lopez, *Sanctions Decade: 1990s*, 46–47.

19 Bryan Early ("Sanctions Busting for Profits: How the United Arab Emirates Busted the U.S. Sanctions against Iran," chap. 5 in *Busted Sanctions*) provides the particularly interesting example of Dubai. Here was the UAE government trying to build closer security relations with the US, with even its soldiers part of the multinational force forcing Iraq to pull out of Kuwait. Yet traders in Dubai cashed in on sanctions busting, in fact doing so through networks it developed in Iran—the enemy in the name of which the US had originally strategized its aid to Iraq in their war, and ostensibly the avowed Shia enemy of Sunni Emirates.

20 Lopez and Cortright, "Containing Iraq."

21 Lopez and Cortright, "Containing Iraq."

22 Lopez and Cortright, "Containing Iraq."

23   1998 Report by the Center for Strategic and International Studies, cited in Lopez and Cortright, "Containing Iraq."

24   Thomas J. Biersteker, Marcos Tourinho, and Sue E. Eckert, "The Effectiveness of UN Targeted Sanctions," in *Targeted Sanctions*, ed. Biersteker, Eckert, and Tourinho, 233–234.

25   European Union, "EU Sanctions Map," https://www.sanctionsmap.eu/#/main; Giumelli, Hoffmann, and Ksiazczakova, "When, What, Where and Why of European Union Sanctions"; Weber and Schneider, "Introducing the EUSANCT Data Set" and "EUSANCT Data Set Case Summaries"; GIGA Sanctions Data Set.

26   Clara Portela and Erica Moret, "The EU's Chemical Weapons Sanctions Regime: Upholding a Taboo under Attack," European Union Institute for Security Studies (EUISS), July 31, 2020, https://www.iss.europa.eu/content/eu%E2%80%99s-chemical-weapons-sanctions-regime; and Erica Moret and Patryk Pawlet, "The EU Cyber Diplomacy Toolbox: Towards a Cyber Sanctions Regime?," EUISS, July 12, 2017, https://www.iss.europa.eu/content/eu-cyber-diplomacy-toolbox-towards-cyber-sanctions-regime.

27   EU Sanctions Map, https://www.sanctionsmap.eu/#/main.

28   For the cases included in the EUSANCT database, 44 percent have had democracy promotion as an objective, 33 percent conflict management, 27 percent post-conflict stabilization, 15 percent international law and norms, 14 percent nonproliferation, and 7 percent terrorism. All of these nest within the overarching goals of the EU's Common Foreign and Security Policy (CFSP).

29   SIPRI, "Arms Embargoes," https://www.sipri.org/databases/embargoes.

30   Moret, "Humanitarian Impacts of Economic Sanctions on Iran and Syria."

31   One of the EUSD goals is to provide the empirical basis for systematic comparable studies.

32   European Union, "Sanctions: How and When the EU Adopts Restrictive Measures," October 20, 2020, https://www.consilium.europa.eu/en/policies/sanctions/; "How the EU Decides and Imposes Sanctions," *DW*, https://www.dw.com/en/how-the-eu-decides-and-imposes-sanctions/a-56515391.

33   Taylor, *Sanctions as Grand Strategy*, 74.

34 Zuzana Hudáková, Thomas Biersteker, and Erica Moret, "Sanctions Relaxation and Conflict Resolution: Lessons from Past Sanctions Regimes," The Carter Center (October 2021), https://www.cartercenter.org/resources/pdfs/peace/conflict_resolution/sanctions-relaxation-10-2021.pdf.

35 "Freed Cuban Dissidents Arrive in Spain," *DW*, July 13, 2010, https://www.dw.com/en/freed-cuban-dissidents-arrive-in-spain/a-5789826.

36 Graduate Institute Geneva and Global Governance Centre, Geneva International Sanctions Network, https://www.graduateinstitute.ch/sites/internet/files/2020-05/GISN%20list%20of%20past%20events.pdf.

37 For some efforts along these lines, see Alex Vines, "The Effectiveness of UN and EU Sanctions: Lessons for the 21st Century (Review Essay)," *International Affairs* 88:4 (2012): 867–877.

Conclusion

1 David Miliband, "The Afghan Economy Is a Falling House of Cards. Here Are 5 Steps to Rebuild It," *CNN.com*, January 20, 2022, https://www.cnn.com/2022/01/20/opinions/afghan-economy-falling-house-cards-miliband/index.html; Erica Moret, "The Role of Sanctions in Afghanistan's Humanitarian Crisis," *Global Observatory*, International Peace Institute, October 14, 2021, https://theglobalobservatory.org/2021/10/the-role-of-sanctions-in-afghanistans-humanitarian-crisis/.

2 Drezner, "United States of Sanctions: Use and Abuse of Economic Coercion," 142.

INDEX

For the benefit of digital users, indexed terms that span two pages (e.g., 52–53) may, on occasion, appear on only one of those pages.